Happy Creek

STOP, LOOK AND LIVE

BY JAMES KELLER

STOP, LOOK AND LIVE

JUST FOR TODAY

GOVERNMENT IS YOUR BUSINESS

ONE MOMENT PLEASE!

YOU CAN CHANGE THE WORLD

CAREERS THAT CHANGE YOUR WORLD

MEN OF MARYKNOLL

Stop, Look and Live

A story for each day of the year to bring out the power within you . . . A new Christopher book.

By

JAMES KELLER, M.M.

HANOVER HOUSE, GARDEN CITY, N.Y.

1954

LIBRARY OF CONGRESS CATALOG CARD NUMBER 54–9585

COPYRIGHT, 1954, BY THE CHRISTOPHERS, INC.
ALL RIGHTS RESERVED
PRINTED IN THE UNITED STATES
AT THE COUNTRY LIFE PRESS, GARDEN CITY, N.Y.
FIRST EDITION

NIHIL OBSTAT: JOHN M. A. FEARNS, S.T.D.
CENSOR LIBRORUM

IMPRIMATUR: ✠ FRANCIS CARDINAL SPELLMAN
ARCHBISHOP OF NEW YORK

FOREWORD

An Oriental prince gave a jester a wand saying: *"Keep this until you find a greater fool than yourself."* The jester laughingly accepted the wand and flourished it on festive occasions.

One day the prince lay dying. Calling the jester to his bedside, he said: *"I am going on a long journey."*

"Where to?" asked the jester.

"I don't know," came the reply.

"How long will you be gone?" asked the jester.

"I shall be gone forever," came the reply.

"What provisions have you made for the trip?" the jester asked.

The prince shrugged his shoulders. *"None at all."*

"Then," said the jester, *"take this."* And placing the wand in the nobleman's hands, he added: *"It belongs to you!"*

They also run a foolish risk who fail to recognize the great purpose of life: 1. why they are here, 2. where they came from, and 3. where they are going, run a foolish and dangerous risk.

On the other hand those who keep themselves reminded from day to day that the longest life here on earth is but a brief preparation for the endless years of eternity usually lead a full and meaningful existence.

The aim of this book is to help you *"stop, look and listen"* for a few minutes of each day so that you may live here on earth more fully for the glory of God and the good of others, and thus prepare yourself for everlasting happiness.

The more you think, pray and work from the point of view of eternity, the more useful your life is likely to be. You will want to do more than save yourself. You will find an urge developing within you to play the role of a Christopher or Christ-bearer by filling your days, months and years with works that will help change the world for the better.

God gives us many reminders of eternity. One of the most unusual is the Grand Canyon. It offers one of the most breathtaking views I have ever seen. It is almost impossible to convey the sheer magnitude and grandeur of this wonder of nature.

Someone said that if the 200 mile stretch of the main range of the Allegheny Mountains could be lifted up and dropped into the Grand Canyon, they would not half fill the colossal cavity.

In width it ranges from 2 to 18 miles. At its greatest depth it lies more than a mile below its rim. In length its winding gorge stretches for 280 miles.

As I stood on the brink of this mighty chasm, I felt drawn closer than ever before to the eternity, infinity and beauty of the Creator Who has fashioned it.

No one has yet done the Grand Canyon justice whether by painter's brush or by pen. The constantly changing colors defy description. The dull red that glows in the sunlight is heightened by the seeming endless diversity of many colored rocks with their great diversity of tints.

For me the almost overpowering lesson of the Grand Canyon was to be found in the river that seemed like a slender silver thread as it wove its way through the narrow gorge more than a mile below me.

Scientists claim that it has taken more than a million years for this Colorado River to carve its course deep into the depths of the earth. Down through countless ages this stream has been relentlessly seeking its objective.

A million years! It is impossible for the average person to comprehend it—and yet a million years is only the beginning of eternity. What a different meaning life takes on when considered in the light of eternity. What is the longest life compared to it?

Life could be compared to running through the Grand Central Station to catch a train. Reaching your distant destination depends on those few seconds. Where you came from—where you are going—why you are there must at all cost be kept in mind.

Down through the centuries that which has spurred on men of good will is the deep-seated conviction that God has given them a life that only starts in time but reaches its fulness and completion in the endless years of eternity.

It is this unquenchable sense of eternity that has brought out of men a yearning desire to make the world a bit the better for the brief time they are in it.

The thought of eternity, therefore, has been stressed in a particular way in this book in the hope that it will stimulate those who read it to take time to think of these ultimates and also to play the missionary role of a Christopher.

Explaining the Christopher Movement

A Christopher* is a bearer of Christ. Individually and personally he carries Christ into the market place. By prayer and work he strives to bring Christian principles especially into the vital fields that touch the lives of *all* people: (1) education, (2) government, (3) literary and entertainment fields, (4) labor, (5) social service, and (6) library work. Much of the tragedy of our times is due to the fact that godless elements have swarmed into these same spheres, while the followers of Christ have remained on the side lines, doing little more than saving themselves. Complaining, criticizing, negative analyzing will accomplish little. Positive, constructive action is needed.

A Christopher spends his time *improving*, not *disproving*. He knows that "it is better to light one candle than to curse the darkness." As soon as there are more people "turning on lights" than there are *"turning them off,"* then—and only then—will the darkness disappear.

1. *No Organization*. There are no memberships, no meetings, no dues—no organization beyond Christopher headquarters at 18 East 48th St., N.Y. 17, N.Y.

2. *Limitations*. The Christopher movement confines itself to one phase of a big problem. It is merely an attempt to supplement, not replace, basic and essential organization. It restricts itself to emphasis on primary truths, while recognizing the importance of all the truths that flow from them.

3. *The Distinguishing Mark*. Love of *all* people for the love of God should be the distinguishing characteristic of anyone who would play the role of a Christopher. In no case should there be a return of hate for hatred. Those

* The word *Christopher* is derived from the Greek word, *Christophoros,* meaning *Christ-bearer.*

who would be bearers of Christ must be ready for all the ingratitude, suffering, rebuffs, and countless disappointments which the Master encountered. Each must strive to be kind while still remaining firm, to be able to disagree without becoming disagreeable. *"Love your enemies, do good to them that hate you and pray for them that persecute and calumniate you."* (Matthew 6:44) With this motivation, the most difficult task can become a labor of love.

4. *Emphasis on the Individual.* Because God has implanted in every human being a desire to be creative, to make a certain contribution to the peace of the world that no one else can make, the Christopher approach stresses individual initiative. Our policy is to point out elementary principles and then leave it to each person to work out his own method of blending, integrating, or incarnating the divine into the human. This allows for greater freedom, within reasonable limits, and encourages that element of originality, imagination, and enterprise which is possible only when the individual feels a personal responsibility in changing the world for the better.

5. *No Placement Bureau.* Despite repeated requests, we have purposely refrained from setting up any placement bureau. We feel that it is better for each to seek endeavors of his own choosing, when and where he likes. Furthermore, we are convinced that it is an important experience in the missionary approach of the Christopher movement for such a person to go through the difficult, and often discouraging, ordeal of discovering for himself the role he should play in helping to restore Christ to the market place.

6. *Dependence on God.* By the very nature of Christopher work, a deep conviction of dependence on God, of

being an instrument, however unworthy, in the hands of God, is absolutely essential. The closer one is to Christ, the more one is bound to accomplish. Competence is needed, to be sure. But ability without godliness can be a great danger even for those who have dedicated themselves to a good cause.

7. *Reaching the Millions.* At present some ten million persons over America are being reached regularly with the Christopher idea through talks, literature, books, movies, radio and television programs. . . . Christopher News Notes are sent monthly to approximately one million persons free of charge. . . . Nearly two million copies of the following seven Christopher books are in circulation: *You Can Change the World, Three Minutes a Day, One Moment Please, Government Is Your Business, Careers That Change Your World, All God's Children* and finally, *Stop, Look and Live.* . . . The Christopher program, reaching 9 million persons a week, is presented regularly over 1000 television and radio stations throughout the country. Our objective is merely to encourage and make suggestions to each and all of these millions. We leave it to each individual to decide for himself what part he shall play.

8. *No Christopher Clubs.* Because we restrict ourselves to developing individual initiative and personal responsibility, *we do not authorize Christopher clubs or groups of any kind,* or the use of the Christopher name in connection with any project that has resulted from the Christopher idea. We leave it to each to decide whether he will work alone or join any one of hundreds of excellent organizations. Each individual speaks and acts for himself, not for the Christopher movement.

9. *Financial Support.* In keeping with our policy of

no memberships, no subscriptions, no dues, we merely announce our needs, while soliciting funds from no one. We depend entirely on God to provide, through voluntary contributions (which are tax exempt), the fifteen thousand dollars a week now needed for our various Christopher projects.

10. *The Christopher Position.* The Christopher movement is under Catholic auspices. By the very fact that it is Catholic, it is deeply concerned, for time and for eternity, with the welfare of *all* men—even of those whose background makes them hostile to religion. In loving solicitude we are bound to include *all* and exclude *none*. Each is a child of God, at least through creation. Each, doing even one thing for Him, can start to be a Christopher, a Christ-bearer. Inasmuch as the movement has no memberships and no meetings, each person participates in the work of the Christophers as far as he can and will.

11. *To One and All.* The role of the Christopher is a simple one. He or she goes into the market place, into a job of his or her choosing, without fanfare, or flag waving, without doing anything sensational. His or her simple task is to insist on truth where others are intent on furthering falsehood, to establish order where others are spreading confusion.

Where there is hate, he tries to bring in love; where there is darkness, he carries light. Always striving to implant more firmly the fundamentals which others are trying to uproot, the Christopher emphasizes the normal rather than the abnormal.

Nothing remarkable may ever be required beyond a generous spirit of courage and daring. He or she expects to do the usual, not the unusual, the ordinary, not the extraordinary, knowing that while the steady fulfillment of duty often requires plodding devotion and day-by-day hard work, even monotonous drudgery, yet this continuing sacrifice is constantly lightened by a driving purpose. The most trivial and tiresome task achieves significance and dignity when done for the sake of Christ, Who said ". . . My yoke is sweet and My burden light." (Matthew 11:30)

STOP, LOOK AND LIVE

STOP, LOOK AND LIVE

Someone recently suggested that a spot be included in every juke box whereby anyone interested in a little quiet could insert a coin and buy three minutes of silence.

The man who made this unusual proposal is fond of music but claims that he values silence still more and that besides a little silence actually helps one appreciate music even more.

How, when and where you find—or even *"buy"*—the bit of silence that is essential for one who would live a meaningful life should be left entirely to you.

But we would respectfully propose to you on this first day of the year that you consecrate at least three minutes each day to that quiet reflection and prayer that is so necessary if you are to have a proper perspective on time and eternity.

There is much food for thought in the old Hebrew proverb: *"Silence is the fence around wisdom."* To protect yourself against the dangers of too much noise and distraction, set aside a brief period in every day when you can think of God and talk with Him.

If you persevere and develop this practice into a daily habit, you are bound to grow in love of God and others. Yes, life itself will take on a new meaning and purpose if you *"stop, look and live!"*

"Hear in silence, and for thy reverence good grace shall come to thee." (Eccles. 32:9)

✥ Help me, O Lord, to learn the blessedness of silence.

HE HEARD MUSIC

The operation was over. The patient was just coming out of the anesthetic when he said, *"I hear music!"*

Seeking to calm him the nurse said, *"Now, now, don't get excited, that's just St. Peter's band."*

Far from settling him, this casual remark stirred him up all the more. With a gulp he shouted, *"Gee, I made it!"*

When he was told that it was St. Peter's High School band that was playing just across the street, he realized that he was still on earth, with quite a bit of work to do before he entered the pearly gates.

Whether you complete your mission in life sooner or later makes little difference. The important thing to remember is that the longest life is short in comparison to the endless peace and bliss of eternity.

It's a great consolation to realize also that there is a place that God has prepared for you individually for all eternity. All you have to do to win it is to follow the rules that the Creator laid down regarding the way to get there.

"Come ye blessed of my Father, possess you the kingdom prepared for you from the foundation of the world." (Matthew 25:34)

⇜ O Author of all life, assist me in keeping always before me the one and only big goal of my existence.

EDUCATION WITHOUT GOD

The story is told of an American explorer coming upon a tribe of cannibals who were about to sit down to a hearty meal of human flesh.

Chatting with the cannibal chief, the American was astonished to find that he had been educated in the United States.

"*Do you mean to say,*" demanded the explorer, "*that you went to college and still eat human beings?*"

"Oh, yes," replied the chief. "*But, of course, now I use a knife and fork.*"

Education without God often does little more than polish up the surface of a man's life. There is always the danger that a person so educated will believe that men are nothing more than animals. But education with God teaches us to see ourselves and all others as made to God's image and likeness. Knowing this, we must treat each other as God's children deserve to be treated.

"*God created man to his own image: to the image of God he created him.*" (Genesis 1:27)

&⸱ Creator of all, help me to see all men as Thy children and to love and serve them for Thy sake.

TAKING ONE'S SELF TOO SERIOUSLY

Danny's father brought his boss home for dinner one evening. The man was quite gruff and self-centered. Nearly everything he said was a pat on the back for himself.

He hadn't paid much attention to young Danny, but the boy never took his eyes off him. Finally, the visitor became so conscious of the absorbing look of the youngster that he turned to him and said: *"Say, sonny, why do you keep looking at me?"*

Danny saw his opening and brightly said: *"My Daddy keeps saying you're a self-made man!"*

Beaming first at the boy's father, the honored guest then turned to the child and proudly admitted that he was.

The answer didn't completely satisfy Danny. With utmost candor, he asked: *"But why did you make yourself like that?"*

God allows us the freedom to help or hurt ourselves. If we use the portion of our thought and energy on ourselves that He intended for others, we not only damage ourselves but we deprive others of the attention that God sent to them through us.

"Before all things, have a constant mutual charity among yourselves, for charity covereth a multitude of sins." (I Peter 4:8)

❧ O Lord, keep me ever reminded that I should not take myself too seriously and others not seriously enough.

4

HOW TO LEAD A RELAXED LIFE

There was much wisdom in the casual comment of a Negro cab driver. He summed up briefly a bit of common sense that anybody could take to heart.

"It looks like rain," I said, as we drove along.

Without a moment's hesitation, he replied: *"Well, if it does, it's all right with me and if it doesn't, that's all right, too. I just leave it to the Lord. He has it all figured out. He sends a bit of rain, a bit of sun, some snow and ice and a lot of other things, that He thinks are good for us. I just take what He sends and thank Him for it."*

Then as a red light brought him to a stop, he turned to me and said with a big, happy grin: *"You know what that all adds up to, don't you? I lead a relaxed life."*

The vast majority of people often make things hard for themselves and everybody else. They, too, could lead a *"relaxed life"* if they would learn to adjust themselves to the will of God.

When you say the *"Our Father,"* pause and reflect a bit on the deep meaning of these words:

"Thy will be done on earth as it is in heaven." (Matthew 6:10)

⋙ O Holy Spirit, grant me the privilege of helping to bring down to earth some of the peace and order of heaven.

YOU PAY THE PRICE

In Washington, D.C., there is a faithful government worker who has served his country well for more than thirty years. His job is an inconspicuous but most important one. It affects the safety and well-being of every American.

Being a man of deep religious principles, this devoted public servant never wavers. No one can deflect him from his sense of loyalty and integrity. Asked one day why he didn't get out of government and save himself the misunderstanding and abuse he was subjected to, he pointed to a motto hanging on the wall. It read: *"No one would have crossed the ocean if he could have gotten off the ship in the storm."*

When he graduated from college, this man deliberately chose a career in government as his life-time work, even though it meant sacrificing a business opening in which he might have gained much financially. He realized that anyone determined to perform a real mission in life for love of God and others must expect to take a temporary beating.

"Through many tribulations, we must enter into the kingdom of God." (Acts 14:21)

&ʒ O Lord, help me to see that what seems to be the hard way is so often the best way.

KEEP THAT SENSE OF PROPORTION!

In Detroit recently, a group of women's clubs started a drive to build more hospitals for the growing number of mentally ill in the state of Michigan.

God bless these good ladies for showing an interest in a problem that is growing more and more serious all over the country.

But we hope and pray that even more will be found to tackle the big job of getting to the *cause* of most mental disturbances.

In many instances, the basic trouble is that a person has become too wrapped up in himself and his own problems.

God never intended it to be that way. The power for good that He gave each of us must be used for others as well as for ourselves if we are to fulfill our purpose in life. Keep that divine sense of proportion and you can't help but have peace of mind, heart and soul even on the darkest days. And the more you have it, the more you will want to share it with others.

Christ put it so simply. Here are His words:

"Thou shalt love thy neighbor as thyself." (Matthew 22:39)

◆§ Lord, help me to keep a sense of balance by being as thoughtful of the welfare of others as I am of my own.

7

REMEMBER THE FUNDAMENTALS

A violent storm in Wisconsin recently caused considerable damage. Communications were disrupted. Telephone and electrical wires were torn from the poles.

In the midst of it all, a farmer made a remarkable discovery. He found that his fifteen helpers were proficient in every way except one. Although they were experts with electrical milkers, not a single one among them knew how to milk a cow by hand.

Gadgets of all kinds are provided these days to make life easier for us. But they can make it more complicated if they dominate our lives. There is always the danger of overlooking *"fundamentals"* by becoming immersed in *"incidentals."*

You can render a great service if you try to remind people of the real purpose of life and thus save them from being deflected by the passing pleasures and allurements that lead nowhere.

Keeping first things first is difficult at times, but if you strive to keep others conscious of this necessary sense of proportion, you are likely to have a better balance in your own life.

"Seek ye therefore first the kingdom of God and his justice, and all these things shall be added unto you."
(Matthew 6:33)

&s Give me the wisdom, O Lord, to see the difference between the more important and the less important things of life.

8

YOUR POWER FOR GOOD

A man in New Jersey worked for four years in his trade union to get more good rank and file members to attend meetings and thus outwork and outvote a small minority who wished to use the union for subversive ends. His job was a discouraging one at first. But keeping ever before him the Christopher slogan: *"Better to light one candle than to curse the darkness,"* he persevered.

God blessed him for it. This one man changed a whole union for the better.

If you are dedicated to God and country, you will find developing within yourself a driving power to push through all obstacles. More and more you will be inflamed with a fire which warms but does not burn. Everything you say or do will reflect that devotion, loyalty, and quiet enthusiasm which is seldom, if ever, the lot of those whose only cause is themselves.

A remarkable transformation can take place in you, once you make the simple adjustment from dull, narrow concentration on self, to the stimulating, vitalizing interest and concern in the general good of all. With God's help, you will be forever buoyed up with the knowledge that the world itself is at least a tiny bit better because you are in it.

"As the Father has sent Me, I also send you." (John 20:21)

▪ O my Jesus, give me the courage to persevere in helping others.

FOR EVERYBODY'S SAKE

Two lawyers in Chicago fell into a discussion one day about the trend away from law and order here and over the world. One lawyer said that our only hope is to get back to the Ten Commandments.

"What have they got to do with it?" his companion countered. *"They're just a set of worn-out customs."*

The first lawyer challenged him to look over the Ten Commandments and see which one among them could be thrown out without endangering our homes, schools, business and normal freedom. The other man picked up the challenge and said he would have his answer ready the next time they were together.

A few days later the two met again at their club. *"You really got me this time,"* said the skeptical one. *"Do you know that I've been racking my brain for several days to find just one of those Commandments that we could do without and still keep things going. I must admit that I haven't found it. For the first time in my life I see that they are the foundation of all law and order."*

You may render a great service by reminding persons who fight against the eternal laws of God that in so doing they hurt themselves as well as everybody else.

"There is no power but from God." (Romans 13:1)

❧ O God, keep me ever conscious that in furthering Thy law I can do much to bring peace on earth to all men.

THE ONLY THANKS THAT COUNTS

A woman in San Francisco shows great perseverance in taking jobs which serve the public good but which bring her little or no thanks.

This zealous lady, now approaching her sixties, gave full credit to her mother. She said that her mother impressed two things on her as a child:

1) *that the best way to be happy in this life was to work not for self but for others;*

2) *that she should neither look for thanks for serving others, but rather leave it to God to supply the reward.*

Parents, teachers and all others who have anything to do with the training of the young could render a great service to God and country by imitating the example of this mother and teaching this valuable lesson frequently and at an early age.

"In your patience, you shall possess your souls." (Luke 21:19)

◦§ Grant me the grace, O Lord, to seek no thanks except from You.

LIFE WITH A PURPOSE

Working in his garden with a hoe one day St. Francis of Assisi was asked what he would do if he was suddenly told that he was to die at sunset that day. The answer he gave is a very significant one.

"I would finish hoeing my garden," he replied simply.

If you live each day as if it were your last day on earth, you will probably find that you will be well prepared to die. In fact, this outlook will do much to make every act a prayer.

If we act sensibly and face the fact that we are here for a purpose, our whole existence can take on a new and refreshing meaning. We shall begin to see that the world itself can be a little better, for our being in it. We shall judge things more and more from the perspective of eternity.

Yes, the more you fulfill the chief purpose of your existence the more relaxed your life will be, the more prepared you will be at all times to report to headquarters.

"Give an account of thy stewardship, for now thou canst be steward no longer." (Luke 16:2)

⊷§ Keep me mindful, O Lord, that life here on earth is nothing more than a stepping-stone to eternity.

OVERCOME EVIL BY GOOD

In Harrisburg, Pa., a man parked his car in front of the City Hall. He hurried inside to pay a fine for illegal parking. By the time he had completed this little transaction, he returned to find that he had been tagged once more for illegal parking.

Many people through neglect go on making the same fault over and over again. As a result, they never make much headway spiritually.

It is possible to follow a negative course and merely try to root out faults. But by doing positive good it is much easier to accomplish that and to make great progress as well.

A sure way to correct a tendency to be unfriendly or abrupt with others is to go out of your way by showing them a thoughtful consideration. An inclination to dishonesty can effectively be overcome by championing the truth. One who neglects to vote, for instance, quickly corrects that fault once he takes it upon himself to be a *"committee of one"* in getting others to register and vote.

Doing good in a positive, constructive manner is an effective means of both curing faults and accomplishing something.

"Be not overcome by evil, but overcome evil by good." (Romans 12:21)

Inspire me, O Divine Master, to be a *"doer"* of good not merely an *"avoider"* of evil.

13

A KEG OF NAILS DID IT

On his way to lunch one day the driver of a truck was hurrying down a cobblestone street in Camden, New Jersey. Suddenly a hundred pound keg of nails tipped over in the back of the truck and started bouncing off the open back. The driver, unaware of what had happened, drove merrily along onto a highway. Thousands of the small, sharp nails spilled over the roadway for several blocks as the driver sped on.

Within a matter of minutes there were punctured tires on twenty automobiles that had been following the truck. On some cars all four tires were punctured.

Irate motorists flooded the Camden police headquarters with angry calls. Police barricaded the street until all the nails had been removed.

The neglect of one man caused considerable trouble for several others. Failure to cover the keg of nails, to fix it so that it would not tumble over, or to keep the back board of the truck up so that the nails would not scatter over the street were faults that could have been prevented.

Few people admit their sins of omission. And yet what one fails to do may cause more harm to others than deliberate malice.

"Lord, that I may see." (Luke 18:41)

✍ Help me, O God, to live up to the responsibility Thou hast placed in my hands.

SHE PAID A 43-YEAR-OLD BILL

Dr. R. J. Shull, of Hugo, Okla., recently received a $50 check for delivering a baby forty-three years ago.

Now seventy-five years old, Dr. Shull tells how he received a long distance phone call from a woman in Shreveport, La., who asked how much she owed him for delivering her child in 1910.

The doctor, both surprised and touched, told the lady that he couldn't recall the amount due and urged her to forget about the old bill.

The sense of responsibility that stimulated the lady to phone the doctor apparently persisted for she immediately airmailed a check for $50.

The voice of conscience is the last thing to die in man's soul. It is the stirring of God's law within. Even after neglect of its inspiration for many years, it will save us in the end if we will heed it.

Cultivate a devotion to that honesty and integrity which God expects of each of us and which is so much needed in all spheres of life today. To be sure, it is difficult, but it is a sure way to peace of soul for time and for eternity.

"If thou hadst known . . . the things that are to thy peace." (Luke 19:42)

◄§ Help me, O Divine Truth, to be honest with Thee and every man.

NO MONEY CAN SUPPLY

In 1929 a man in Racine, Wisc., left home telling his wife and six-year-old son that he was going out to look for work. They never heard from him again.

Twenty-three years later, and just a few days before his death, the missing man, now living in Buffalo, summoned a lawyer to draw up a brief will. In it he left all his possessions to his wife and son

"I have a family somewhere," he told the lawyer. *"You find them."*

This belated expression of interest in his family revealed a lingering sense of responsibility in this man. Many wait until it is too late to make up for omissions of a life-time. Material support is necessary, but no money can make up for the devotion and love that a husband and father owes to his very own.

There are countless persons who are being deprived of the love and peace that God wishes each of us to have in this life as a foretaste of the greater and endless joys of the life to come. You can reach some of the many who are broken in spirit and lead sad, unhappy lives.

"Bear ye one another's burdens and so you shall fulfill the law of Christ." (Galatians 6:2)

~§ Let me learn, O Lord, the joy of sharing with others the peace of soul Thou hast bestowed on me and which no money can buy.

THE PRICE OF PEACE

Because he showed "complete disregard for his personal safety" in order to carry seven wounded men to the shelter of a ravine in one of the worst battles on Heartbreak Ridge in Korea, Lt. Eugene F. Kelly of Tuckahoe, N.Y., was presented with a Silver Star.

The fighting in this engagement was so bloody that in many companies all the officers were killed or disabled. Lt. Kelly said he felt obligated to help those who could not help themselves. Seven times he crawled over the rough terrain, often as much as 100 yards, and dragged the wounded back to the ravine. One of those he helped was Captain William Clark, son of General Mark W. Clark.

When asked why he dared to take such a risk for others, the 31-year-old hero gave as his modest reason *"someone had to do it."*

The real test of love of one man for his fellowman is revealed in how much he is willing to suffer for him. If more could be found to be other Christs and live for others, regardless of the sacrifice involved, fewer might have to die at war.

"Thou shalt love thy neighbor as thyself." (Matthew 22:39)

⇒ O Jesus, let me learn to live for peace, regardless of the cost.

BIG HARM FROM LITTLE MISTAKES

In San Antonio not long ago a lady brought her car to such a sudden stop on a rainy day that eight other autos plowed into each other. Traffic was snarled for hours.

While the eight drivers sized up the damage to their cars, police began issuing traffic summonses to each of them for "negligent collision." The officers started with the last driver and worked their way forward. By the time they had reached the head of the line, they found that the driver who had caused all the trouble had quietly driven away.

Many a person does serious damage to the reputation, business or profession of others by a thoughtless remark or deed that spreads misunderstanding, with chain-reaction effect. In more instances than not, the one who originates the mistake has little idea of the far-reaching harm that results. The least he can do is to repair the harm caused.

"He that thinketh himself to stand, let him take heed lest he fall." (I Corinthians 10:12)

⊸§ O Lord, let me learn and relearn Thy great lesson of doing unto others as I would have them do unto me.

VALUE MAKES THE DIFFERENCE

A woman found a ring on a New York street. *"It was dirty,"* she said, *"and it shined so much and was so big I thought it was a cheap one—the kind you get in the dime store."*

She didn't think much about it until she read the sad story of an Air Force sergeant who had lost the $1000 diamond ring he planned to give to his fiancee. Thinking he had dropped it in a trash can, he went to one of the city's sanitation dumps and sifted and combed three tons of garbage—but his search was fruitless.

When the woman read this story she began to wonder if the ring she found might be worth more than she had thought. She got in touch with the sergeant. He came to her home and identified the ring. She got a cash reward—and learned a good lesson.

Value makes the difference. When men think of human beings as worth little more than animals, they treat them either with indifference or brutality. But, more often than not, when they realize the true worth of the least person—that he is made to the image and likeness of God—their whole attitude changes. Their life takes on new meaning. And they get a reward here which is a foretaste of their reward in heaven.

"Thou hast made him a little less than the angels." (Psalms 8:6)

&§ O Divine Master, never let me forget the true value of even the least of men.

TO SAVE FORTY CENTS

One day the Coast Guard operating in the waters off the coast of Washington received a report that a 26-foot fishing boat was overdue on the 80-mile voyage from Neah Bay to Port Townsend.

In a search of over eleven hours, three Coast Guard planes spent nine hours in the air covering an area of 2000 square miles. Two Coast Guard ships cruised over 900 square miles. Forty crew members of the ships and planes put in 250 man hours. Seventeen telephone calls were made, eight teletype and twenty-nine radio messages transmitted.

When it was all over, the Coast Guard learned the missing boat had been in Port Townsend since mid-morning. The man whose responsibility it was to report the fishing vessel's safe arrival refused to do so when a telephone operator told him the telephone call would cost forty cents.

Little "refusals" to make sacrifices for others often add up to a very high price. In many ways selfishness is what prevents peace for which all men yearn. If you do your part, regardless of the cost, you may be doing more than you think to bring Christ's peace to the world.

"Blessed are the peace-makers: for they shall be called the children of God." (Matthew 5:9)

&5 O Prince of Peace, grant that my every thought, word and deed may help others, not hurt them.

HIS OWN FAULT

A man in St. Joseph, Missouri, recently was fined $25 for smoking in bed. The Fire Department had charged that his smoking in bed had started a blaze in a hotel room.

He was asked whether he knew it was against the law to smoke in bed. He replied, *"I'll say that I did. I was the one who painted these signs saying that it was against the law to smoke in bed in hotel rooms."*

Often we find ourselves in trouble like this man, not because we are unaware of what the warning signs say, but because we deliberately do not heed them. It is obvious then, that when we are justly punished, we have no one else but ourselves to blame.

It is not a mark of wisdom to choose wilfully to do those things which God has directly commanded us not to do. Particularly, when we are well acquainted with the fact that we must reap what we sow. Unfortunately, most of us have to prove this for ourselves many times, before we are fully convinced.

"He hath struck them as being wicked, in open sight. Who as it were on purpose have revolted from him, and would not understand all his ways." (Job 34:26, 27)

⋘ Holy Spirit, give me the grace to resist sin.

A BRUSH WITH DEATH

Watching television is not generally dangerous. But it might have turned out that way for a woman in Van Nuys, California.

She was in her motel looking at a movie on television. During an intermission in the movie she went out to fix herself a snack in the kitchenette.

While there, she was startled by a tremendous roar. The apartment shook. She found herself staring at the hood of a car that had crashed through the wall, run over the television set, and smashed to bits the chair in which she had been sitting just a few minutes ago.

Very few people have any idea how, when or where they will get the summons to appear before the Judgment Seat of God.

It may be today, tomorrow or twenty years from now for some who are reading these few lines.

The time is incidental. The main thing is to be prepared to report at "headquarters" on how we have performed the mission in life assigned to us by God Himself.

"Give an account of thy stewardship!" For now thou canst be steward no longer." (Luke 16:2)

ᐳᔞ Grant, O Lord, that I may be better prepared to answer for my life by making each day count for Thee and others.

THE VOICE THAT CANNOT BE STILLED

The owner of a stationery store in Maplewood, N.J., received an unsigned letter containing $1.55.

The anonymous letter said that the money would pay for several articles which had been stolen from the store over a period of months explaining *"My conscience bothers me so I am returning the exact value of all that I stole."*

The saving thing about a right conscience is that it is a constant reminder that we should right what is wrong in our lives. The hope of a conscience kept alive is the hope of freedom. It helps us get things straightened out that are crooked, in both individuals and nations.

There is always hope for peace and recovery—no matter to what depths we have fallen—if we will only listen to the voice of conscience that God has given to each one of us.

"I endeavour to have always a conscience without offense towards God, and towards men." (Acts 24:16)

❧ O Judge of all, help me to follow promptly and cheerfully the reminders Thou dost send me.

DON'T SELL YOURSELF SHORT

Some years ago a young man of 16 left Greece and went to South America. He was homeless, stateless, penniless. His first job in the new world was as a night telephone operator.

Today his assets are 300 million dollars. He owns 91 ships, has offices in 6 countries, and homes in New York, Paris, Athens, and Montevideo.

Finding that he needed another office building in which to house about 100 of his staff, he tried to rent one of the unused resort buildings in famed Monte Carlo. The owners refused.

So this man did something else. He spent a year and a half patiently purchasing shares from 2000 Monte Carlo stockholders. Now he has control of the building he sought to rent—and a lot of other Monte Carlo property too.

Men who set their hearts on making a niche for themselves in this world show a never-say-die perseverance. Their patient persistence in achieving their goal should be a forceful reminder to us to continue our efforts in trying to make this world a better place in which to live.

"For what doth it profit a man, if he gain the whole world, and suffer the loss of his own soul? Or what shall a man give in exchange for his soul?" (Matthew 16:26)

❧ Stimulate me, O King of Kings, to make any sacrifice in this life that I may be assured of the only lasting good.

AS THEY SEE US

A group of young Americans between the ages of 18 and 22 upon returning from a survey of other countries, told of some of the strange conceptions of America they had met with abroad. Here are some of the comments:

"A family in rural England expected that I would be a heavy drinker. What a shock it must have been to them when they discovered I didn't drink at all!"

"The family I lived with thought I would be toting a six-shooter."

Arabs thought Americans went around like cowboys fighting Indians.

It is easy to see how these impressions get abroad through some movies and magazines. The young people themselves claimed it was due to the influence of *"Class C Hollywood movies."*

One of the best ways to change these bad impressions abroad is to do all in your power to raise the standards of our movies, books and magazines. You would do well to pray that those in the creative fields whom God has blessed with talent realize their responsibility by giving the world a true picture of American life.

"Be thou an example of the faithful in word, in conduct, in charity, in faith, in chastity." (I Timothy 4:12)

⋐ O Lord, help each of us to reach the world with ideas that elevate men's minds, not debase them.

LITTLE THINGS ADD UP

A thief, thinking he was getting something of value, stole some vials of tuberculosis and anthrax germs from a scientist's automobile. The scientist was going to use them for experiments.

Said the scientist: *"I only hope that the person who took them will not break the vials and infect himself or let them fall into the hands of children."*

Fortunately, the germs were encased in tough little vials which protected the thief against infection.

Often things we do which are seemingly harmless—the friendship we have no right to encourage, the small lies that finally add up to big ones, the unkind words carelessly repeated over and over—can result in much trouble for ourselves and others.

You can avoid doing great wrongs by asking for God's help in avoiding little ones.

"From all appearance of evil refrain yourselves." (I Thessalonians 5:22)

✑ O God, help me avoid committing little sins that I may please Thee in everything I do.

SECRET OF HAPPINESS

A woman in Elizabeth, New Jersey, who quit her job at the age of 98 is still going strong at the age of 104.

She has lived a life full of meaning. Not only did she rear a large family and take care of her home, but until she was 98 she worked through the day picking vegetables. She never sought pleasure for pleasure's sake. She learned early that deepest happiness comes from hard work.

People who have no purpose or who try to shirk responsibility seem to drag along through life. They lack spark and initiative. They get sick easily and grow old before their time. In fact, they begin to die even while living.

One of the best ways of staying young is to fulfill, in as cheerful a way as possible, the mission God has given you to perform.

"They that hope in the Lord shall renew their strength." (Isaias 40:31)

&§ O Lord, teach me the difference between pleasure and happiness.

NO SUBSTITUTE FOR YOU

You—whoever you are—can do something that no one else can do to change the world for the better. There is no substitute for you. Without joining an organization, paying dues, attending meetings, you can start to be a Christopher or a Christ-bearer.

The role of a Christopher is a simple one. He goes into the marketplace, into a job of his own choosing, without fanfare, or flag waving, without doing anything sensational. His simple task is to insist on truth where others are intent on furthering falsehood, to establish order where others are spreading confusion, to bring love where there is hate.

Nothing remarkable may ever be required beyond a generous spirit of courage and daring. He expects to do the usual, not the unusual, the ordinary, not the extraordinary. Knowing that the steady fulfillment of duty often requires day-by-day hard work, even monotonous drudgery, he also knows that this continuing sacrifice will be lightened by a driving purpose. The most trivial and tiresome task achieves meaning and dignity when done for the sake of Christ, Who said:

"My yoke is sweet and My burden light." (Matthew 11:30)

∾ O God, help me to be a *"doer,"* not merely a *"complainer."*

EXPECTING THE BEST

A restaurant owner in Victoria, B.C., Canada, wanted to test the honesty of his customers. He invited them to set their own prices on the food they ate, ring up their own bills on the cash register and take their change out of it.

Fully expecting *"to lose his shirt"* in the experiment, he was pleased and surprised to find that people paid more than he would have charged. Few gave less than $1 for meals priced at 80 to 90 cents. In some cases they over-charged themselves as much as 150 per-cent.

Those who would be Christ-bearers should remember that there is good in everyone—without exception. Our aim should be to find the good in even the least person and try to build on that.

If you get someone to take only one step in the right direction you have done a great deal. It may require perseverance but if you try to do your best the Lord will bless you.

"Trust in the Lord, and do good, and dwell in the land, and thou shalt be fed with its riches." (Psalms 36:3)

ᴇᴈ O God, open my eyes that I may see the great possi-bilities for good that are all around me.

THE HOPE OF THE FUTURE

Back in 1750, Benjamin Franklin made a wise comment that has a special bearing in these days when juvenile delinquency is on the increase.

"Nothing is of more importance for the public weal," Franklin stressed, *"than to form and train youth in wisdom and virtue. Wise and good men are, in my opinion, the strength of a state far more so than riches or arms."*

Anyone who wants to do a little investigating for himself can quickly discover that during the last few decades we have allowed spiritual values to be sidetracked or eliminated from the home, the school and the work-a-day world.

As a result tens of millions of young Americans have little more than a *"bowing acquaintance"* with God's law and the cultural values of the ages that have gradually elevated the human being despite the debasing influences on all sides that have conspired to drag him down to the level of the beast.

In your own way, you can do something to change this downward trend. If you do, you may be playing a significant role in shaping the future for generations to come. But to do this you must be a *"doer."* It is a challenging task in which you will have God's blessing and aid.

"A young man according to his way, even when he is old he will not depart from it." (Proverbs 22:6)

&3 O Jesus, help me to do my part in seeing that young people are given the fullness of training that is their due.

MORE POWER TO YOU

The sloth is known to be one of the slowest of all animals. But, according to the National History Magazine, it deserves credit for being perhaps the most tenacious too.

Sloths have a great capacity "to hang on." The magazine describes as *"almost unbelievable"* stories about how they cling to life—refusing to let go. It says they have been known to recover after respiration has been suppressed by ether for as long as thirty minutes—yes, and after they have been immersed in water for forty minutes. And they can endure wounds that would kill other animals.

God has given you power which He expects you to use for the good of all.

But those who would change the world for the better, must learn the lesson of patience and even tenacity. No worthwhile change takes place overnight. God will aid the one who persists. The important thing is to make a start—then to persevere in spite of difficulties and discouragements.

"He that shall persevere unto the end, he shall be saved." (Matthew 10:22)

◄§ O God, grant that I may use my powers for Thee and for the good of all men.

SHE TOOK RESPONSIBILITY

One night while sweeping the floor of a bank in Syracuse, New York, a cleaning woman found $40,000. Startled and a bit scared at first, she didn't know what to do with so large a sum of money.

Finally, she put it in a paper bag and took it home with her. First thing the next morning she called the bank and asked that someone come and get it.

"I was sure glad to get rid of that money," she said when a bank officer came for it. *"I couldn't sleep all night."*

Without wishing it, this woman had a heavy responsibility unexpectedly thrust upon her. She discharged it faithfully.

You should continually strive to fulfill your personal responsibilities. There are some things for good only you can do—some things which will remain undone unless you do them.

You may be called upon to endure hardships for the sake of others—maybe to stand alone for the right. Be sure that, with God's help, you can do it.

"Walk worthy of the vocation in which you are called."
(Ephesians 4:1)

  O Saviour, give me the strength and courage I need to shoulder my responsibilities.

THROWING CAUTION TO THE WINDS

It was 40 below zero and a B-29 with its crew of 13 was flying back to Okinawa from a bombing mission over North Korea. An alert gunner suddenly discovered that a live bomb was stuck in the bomb rack. Its time fuse was ticking away. In seconds it would explode. With no regard for his own safety the gunner disarmed the bomb thus saving the lives of the entire crew.

It is inspiring to see the heroism of men and women that goes on all around us every day. Toiling, sacrificing, sometimes dying for loved ones, they are living proof that God has given every one of us a real capacity for greatness.

Chances are you'll never have the opportunity to disarm a live bomb. But sometimes it is just as heroic to make the constant little sacrifices necessary in daily life. And yet if you do your best to help others for love of God, the Lord will bless you.

Even the tiniest efforts can take on heroic proportions and have far-reaching effects for good.

"Greater love than this no man hath, that a man lay down his life for his friends." (John 15:13)

⇜ O Jesus, help me to realize that through my little efforts I can do big things for love of Thee.

33

ENDURING HARDSHIPS

When a young mother in New Orleans first learned that her twin babies, born blind, could probably not be helped by an operation, she wept. Next she took them to a specialist in New York to see if something more could not be done.

At the hospital she met another woman whose baby had the same eye disease. There would be an operation, said the woman, but it would not help. Then, in her discouragement, she expressed the wish that she could *"do away"* with her baby.

Shocked, the New Orleans mother said, *"I can't understand people who take the view that everything is lost when something like this touches their lives. We have felt all along that our babies will see some day. Even if they don't, we plan to give them as normal a life as possible."*

One of the lessons of life is to learn that we must get used to hardships. With faith in God, we can always hope and work hard, regardless of discouragements. God will do the rest. Should He withdraw certain of His gifts, He will give us the gift of acceptance and peace of soul, if we love Him.

"Be ye steadfast and unmovable; always abounding in the work of the Lord, knowing that your labour is not in vain in the Lord." (I Corinthians 15:58)

◦§ O Father, grant me strength of will to work hard for Thee in the service of men.

34

THE FOLLY OF ANGER

The board of education sent an inspector to visit one of its schools.

Everything was going along nicely, when he heard a lot of noise coming from one of the rooms. Angered by the disturbance, he rushed towards the room, pulled open the door, reached in, dragged out a tall fellow who was doing most of the talking, took him to the next room, and made him stand in the corner.

Shortly afterwards, a little boy timidly approached the inspector and said, pointing to the figure in the corner, *"He's our teacher. We want him back."*

Anger sometimes makes us do foolish and harmful things that we afterwards regret.

It is far better to cultivate an attitude of calmness in the presence of even the most trying circumstances. It will save us and others much trouble and embarrassment.

"The anger of man worketh not the justice of God." (James 1:20)

♊O Lord, keep me from giving in to anger no matter how hard I am tempted.

TRYING TO GET AWAY WITH IT

For five years a young business executive in St. Joseph, Michigan, stole one or two checks almost daily from his company's mail, juggling entries in the books to cover the shortages.

One day the company received a bill for 42 cents from an out-of-town bank for handling a check the thief had cashed. An examination of the books showed that the company had never received the amount of the check. An investigation followed which led to the arrest of the thief.

God has established a moral order in the world which no man can violate without paying a penalty. It is a matter of time for the evil-doer to be brought to justice. Rarely does he have to wait until eternity overtakes him before he gets his just deserts.

We should remember always that our only true happiness comes from serving God and obeying His law. In that way alone do we have peace within ourselves which we can both enjoy and also share with others.

"Not defrauding, but in all things showing good fidelity . . ." (Titus 2:10)

O Lord, grant that I may always have that peace which comes from loving and serving Thee.

GOD ALONE SUFFICES

In Akron, Colo., an insane man barricaded himself in his farmhouse. When the sheriff and his deputy came to take him to the psychopathic hospital, he shot and killed them both.

The next morning a posse closed in on the house. But they never captured the crazed killer. He shot himself before they could get to him.

Going through his house, a member of the posse found a piece of cardboard on which the man had written his last will and testament: *"I want my land to go to the families of the sheriff and his helper's family. It won't pay for their lives, but it is the best I can do."*

It requires little knowledge to realize that no amount of this world's riches can ever make up for the loss of a single human life. Yet, how often in our search for happiness we forget this truth.

You can do much to teach men that lasting happiness here and hereafter is found only in God and His service.

"A man's life doth not consist in the abundance of things which he possesseth." (Luke 12:15)

⁕ O Lord of all, grant that I may teach men to love Thee above all things.

37

NO BED OF ROSES

A prominent scientist said recently that lifeless deserts once formed a natural barrier to the destructive powers of insect pests. They simply couldn't spread across the barren areas.

But a change began to take place with the increase of desert caravan travel. The insects *"hopped"* rides on the man-made transports and were carried across desert places without any effort on their part. They thus landed in portions of the world where their natural enemies were few and where plants had not developed resistance to them. They were able to multiply and do much damage in places once beyond their reach.

In the case of every blessing there is usually some hardship or challenge that confronts us. Life is not a bed of roses because in the roses there are always thorns.

God's purpose seems to be to remind us that this earth is not our lasting home. With every advance there will be a difficulty. He who faces up to these difficulties, instead of complaining, will triumph in the end.

"Do ye manfully, and let your heart be strengthened, all ye that hope in the Lord." (Psalms 30:25)

&5 O Lord, grant that I may face up to my difficulties and with Thy help conquer them.

LEADERSHIP FOR GOOD

In connection with a public safety contest, the Junior Chamber of Commerce of Jacksonville, Florida, had one of its members do nothing else but jaywalk during all of his lunch hours for an entire week.

Prizes valued at $75 awaited the person who would attempt to stop him. No one did. On the contrary, whenever he jaywalked or crossed a street against a red light, people followed his lead. They did the same thing he did.

Little do we realize the tremendous influence for good each one of us can have on the millions who drift aimlessly—following any leader, grasping at any and every panacea that promises them some temporal happiness.

If those who believe in God would work as hard in leading men to His Truth as others do to keep it from them, how much more real happiness and peace there would be in the world.

God has given you the power to do something—however small—towards providing the right kind of leadership for men who need it and want it so much. Begin today to do your part.

"Follow not that which is evil, but that which is good." (3 John 1:11)

↝ O Lord, help me to lead men to know and love Thee.

AN AFFAIR OF THE HEART

A University of Alabama professor said that the human heart is much more efficient than any machine man has ever invented.

The heart, he said, can use almost everything in the blood and is not dependent on any one thing or combination of things to produce energy. If something is lacking it can use something else.

Heart failure is brought on when, due to old age or certain diseases, the heart's muscle fibre stretches like a rubber band, loses its ability to expel the used blood, and reduces its efficiency to a dangerously low level. This trend cannot be reversed unless it is caught early and dealt with skillfully.

Everyone would agree that America is a strong, great country and efficient in the production of the material goods of life. But all too few are alert to the forces of evil that work day and night to weaken her moral and spiritual fibre which is the very heart of our nation.

You can help keep America free by taking personal responsibility for starting a trend for the better—by working just as hard to bring Christ into the marketplace as the godless do to keep Him out.

"Labour as a good soldier of Christ Jesus." (2 Timothy 2:3)

✋ O Lord, grant that I may work hard every day to bring Thy Truth into everything I do.

VICTIMS OF PRIDE

Two boys, 16 and 17 years old, lost their way for 24 hours during a hunting trip near San Jose, Calif. While a posse of 40 men was searching for them, the boys walked sheepishly into town.

They said that they had passed several farmhouses where they could have asked for directions. But, considering themselves to be experienced hunters, they didn't want to admit that they were lost.

Few of us realize how much trouble and anxiety we cause others by being too proud to admit our mistakes and to change our ways.

Human frailty will cause all of us to make mistakes sooner or later. At such times it is wise to admit our mistakes, and try to do better the next time. If you wish to depend entirely upon yourself, God will let you. He won't interfere. But He is waiting for you to ask His help. And if you do, He will give you the wisdom and courage to do what is best.

"God resisteth the proud, and giveth grace to the humble." (James 4:6)

✍ Dear Father of all, help me to depend on Thy wisdom and strength in everything I do.

41

DISGUISED BLESSINGS

A young woman was having difficulty crossing a street in Chicago in a blinding snowstorm. A gallant traffic policeman spotted her difficulty, and stopped traffic. He then gathered her up in his arms, carried her across the snowladen street and set her down.

In a blaze of temper, the young woman kicked the policeman for being forward. Whereupon, without a word, the officer swept the young woman up in his arms, carried her back and deposited her in her original position. He then waved traffic on.

So often blessings come to us, and we fail to recognize them for what they are. Particularly is this true when we want something very much, and we cry and plead to God to give it to us, and He does not seem to answer. We are apt to forget that He knows what is best for all of us, and He will work everything out to our advantage.

When we reproach God for not granting our wishes, we may find ourselves back where we started or worse off than before. When we pray let us first of all realize that God hears our every prayer, and secondly that He knows best, and will do all for our good when we trust in Him.

"Blessed is the man that trusteth in the Lord." (Jeremiah 17:7)

O God, help me always to trust in Thy wisdom.

WORK LIKE HE DID

The Lincoln Memorial in Washington, D.C. is a nation's tribute to its martyred Civil War President. This massive shrine pays tribute to the greatness of a simple and heroic man whose very life was offered in the name of liberty.

Seated in a great chair 12½ feet high, the gentleness, power and determination of Lincoln come to us clearly through the features chiseled in granite by the sculptor. We can almost hear him speak the words with which he closed his famous Gettysburg Address: *". . . that this nation, under God, shall have a new birth of freedom, and that government of the people, by the people, for the people, shall not perish from the earth."*

There is something that you can do to preserve the God-given liberty with which America is blessed. Do more than complain about those who are striving in a hundred different ways to destroy it. They are on the job, not sitting on the sidelines. If your heart is in truth, you will work as hard for good as they do for evil, you will be acting like Lincoln did.

"For where your treasure is, there will be your heart also." (Luke 12:34)

O God, help me to be a *"doer"* not just a talker.

43

YOU DECIDE THE RESULTS

The parents of a 15-year-old boy wanted to give him a gift he would appreciate. After thinking about it for some time, they bought a lead-soldier molding outfit for him.

But instead of using it to make soldiers, their son made counterfeit nickels to feed the juke boxes!

Most of the things which God has given us can be used for good or for evil. It all depends on who uses them.

For example, a criminal wielding a knife can destroy life. A surgeon's skillful use of a knife can be the means of saving life. Atomic energy can be used for research into medicine, agriculture and industry—or it can blow us off the face of the earth. Television can benefit all of mankind—or it can be used to spread ideas which would wreck America.

These fields can be no better or worse than the people in them. God expects you to play a part in seeing to it that they are staffed by those who are filled with a love of God and country.

"Whether you eat or drink, or whatsoever else you do, do all to the glory of God." (I Corinthians 10:31)

&ゞ O Creator of all, help me to do my part in seeing to it that the vital fields are an influence for good.

44

MUCH DEPENDS ON YOU

"The Turnpike," said the head of the Pennsylvania Turnpike Commission, *"is only as safe as the drivers who use it."*

But one newspaper thought more had to be done to cut down the traffic fatality rate than to depend on the honor of motorists. Pointing out that 47 per-cent of the trucks using the famous Pennsylvania highway exceeded the speed limit of 50 miles per hour, it proposed that additional state troopers patrol the highway to enforce the speed laws.

Too many go through life with a "let George do it" attitude. *"What harm is done if I disobey them? I am only one,"* they say. When enough people take this attitude it adds up to trouble for everyone.

The same thing is true in exerting your power for good. We all want good government, good education, good television, good everything else. But too often we expect others to provide it for us. Much depends on you —individually. The next time you are tempted to say, *"Why don't they do something about it?"* ask yourself this question, *"Why don't I do something about it?"* You will be amazed to find out how much you, personally, can do.

"These things I will have thee affirm constantly: that they, who believe in God, may be careful to excel in good works." (Titus 3:8)

⪧ O my Jesus, help me to be Thy instrument of peace.

CROWDING OUT THE GOOD

An old Arabian fable says that one cold night a camel thrust his nose under the flap of an Arab's tent. *"Let me keep my nose in your tent,"* he said. *"It's so cold out here."* The Arab gave his consent and went to sleep.

Awakened a short time later, he found not only the camel's nose, but his head and neck as well, inside the tent. At the camel's further request the Arab permitted him to place his forelegs inside. The camel had one more favor to ask: *"It's so cold. May I stand wholly within?"*

"Yes, yes," said the Arab. *"Come wholly inside."*

The Arab went to sleep again—this time with difficulty because there was so little room. When he woke up he was out in the cold. The camel had the tent to himself.

Often some small failing begins to grow. If we do nothing to counteract it, the time may come when that one sin has grown so large as to crowd out of our lives much, if not all, of the good. The more you are aware of this danger the more you will rely on God's help against little faults and failings and try to overcome them before they become fixed habits.

"Be sober and watch: because your adversary the devil, as a roaring lion, goeth about seeking whom he may devour." (1 Peter 5:8)

‌ O God, help me to resist the beginnings of evil.

ONLY YOU CAN DO IT

Fifteen miles above Gay Mills, Wisconsin, the Kickapoo River overflowed its banks and swept towards a little town.

Hearing the news, the town's chief telephone operator —a woman—set off the village fire alarm by pressing a button on her switchboard.

Calls began coming in, *"Where's the fire?"*

"It's not a fire," she replied. *"It's a flood. The river's over its banks, and it's coming this way."*

She notified the Red Cross, National Guard, and Army. Outside the telephone office, flood waters were almost five feet deep. But the switchboard operator stayed at her post —keeping telephone lines open, protecting the lives of her neighbors at great personal risk, doing her job faithfully and heroically. She was in a position to help others and she didn't hesitate to do her part.

God has placed in your hands a contribution to make to the peace of the world. It is something only you can do. No one else can do it for you. A million dollars couldn't buy it. If you fail to make your contribution the world will be just that much further away from peace.

"Now is the acceptable time; behold, now is the day of salvation." (II Corinthians 6:2)

◄§ O Lord, help me to use all my talents in bringing Thy peace and love to all men.

DANGER! NO STOPPING!

In the late winter of last year, a midwestern city had its worst fog in eighteen months. It was so thick that the motorists moved slowly and cautiously over one of the city's main highways.

One careless motorist, driving too fast, suddenly stopped in order to avoid ramming into the car ahead of him. A chain reaction crash followed in which twenty-five automobiles piled up.

It is all too easy for us to consider our actions solely in reference to our own purposes, or our own good. In justice and charity, however, we must consider their results or consequences, which touch the lives of others.

Sometimes we start off a *"chain reaction"* on which we had not counted. Why not make sure that these *"chain reactions"* will only be of the beneficial kind?

"And in doing good, let us not fail. For in due time we shall reap, not failing." (Galatians 6:9)

✍ Heavenly Father, strengthen us to persevere in ever serving Thee.

RENEW YOUR STRENGTH

Civil defense officials in Peckham, England, were surprised one day when a 91-year-old man told them that he wanted to enlist.

"You're too old," they said.

But the old man insisted that he wasn't. To prove his point he told them that in World War II he was offered the job of escorting children from much-bombed London to the country. He turned it down. *"I've always been a fighting man,"* he said, *"and I'm not going to become a nursemaid."* He was given a job as firewarden.

After hearing that story, the Peckham officials enrolled him.

Your ability to serve others is not determined by years or even by strength. The only thing necessary is that you be filled with love of God and country and a desire to do something positive regardless of your station in life. No matter what your age, your job, or the circumstances of your life, you can do something, with God's help, to change the world for the better.

"They that hope in the Lord shall renew their strength, they shall take wings as eagles, they shall run and not be weary, they shall walk and not faint." (Isaias 40:31)

◦§ Dear Lord, teach me that with Thee I can do anything.

GOD CARES FOR YOU

For the first time a little child heard the psalm from the Bible which likens God's Providence in men's lives to a shepherd's care of his sheep.

The psalm says the Lord rules us, sets us *"in a place of pasture,"* brings us up *"on the water of refreshment,"* and concludes:

"Thy mercy will follow me all the days of my life
And that I may dwell in the house of the Lord unto
length of days."

The child listened carefully to the reading of the psalm. When it was all over he said in a simple and direct way: *"The Lord is my shepherd. That's enough for me."*

Life would be much happier for all of us if we had the simple faith of this child. God loves you regardless of your failings and weaknesses. The very fact that you know the Lord watches over you during every moment should give you courage to push on in spite of temptations, discouragements and failures.

"We know that to them that love God, all things work together unto good." (Romans 8:28)

⊷§ Dear Lord, grant that I may place my wholehearted trust and confidence in Thee.

KNOW YOUR GOAL

A man in Florida wanted to make a quick round-trip by plane between Miami and West Palm Beach. He got to West Palm Beach, transacted his business, and returned to the airport for his flight back to Miami.

By accident he was directed to a plane which took him to New York. A blizzard was raging there, the temperature was below zero. The Miami man, attired in summer clothing, caught a cold that kept him in bed for three days.

He sued the airline for $3500.

Many people are headed in the wrong direction in life, because someone wasn't careful enough to start them off on the right road. Sometimes it's because they just don't know which way to turn.

Whatever it is, those who know the right road have a personal responsibility to lead the way and to point out to those who are lost that, the short time we spend on earth is merely a preparation for life after death. And if we follow the right path it will lead us to everlasting happiness.

"This is eternal life: that they may know thee, the only true God, and Jesus Christ, whom thou hast sent." (John 17:3)

&⸱§ O Father of all, help me to guide others to the road that leads to Thee.

51

TAKING RISKS FOR EVIL

After examining the scene of the crime, Sheriff Shultz of Gettysburg, Pa., said that it was an *"outside"* job. Robbers had broken through the coal chute and taken $45 from the open safe.

Scene of the crime? The Adams County jail!

What chances evil-doers take! What daring they display! They will go anywhere and suffer anything to accomplish their evil purposes. They take any risk and greatly inconvenience themselves to spread their ideas.

On the other hand, the average person with good ideas usually keeps them to himself.

The only way to overcome evil is by being zealous and enthusiastic for good. Over 1900 years ago Christ commanded that the Gospel be preached to all men. If the people who believe in God would take Him literally and reach as far as possible with His love and truth we would be well on the road to peace.

"Be not overcome by evil, but overcome evil by good." (Romans 12:21)

Lord, make me zealous for good so that I may be an instrument of Thy peace.

PRICE OF FREEDOM

When Robert A. Vogeler, an American businessman, was released by the Communists after seventeen months in a Budapest prison, one of his first statements to American reporters was: *"You never know what freedom means until you lose it."*

Because America has always been a land whose very foundations are representative of liberty, we, its citizens, rather take that liberty for granted. And certainly, that liberty is our right. Yet most of us forget that *"the price of liberty is eternal vigilance."* If we are to remain a free and strong people we must learn to guard that freedom, lest somehow it is taken away from us.

The best way to safeguard our freedom, is to make sure that we remain true to those principles on which our freedom was founded. A nation that is comprised of an individually strong and fine people must of necessity be a free people. On the other hand, a nation that is comprised largely of moral and spiritual degenerates cannot hope to escape collapse.

It is up to us then to do all we can as individuals so to use our influence for good that we may help to morally strengthen and uplift all our fellowmen.

"Now the Lord is a Spirit. And where the Spirit of the Lord is, there is liberty." (II Corinthians 3:17)

⊷ O Lord, let us know that true freedom is found only in Thee.

NOT BY BREAD ALONE

A man in Frankfurt, Germany, recently fasted for 79 days, earning a total of $6000 in fees from spectators and losing 78 pounds. He had planned to break his fast sooner, but hearing that an Indian fakir had just set a fasting record of 78 days, he wanted to exceed it.

We often wonder at the things some people will do, the hardships and sufferings they will endure to acquire the fame of having set a record. Yet, how few of us are willing to endure or suffer anything for love of God. Who can give us the only lasting reward of eternal life. If we could learn to discipline ourselves, physically, mentally and spiritually, we would grow more and more in strength and character. Christ knew the necessity of self discipline for spiritual growth, and set us a lasting example when he voluntarily went into the wilderness and fasted for forty days.

Self discipline always means that one will meet with temptations, and Jesus was sorely tempted by the devil. Yet He resisted the temptations, and we are told that afterwards, *"angels came and ministered to him."* We can be sure that when we discipline ourselves for love of God, He will assist us in all our trials.

"And every one that striveth for the mastery, refraineth himself from all things." (I Corinthians 9:25)

≈§ Holy Spirit, teach us to discipline ourselves so that we may be more filled with Thee.

54

TO LOVE MEANS TO GIVE

"I hope they all get me something nice for my birthday," said the little girl to her mother as she awaited the arrival of her friends for her fifth birthday party.

"You mustn't always talk about 'getting,' darling," corrected her mother. *"You must think about 'giving,' too."*

"Well, then," replied the little girl. *"I hope they all GIVE me something nice!"*

Without being aware of it, many of us carry childish ways over into adult life. So many of us want *to be loved* rather than *to love, to receive* rather than *to give.*

We could fill our own and others lives with happiness if we would only try to fulfill the demands of love even when they cause us inconvenience and suffering—if we would try to be *"go-givers"* instead of *"go-getters."*

Christ didn't say that the life filled with love would be easy. He said,

"If you love me, keep my commandments." (John 14:15)

 Dear Lord, teach me to show my love for Thee by loving and serving others.

ARE YOU HALF ALIVE?

A coal miner in Yorkshire, England, suddenly found himself heir to a $45,000 fortune. It was more money than he had ever seen—more by far than he would ever earn in the mines.

He decided to quit mining and to spend his time in comfort doing all the things he had dreamt about so long. He bought a new house, a new car, new clothes. He lived a life of ease, and for a time he liked it.

Then one day, soon after with plenty of money still in the bank, he went to the mines to ask for his old job back. He had found the *"pot of gold"* only to discover that it was filled with boredom.

By divine decree man must work, and *"earn his bread by the sweat of his brow."* Whoever ceases completely to work disobeys both God and nature. He soon stagnates, and eventually arrives at a state in which he is only half alive. The result is that he is at peace neither with God nor with himself.

We should find much more satisfaction in living if we tried to use all our thought and energy to make the world a better place in which to live.

"I am come that they may have life, and may have it more abundantly." (John 10:10)

&ε; O Lord of all life, inspire me to use all my thought and energy in Thy service for the good of men.

56

AN HONEST MAN

In Peoria, Illinois, a man came into a police station and asked how much the fine was for going through a stop-light.

"*Ten dollars*," the sergeant answered.

"*Well*," said the man, "*I just went through a stop-light. No one saw me, but I want to pay the fine anyway*."

The sergeant told him that he couldn't be fined because no one had filed a charge against him. The man had to keep his ten dollars.

This man may have gone to an extreme in being honest. Some would say he was more than honest. But nations don't fall because of people like that.

Small dishonesties, practiced over and over again, on an ever-wider scale have wrecked whole nations. The corruption and graft that afflicts many important spheres of American life today, is nothing more than countless dishonesties of individuals multiplied many times over. Shakespeare spoke an eternal truth when he said, "*No legacy is so rich as honesty*."

"*He that is faithful in that which is least, is faithful also in that which is greater: and he that is unjust in that which is little, is unjust also in that which is greater*." (Luke 16:10)

&s O Lord, help me to be honest in all my ways, that I may truly serve Thee and be acceptable in Thy sight.

A MODERN SAMARITAN

A telephone operator in Detroit collapsed one night while taking a call from California. The operator in California heard her moan, and when the line went dead she got in touch with the operator at the main Detroit switchboard who notified the police. The stricken operator was rushed to the hospital in a quite serious condition.

This woman's quick, unselfish thinking possibly saved a life. She was able to be of service, because she was thinking *"outside herself."* Thinking about others, especially those who are not immediately connected with us, is not something that *"comes naturally."* We learn to love in the truest sense of the word by daily practice of kindness and consideration for others.

When we seek to share God's love with *all* His children without distinction, then we are showing Him in the very best way possible that we do love Him.

"I also in all things please all men, not seeking that which is profitable to myself, but to many, that they may be saved." (I Corinthians 10:33)

≈§ O God, teach me to serve Thee by reaching as many as I can with Thy love.

NO SUBSTITUTE FOR THE REAL THING

A father was trying to get his ten-year-old son interested in astronomy. He learned that there was to be an eclipse of the moon one night and immediately phoned his son from the office to tell him about it.

Arriving home late that night, after the boy had gone to bed, the man asked his wife if their son had enjoyed seeing the eclipse.

She replied somewhat wearily, *"I couldn't get him to go outside to see it. They were showing it on TV."*

It has been said that one proof of God's boundless love for man, is that He made His earth so beautiful. An unhappy aspect of a mechanical age is that we become so impressed by man-made wonders that we cease to be impressed by the wonders of nature. As worthwhile as our mechanical inventions may be, there can be no adequate substitute for the beauty and wonder of God's universe.

There is no painting, however painstakingly done, that can completely capture the beauty of a sunset . . . no fabric however delicately woven or skillfully dyed that can rival the brilliance and texture of a rose . . . no book written by mere man that can teach as great a lesson on Infinity as a cloudless star-filled sky.

"The heavens shew forth the glory of God, and the firmament declareth the work of His hands." (Psalms 18:1)

꙳ O Creator of all, open my eyes that I may see and rejoice in Thy marvels.

A TIME TO BE STILL

One rainy day an electrical worker was driving his truck in Morrisville, Pennsylvania, when a raised ladder on the truck struck two high-voltage wires and broke them.

The deadly electricity coursed through the truck's metal body. But the driver, insulated by the rubber floor matting and his seat cushion, saved his life by sitting still until an emergency crew arrived and shut off the current.

There are often times when we find ourselves surrounded by innumerable dangers. It is at times like these that we may be so overcome by fear as to be sorely tempted to rush headlong towards what may seem to be the nearest exit. But a false move in time of crisis may mean the difference between life and death.

It is then that we need to know the value of *"sitting still,"* and seeking God's guidance. God is our *"emergency crew"* Who will always arrive in time to shut off the current of danger and inform us what to do whenever we call upon Him.

"Be still, and see that I am God." (Psalms 45:11)

⨾ O God, help me in all times of trial to seek Thy guidance, and to fully trust in Thy protection.

BREAD UPON THE WATERS

When Franz Lehar was a young, unknown composer he dined one night in a small, obscure restaurant in Paris. After dinner he found to his dismay that he could not pay his check because he had lost his pocketbook.

The manager, impressed by his sincerity, overlooked the matter and even offered to lend him the money with which to buy a return ticket to Vienna.

Lehar never forgot this act of kindness. Later, when writing *"The Merry Widow,"* he made the little restaurant famous by putting it into his popular operetta with its Café Maxim song.

We often wish that we could do some wonderful thing for God. In seeking the *"big service"* we may forget that we are constantly being given opportunities to show our love for God by helping others. For what we do for others, we really do for God, and God always rewards those who serve Him.

There is no act of kindness, however small, that is not seen and remembered by our Heavenly Father.

"Whosoever shall give to drink to one of these little ones a cup of cold water only in the name of a disciple, amen I say to you, he shall not lose his reward." (Matthew 10:42)

⤳ O Holy Spirit, inspire me to look only to Thee for my reward.

HOPE FOR THE FUTURE

A 58-year-old widow in Chicago was walking along the street one evening when a thief snatched her pocketbook and sprinted off. In it was $10,000, her life savings.

A few days later she received a bulky envelope in the mail. When she opened it a quantity of well-worn bills dropped out—and with them a note from the thief which read: *"I'm sorry for causing you a lot of trouble. But when I opened the purse I was just as scared as you were. I never expected to find that much money. If I did I never would have taken it. I learned my lesson."*

Upon counting the money, the woman found that all of it had been returned except $20.

The man in this story wanted to be honest, but he didn't quite make it. We would all agree that men are never going to be without some defects, as much as they may try to avoid them. But it's important to remember that the more we know God's law and try to keep it, the less likely we are to do wrong in a big way.

"Turn thou to thy God: keep mercy and judgment, and hope in thy God always." (Osee 12:6)

     ᴇᴇ O Father of Mercy, help me to keep Thy law even in little things.

DARING MAN WANTED

An advertisement in a French newspaper read: *"Man wanted to work in dynamite factory. Must be willing to travel."*

We often wonder who it was that took this job. He must have been a man of some daring. He certainly had to be prepared—if not willing—to *"travel"* in more ways than one.

We would have peace almost overnight if enough people could be found to show the same daring for God. Most of us, at some time or other, have had secret yearnings for a life of brave adventure. Yet often, when this opportunity presents itself to do some daring thing we fail to take advantage of it. Perhaps this is because we are fearful or unduly cautious. Could it be, too, that we do not love God enough?

In our day, the *"children of darkness"* are more willing to accept a dangerous assignment than are the *"children of light."* The zeal displayed by those following evil often puts Christian people to shame, for we are given the same opportunity to work with equal fervor for Our Lord.

"I press towards the mark, to the prize of the supernal vocation of God in Christ Jesus." (Philippians 3:14)

❧ O Divine Savior, make me zealous for Thy Truth, no matter what it may cost me.

HASTE MAKES WASTE

A California highway inspector claims that 90 per-cent of automobile accidents are directly or indirectly due to speed.

If speed were reduced even moderately, 50 per-cent of lives lost in highway accidents would be saved—many more if speed were cut down drastically.

Defective brakes frequently cause accidents that could have been avoided if drivers had been willing to take a little time to shift into second or low gear instead of depending on their brakes.

Accidents often do serious harm to innocent people as well as to those causing them. The driver's late remorse is of little use in restoring smashed bodies.

Haste can make a lot of waste especially in driving a car. If the average motorist would realize that driving carefully is an expression of love and consideration for his fellow man, he would be inclined to show the same restraint that he would expect from others.

"The love of our neighbor worketh no evil. Love therefore is the fulfilling of the law." (Romans 13:10)

⊷ O God, help me to control myself so that my life may be of benefit to others.

TEST OF LOVE

An Army patrol in Korea was caught in a Red ambush. There was bitter fighting with hand grenades and small arms.

When an American soldier fell wounded to the ground, the patrol's corporal threw himself over his body to shield him from bursting Red grenades. Said the corporal: *"He'd have done the same for me."*

Most of us act readily enough when we are approached to give to a charity drive, or when we are pressed into doing a good deed.

But all too few of us do good works spontaneously out of a deep love for God and man—not because we have to, but because we want to.

The secret of a happy life is in serving men—even to the point of sacrificing your life—solely because your love of God prompts you to.

"Greater love than this no man hath, that a man lay down his life for his friends." (John 15:13)

❧ Lord, teach me to do everything for love of Thee.

WELL ANYWAY, HE READ THEM!

A poor man, who became suddenly rich, had little knowledge of literature. He thought that he ought to have some good books in his house, and asked a friend to buy some for him. Soon his library was stocked with the best works in English literature. He was most pleased, and wrote a letter of thanks to his friend in which he said:

"Thanks for the fine books you got me. I like very much those plays by Mr. Shakespeare and the poems by Mr. Browning. Do me a favor. If these authors put out any new books, please get them for me."

Though we may laugh at this man and his limited knowledge of literature, we must concede that it was better for him to try to learn something about this subject than to completely ignore it.

Many of us don't try to do something new, because we are afraid that we will make mistakes and be laughed at. But unless we are willing to risk mistakes, we will never be able to accomplish anything worthwhile. God's children may venture fearlessly into the untried and unknown, for we know we are in His unfailing care and under His everlasting protection.

"What shall we then say to these things? If God be for us, who is against us?" (Romans 8:31)

〜§ O Lord, teach us not to be afraid of the new and the different in serving Thee.

HIDDEN TREASURE

Twenty years ago, a doctor in South Bend, Ind., found a ring. Its stone and setting were so discolored that he tossed it into a drawer considering it of little worth.

Recently his daughter went to work in a jewelry store, where she learned to evaluate precious stones. Remembering the ring her father had found, she cleaned and examined it. To her amazement she discovered that it was worth not $50 or $100 as she had thought, but $1500.

Isn't it quite possible that you have an undetected diamond of great worth in the form of a talent that you somehow never got around to developing; a field of endeavor you always wanted to explore, but lacked the courage; a service you could render for the love of God that you never made the time for?

It's amazing, how once we begin to search for worth in the things we always had, how many more we discover that we didn't know were there.

"The kingdom of heaven is like to a merchant seeking good pearls. Who when he had found one pearl of great price, went his way, and sold all that he had, and bought it." (Matthew 13:45,46)

◦§ O Lord, help me to discover and use all my talents for Thy service.

67

IT'S QUALITY THAT COUNTS

Shakespeare said, *"Brevity is the soul of wit."* It is certainly true that the wisest and deepest thoughts have been expressed in few words.

For instance, the Book of Genesis in the Bible tells the story of creation in 400 words.

The Ten Commandments, found in the Book of Exodus—also in the Bible—contain only 297 words.

The Declaration of Independence, which set forth the basic principles upon which America is founded, used but 1321 words.

And Lincoln delivered his famous Gettysburg address in 266 words.

We may sometimes forget that, as with words, it's the quality of our deeds—not the size of them—that counts.

God doesn't expect most of us to do spectacular things. But He does expect us to do as much as we can to spread His love and truth. He has given each of us a share in His love and wants us to pass it on to those who need it so much. Any little thing you do may have far-reaching effects for time and for eternity.

"Ever follow that which is good towards each other, and towards all men." (I Thessalonians 5:15)

&§ O Divine Savior, teach me to share Thy love with others in everything I do.

ALL GOD'S CHILDREN

The proprietor of a grocery store in San Francisco was about to close up for the night when a customer came in and made a purchase. As he was about to leave, he pulled a gun from his pocket, ordered the grocer into a back room, and fled with a large sum of money taken from the cash register.

A moment later, as the grocer was telephoning the police, the thief rushed back into the store, tore the phone from the wall and shouted to his victim, *"I knew I couldn't trust you."*

It is strange how in the affairs of men and nations, even the most dishonest expect others to be trustworthy.

How much more necessary it is for the children of light, to consciously respect all men, and to render good-will to each, even those we do not particularly like. We can do this just by heeding our basic instincts, but we can also do it in His name, as He invited us.

"And as you would that men should do to you, do you also to them in like manner." (Luke 6:31)

❧ Heavenly Father, help me to regard all men as Thy children.

ABANDONED PROPERTY

In a recent edition of a New York newspaper, there appeared a long list of names. The persons whose names were listed were being notified by a large insurance company that they were entitled to abandoned property in amounts of twenty-five dollars or more, which if unclaimed by a certain date would be paid to the Comptroller of the State.

Maybe your name wasn't among those listed in the newspaper, but every person on earth is entitled to a share in God's kingdom. All you have to do is step up and claim it.

God has put a great fortune at our disposal in giving us unlimited talents. When we fail to use them, either through ignorance of their existence, or through indifference, like the property belonging to those people, these blessings become lost to us altogether.

But if every one of us took full advantage of all the wonderful things God gives to us, to benefit both ourselves and others, wouldn't we practically overnight realize a miracle of peace and prosperity?

"Behold, I say to you, lift up your eyes, and see the countries, for they are white already to harvest." (John 4:35)

Grant, O Lord, that I may see and use for good the countless advantages that Thou dost put at the disposal of those who love Thee.

THE STRENGTH OF LOVE

In Astoria, Oregon, a young boy was driving a 3000 pound truck when it skidded off a road and overturned on the bank of a river. The boy was pinned face-down by the truck under two feet of water.

His father, a forty-two-year old man, five-foot eight-inches tall, and weighing only 165 pounds, saw the accident from a nearby farmhouse. He rushed to the scene and with tremendous effort pushed the truck from its side onto the wheels. Then he administered artificial respiration until a State Patrolman came to his aid. The doctor who attended the boy said that the father's feat was "superhuman."

The father's love for his boy provided him with the necessary strength to rescue him. The love of a parent for a child is perhaps the most powerful of human emotions.

It should bring us great comfort and courage when we think about the fact that God loves us more than it is possible for any earthly father to do. There can be no danger too great for Him to save us from, and no need too large for Him to meet.

"But in all these things we overcome, because of Him that hath loved us." (Romans 8:37)

ﾍ§ O Lord, help us always to trust in Thy boundless love.

GENIUS IN TAKING PAINS

In Amarillo, Texas, an armored truck was robbed of $8652 less than 50 feet from offices of the F.B.I., the U.S. marshal and the sheriff.

Investigation proved that somehow the thieves had obtained the lock from the truck's door some days prior to the theft, and had *"fixed"* it so that it could be opened with a skeleton key. They then replaced the lock, and waited patiently many days for the opportunity to pull the robbery.

We are often astounded at the infinite pains criminals take in perpetrating their crimes. They will go to any lengths to obtain what they want.

We who wish for the really good things are usually not so apt to be zealous. Is it that we do not *want* as intensely as they do? It would be good to realize that we cannot force zeal.

To really persist in finding or doing something, we must love what we are seeking with all our hearts. When we learn to love God with our whole hearts we will find it easy to follow in His way.

"I know thy works that thou are neither cold, nor hot. I would thou wert cold, or hot." (Apocalypse 3:15)

&§ O Holy Spirit, inspire us with the zeal of Thy love.

A NECESSARY SOLUTION

A woman went to visit a friend who lived in a beautiful part of the countryside, but in a rather primitive cottage.

As she was preparing to retire for the night, the hostess appeared at the door. *"If you should want anything that you don't have,"* she said, *"just ask for it. We can show you how you can do without it."*

There are times when it is necessary for all of us to know how to *"make do."* To neglect a duty because we don't have all the things needed to do it, may cause us to miss a glorious opportunity to further God's kingdom.

When we truly want to do God's will, we are prepared to use whatever we have on hand to do it with, trusting in Him to provide for our needs as they arise. Those who have done this can vouch that God never fails.

"Better is a little to the just, than the great riches of the wicked." (Psalms 36:16)

O Lord, show me how to use the things I have now, and trust in Thee for the rest.

OF SUCH IS THE KINGDOM

The parents of a tot in Chicago taught him to swim when he was only 18 months old. Six months later, in company with his older brother, he was playing near a deep water-filled excavation when he slipped and fell in. He thrashed around and kept himself afloat while his brother ran home to get their mother. Upon arriving on the scene she pulled her little boy out of the water.

Often we neglect to teach our youngsters important things because we feel that they are too young. But if the parents of this child had failed to afford him the opportunity to learn to swim they would have been faced with a bitter tragedy.

How often the moral collapse or tragic end of some are attributable to a failure of their parents to develop their moral or spiritual sense. How many saints, statesmen, writers, and the like, are lost to the human race because the talent they had was never activated by short-sighted parents?

"Suffer the little children to come unto me, and forbid they not; for of such is the kingdom of God." (Matthew 10:14)

⋅⊰ O God, help me never to neglect an opportunity to help a little child develop in the right way.

AFTER FIFTY YEARS

An Atlantic City newspaper, with a rare streak of nostalgic sentimentality, recently devoted an entire page to photographs of several men who had attended the same public school, showing them as they appeared fifty years ago and as they are today.

It was interesting to note the diversity of occupations that have claimed these schoolboys of half a century ago. There were listed: doctor, lawyer, former city magistrate, conductor and composer, dentist, writer, teacher, salesman, manufacturer, to mention only a few. Certainly a class of which their former teachers could have been proud!

We wonder if many present-day teachers wouldn't be surprised if they could look into the future and see what the youngsters now entrusted to their care will become.

Most teachers never know the quality and degree of the influence they have had upon their students. But it is certain that each one contributes in some measure to the development of each student, whether good or bad. This knowledge bears a grave responsibility, but also offers an exciting challenge. We can't all be teachers, but we can each help to see that our children have good ones.

"Call together the people unto me, that they may hear my words, and may learn to fear me all the time that they may live on the earth and teach their children." (Deuteronomy 4:10)

⋖ O God, help us be better teachers to our children.

A REASON TO LIVE

When Joseph Jefferson, the noted actor, was past 70, he suddenly acquired a great enthusiasm for gardening. On being asked the reason he replied, *"The saddest thing in old age is the absence of expectation. Now a garden is full of expectation—and you get a lot of things you don't expect, too."*

There's a magic in expectation. Anyone who has seen a dream through from conception to realization will tell you that the greatest pleasure has been not so much in the final success as the working and planning towards it.

This expectation is the basis for the virtue of hope. Just as we can expect things and projects to succeed, similarly we can hope that God will bring our whole life to a happy conclusion.

All we have to do is to do our best in the small things and then hope and trust that God will bring all to fruition.

"A good tree cannot bring forth evil fruit, neither can an evil tree bring forth good fruit." (Matthew 7:18)

O Lord, help me to be good, think good, and do good.

NEVER OUT OF RANGE

A burglar in Syracuse, New York, was caught red-handed. He had unfortunately chosen to rob a mechanically-minded storekeeper who had rigged up a device attaching a camera to his cash register, so that anyone trying to steal its contents would immediately be photographed, and would set off a burglar alarm as well.

No doubt this burglar had the surprise of his life at being caught and so unmistakably identified.

Because we can't see Him, we often forget that God sees us. If we could remember this fact all the time, we would certainly live different lives. It is because we think we are alone, separated from God, that we so often fall into sin; that we so often neglect to do the things we should do.

But Jesus told us that the very hairs on our heads are numbered, and nothing about us is hidden from God. When we are tempted to wrong, it would be good if we would remember that we are never out of range of the camera of God's vision.

"Neither is there any creature invisible in his sight: but all things are naked and open to his eyes, to whom our speech is." (Hebrews 4:31)

⇜ Holy Father, help me to always remember that You see me.

77

PROOF ENOUGH

A mechanic was called in to repair the mechanism of a giant telescope. During the noon hour the chief astronomer came upon the man reading the Bible. *"What good do you expect from that?"* he asked. *"The Bible is out of date. Why, you don't even know who wrote it."*

The mechanic puzzled for a moment. Then he looked up. *"Don't you make considerable use of the multiplication tables in your calculations?"*

"Yes, of course," returned the other

"Do you know who wrote them?"

"Why, I guess I don't."

"Then," said the mechanic, *"how can you trust the multiplication tables when you don't know who wrote them?"*

"I trust them because they work, of course," the astronomer explained testily.

"Well, I trust the Bible for the same reason. It works."

The Bible works because it is the truth. And the truth works because God is its Creator. Since God is in last analysis the Author of the Bible, and since He is Creator of the world, the principles of the Bible and those of human life must agree. God cannot contradict Himself. He could not author a book that did not *"work."*

"You shall know the truth, and the truth shall make you free." (John 8:32)

⋙ O Lord, strengthen our trust in Thee.

NO ROSES WITHOUT THORNS

In a General Motors laboratory hangs this motto: *"The price of progress is trouble."*

Anyone who expects to make a great success out of anything without some difficulty is in for a great disappointment. Not only do we have to work hard for the goal we are trying to attain, but we also have to be prepared to face many set-backs, and to overcome unforseen difficulties. It would seem that the greater the reward we seek, the greater the problems.

We should remember too that we do not work alone. God comes more than half way. And even if we fail, He can turn our failure into victory. God wants our efforts more than He wants our results.

So when it seems that the troubles we face in doing the things we want are more than we can bear, we can remind ourselves that if we are faithful in the end we shall receive our reward.

"And he that shall overcome, and keep my works unto the end, I will give him power over the nations." (Apocalypse 2:26)

 O Lord, help me not to become discouraged by difficulties.

IF HE ONLY HAD!

A wealthy recluse grew very fond of the night elevator operator in her hotel. Confined mostly to her room, she did not see a great deal of him, but when she did she never failed to stop and have a pleasant chat. One day she asked him to write down the names of his children on a sheet of paper, put it in an envelope, and leave it in her mail-box. She indicated that she wanted to remember them in her will.

The elevator operator became so busy that he forgot all about it.

A couple of months later the woman died, leaving quite a fortune to about four people. The operator's children were not included.

Often the great opportunities, the "big breaks," depend upon our doing one small action, or saying one little word at the right time. To open the way to big opportunities, we must try to consider even the smallest task as important. If it is worth doing at all it is worth doing well and on time. We never know what wonderful good may come to pass as a result of doing one small thing well for God.

"Well done, thou good servant, because thou hast been faithful in a little, thou shalt have power over ten cities." (Luke 19:17)

≈§ O God, help me never to miss the slightest opportunity to serve Thee.

CARRYING A GOOD THING TOO FAR

An elementary teacher in Houston, Texas, instructed her students to be quiet while she was out of the room. The students obeyed. No one said a word when a strange man came into the room and spoke to them. *"You children must be awfully good for the teacher not to be here,"* he said. He went to the teacher's desk, stole her purse containing $7, and departed, smiling at the still silent children.

The teacher had done a good thing to teach her children obedience, but she had failed to teach them the equally valuable lesson of using common sense.

Blind obedience can be a very harmful thing. God gave us free will and the right to exert it.

We do children a great disservice when we stifle their initiative. How much better if we train them to direct their energies into good constructive channels and thus train them for lives of service and dedication.

"When I was yet young, before I wandered about, I sought for wisdom openly in my prayer." (Ecclesiasticus 51:18).

&§ O Lord, teach us to keep our minds open to Thy wisdom.

THE LONG VIEW

Ben Hogan, famous golf champion, was asked in the course of an interview what it took to make a champion. Among other things he said that many fine golfers failed to do well at tournament golf because they were unable to take the *"long view."*

In tournament golf, the golfer must prepare himself both physically and mentally to play for many days. He must not permit himself to become discouraged by a day's failure, however bad, because he must realize that in the final count it will be the average of many days' scores that determines whether he has won or lost. Many golfers, Hogan says, become discouraged when there are no immediate signs of victory and give up.

Having the *"long view"* in any undertaking is most important to ultimate success in anything. Many important schemes have fallen through because those involved became disheartened by seeming failure, and were unable to see that in the long run those same failures could contribute to success.

To give up when the "going is rough" is truly to fail. Let those who work for God's peace on earth and good will among men, learn to take the "long view" when it seems least promising and then refuse to give up.

"But he that shall persevere to the end, he shall be saved." (Matthew 24:13)

ₑ§ Dear Lord, fill my heart with courage to complete all I undertake.

NEVER TOO LATE

In a Greenwich Village apartment lives a woman who reached sudden fame as a writer. She is 70 years old.

This woman has been a writer for many years, but her works received little recognition until she decided to begin a completely new style of writing.

Recently, she was given a coveted award for outstanding work in the field of literature. She told interviewers, *"I feel that at last I have found my way. I have a great deal to say and not much time to say it."*

Many people recognizing that at 70 there is *"not much time to say it,"* would not have attempted to say it at all, and would not have reaped the unbelievable success this woman has.

She is only one of the many examples to prove that it's never too late to begin doing something worthwhile. If you have been thinking that it is too late in your life to begin doing something constructive for God, remember that it is always "better late than never."

"But about the eleventh hour he went out and found others standing, and he saith to them: Why stand ye here all the day idle? They saith to him: Because no man hath hired us. He saith to them: Go ye also into my vineyard." (Matthew 20:6, 7)

✒ Holy Spirit, teach me not to seek excuses for failing to serve Thee.

WHERE'S THE FIRE?

An editor of a newspaper in New Jersey lifted his telephone one day to find out where the fire engines he heard were heading. He never completed the call. The engines stopped outside his office. The fire was in the newspaper's press room.

It seems a human failing to "look for fires" anywhere but close to ourselves. Individuals blame their neighbors for any unpleasantnesses in the neighborhood. Nations blame each other for the world's unrest. No one willingly assumes the burden of blame. Yet thinking people must realize that the responsibility for solving problems lies with every one.

If we would learn to face up squarely to issues, and then to resolutely go about correcting them, we would find the *"fires"* immeasurably easier to put out. Moreover, it would avert much resentment, if we could remember that criticism, like charity, begins at home.

"And why seest thou the mote in thy brother's eye: but the beam that is in thine own eye thou considerest not?" (Luke 7:41)

ò O Lord, help us to see ourselves as Thou seest us.

WHY DO I LOVE YOU?

After rescuing a fellow-townsman from his burning home, a Moffat, Ontario, grocer declared modestly: *"Anyone would have done the same thing. He was a very good customer."*

Every imaginable sin is the result of selfishness. The reason we stray away from God, and hurt ourselves and others, is that we love ourselves more than anyone else.

Although possibly, this grocer did not mean to attribute his saving of his neighbor to the fact that the man was a good customer of his, yet we cannot help but see a sort of mental connection there.

Doing something for others with an eye to their value to us, means of course that we really love ourselves more than them. Being unselfishly loving is perhaps the most difficult of virtues to acquire. If we honestly search ourselves we will see that we love mostly because we are in some way repaid by that person. But a persistent effort to practice unselfish love is really worthwhile, for we will find that we are rewarded by a far greater intimacy with God. And that is the one thing that all men, whether they recognize it or not, hunger after.

"He that loveth not, knoweth not God: for God is charity. (1 John 4:8)

&⸹ O Heavenly Father, give me grace to love only for Thy love's sake.

A CHANGE FOR THE BETTER

The highly responsible position of assistant Cabinet member was offered to a businessman. He was about to refuse the job when his wife reminded him that he was among those who always complained that there should be better people in government. Now, she pointed out, he had the chance to do something positive about it. The man began to realize the truth in his wife's persuasive arguments. He changed his mind, accepted the job, and started to work hard for the benefit of all Americans.

So often we shrink from responsible positions because of the great demands they make on our time and energies. This, however, does not usually hinder us from criticizing those who occupy these posts. If we really loved God and our fellow men, we would welcome these positions even when they involve sacrifice, knowing that by doing what is our duty we are being pleasing to God.

If there is no such position that you can take, maybe you can be of great influence in helping someone else see his obligation to serve where needed.

"Jesus saith to them: My meat is to do the will of him that sent me, that I may perfect his work." (St. John 4:34)

❧ O Lord, let me never fail to accept a responsibility to serve others better for love of Thee.

IT'S THE LAST ONE THAT COUNTS

Big powerful Jim Jeffries was one of the great prize-fighters of all time. His ring career lasted nineteen years, and in that time he chalked up an astounding record as a boxer.

In nineteen years Jeffries lost only one fight—his last one. The one oddly enough, for which he is most remembered. Until the time of this bout with Jack Johnson, Jeffries had been retired for many years. But his record of undefeated champion was tarnished by this one last bout into which he had been forced by public demand.

The strangest thing about the adulation of the crowd is the way it's here today and gone tomorrow. As long as the hero is a winner, he may count on the glitter and the gold. But as soon as he loses, as soon as a success "flops," in the eyes of the world he ceases to be of interest. As far as worldly success goes, it is always the *"last one"* that counts.

It is a comfort to us that God does not reckon success as men do. In the sight of God, what matters is not whether we are winning or losing, but whether or not we are doing the very best we can. If we are, in the sight of God we are always winners.

"And behold, they are last that shall be first: and they are first that shall be last." (Luke 13:30)

✑ O God, help me not to work for worldly honor, but for Thee.

HOW NOT TO DEVELOP ULCERS

A doctor in Dallas, Texas addressing a convention of the Southern Medical Association, said that more than 15 million persons in the United States either have, or will have ulcers before they die.

Doctors now understand that stomach ulcers are the result of varied mental tensions. Persons free from anxieties and resentments of any kind, who are happily and fruitfully employed, are not known to develop ulcers. For that matter they are not apt to develop any serious illnesses. But in a world that makes so many constant demands on our nerves and energies, it is difficult to maintain the perfect mental health required to be perfectly healthy physically. However, we can try.

How, you ask? Well first of all, we can take our worries to God, and believe with our whole hearts that He is going to help us to solve them. Then we can "spring-clean" our hearts, to make sure that there isn't any ugly hate or resentment eating at them. Then we can start loving everybody so much that we want to get out and do something to help them. However you choose to show your love for others, you'll find that it will make you so happy that you won't have time to worry.

"For all healing is from God." (Ecclesiasticus 38:2)

&§ O God, heal us by Thy Love.

WELL, THAT FIXED IT!

In Oakland, California, a man's car broke down one time too many. He picked up a .22 rifle, pumped several shots into the tires, smashed the radiator and spark plugs with a rock, tore out the upholstery and set fire to the remains.

All of us, who at some time or other have been sorely tempted to lose our tempers, feel a sort of amused sympathy for this man. But we are sure that when his temper subsided, and he viewed the damage he had done he must have felt rather ashamed of his childish outburst, and the result to his own property.

Giving in to temper never accomplishes anything. Rather, it can cause great damage not only to the object or person on which it is vented, but also great physical and mental suffering to the person who loses self-control. The old injunction given to children, *"count ten,"* holds doubly true for adults, for we are unable to do anything constructive at all when dominated by temper.

"And let every man be swift to hear, but slow to speak, and slow to anger. For the anger of man worketh not the justice of God." (James 1:19, 20)

⇜§ O Lord, teach us self-control.

TOO MUCH OF A GOOD THING

Three teen-age boys in Canada broke into a factory which manufactured chocolates and devoured fifty pounds of candy. Hailed into court they told the judge, *"We'll never eat another chocolate."*

Striking a happy medium is not an easy thing for many people to do. Most of us tend to excesses in some form or another. Some play too much and work too little, while some work too much and play not at all. This leads to a character imbalance that eventually distorts individual personality. Particularly is this true of the insatiable pleasure-seekers. Their orgies of enjoyment leave them ill and unhappy, but so ingrained does the habit become that they seek solace in further excesses.

True contentment is the reward of the man who learns that all things, if used wisely, have the power to bless him, but if permitted to dominate him, will curse and destroy.

"By surfeiting, many have perished: But he that is temperate, shall prolong life." (Ecclesiasticus 37:34)

⚜ O Lord, help us to be temperate.

MARATHON!

A French pianist recently set a new record of 245 hours of steady piano playing. This sets a new world record for marathon piano playing, capping by one hour the last record which was set by a German pianist.

We read of many instances of people entering marathon contests, and are often puzzled as to the motives. There would hardly seem to be much point to people driving themselves unnecessarily to the point of exhaustion. To eat more than the other fellow, to circle a dance floor longer, to walk further, would seem to most of us to be the height of stupidity. We say instinctively, *"Why?"*

The instinct which urges us to excel can be a great blessing or a useless thing. It all depends on what we try to excel in. Let us harness this energy to the highest and most useful goals.

Wouldn't it be a wonderful thing if we could all become marathon God-lovers? That would be the one marathon that could never exhaust us, but turn us into glorious, powerful creatures.

"And God created man to His own image: to the image of God he created him: male and female he created them." (Genesis 1:27)

⊷ O God, help me to love Thee, Who art my Creator.

IT DOESN'T TAKE MUCH

A raccoon climbed a power pole and short-circuited a high-tension electric line in a small town in New York. Scorched fur was found at the spot. For half an hour service was interrupted for 1,200 customers.

So often when we trace the reasons for immense disasters we discover that they arose from trivial things . . . A raccoon, enough to discomfort a whole town . . . one small rotted apple, enough to ruin a full barrel . . . a trifling personal defect, enough to degenerate a character . . . one evil citizen, enough to devastate a nation.

Happily this also works in reverse. A small cake of yeast, enough to leaven many loaves of bread . . . one minute seed, enough to grow a tall magnificent tree. One fine person, enough to spread his influence to the far corners of the earth. . . . It doesn't take much. Though each of us is only one out of many millions, we count!

"So I say to you, there shall be joy before the angels of God upon one sinner doing penance." (Luke 15:10)

✍ Holy Spirit, teach me the importance of little things.

SO THEY LAUGHED

Alexander Graham Bell began making experiments when he was a child, often to the great amusement of his parents. Once when visitors came to call his father told them: *"Alexander is in the kitchen. His mother gave him a glass of water, and he put a piece of wire in it. He thinks he's talking through it."* Everybody laughed.

Somehow, people are always amused at the new and the different. Respect for inventors and discoverers is hard won. Yet, in the cases of those who have proved their point, the scoffers have served the unexpected purpose of adding a deeper incentive for the ridiculed person to succeed.

Those who work conscientiously to serve God, even when it means departure from the beaten tracks, are usually regarded as "strange" to say the least.

If the dictates of your heart and conscience have led you into some "different" activities, don't permit the "wet blankets" to discourage you. Remember that Our Lord was continually being mocked and discounted.

"Blessed are they that suffer persecution for justice' sake: for theirs is the kingdom of heaven." (Matthew 5: 10)

&s Dear Lord, help us to persevere in serving Thee, no matter what others may say.

93

SUFFERING IS REWARDED

A waterfront worker in New Jersey invented a *"grain trimmer."* It was a machine which shot grain into the hold of a ship in a fine, even spray. With the grain thus evenly distributed, the cargo no longer shifted with the movement of the ship, which in the past had actually covered up men working in the hold and smothered them.

The inventor's employer gave him $10 for the idea and promised to protect his interests. But the U.S. District Court in Philadelphia decided otherwise when it awarded the inventor 50 per-cent of the profits earned by his machine. They amounted to $96,969.

Often we don't receive our just returns in this life. We are misunderstood, criticized and laughed at, even when doing things for God and others. But never fear—the real reward will come after death. The more you suffer here for love of God and others, the greater will be your reward in heaven, which will last for all eternity!

"Give, and it shall be given to you: good measure and pressed down and shaken together and running over shall they give into your bosom." (Luke 6:38)

⚓ O Heavenly Father, give me the courage to endure anything for Thee, knowing that Thy reward will be far greater than anything the world can give.

ALIVE OR DEAD?

Nicholas Murray Butler once said that the tombstone of a great many people should read: *"Died at thirty, buried at sixty."*

It would be a good thing if everyone now and then stopped to take an inventory of himself to discover whether or not he is really alive. If one is miserable and tense and bewildered he is not really alive. Being alive is enjoying life to its fullest; living so that each moment is a glorious experience, active, happy, purposeful.

Yes, you say, but how? Well the quickest way to make living so unpleasant that it is more death than life, is to make self your exclusive concern. The more you turn your attention inward to self, the more negatives you discover. The secret of full living is to apply the magic potion of love. This means, first of all, loving God with all your heart, and mind, and strength. It follows that loving God means loving all His children without exception: Loving them so well that your attention is centered on ways to help them. Real love always finds ways to express itself, and soon life becomes a living moving joyful force.

"My dearest, if God hath so loved us, we also ought to love one another." (1 John 4:11)

⇜ Holy Spirit, teach me true love for others.

GOD TO THE RESCUE

A woman trapped on a trestle in Alton, Illinois, flattened herself between the rails while a passenger train thundered over her. She escaped with nothing more than a few scratches, still clutching a paper bag which contained her lunch. Later she said: *"It's a miracle. I guess God was with me."*

You know, if you asked the question, *"Where is God?"* practically everyone would answer, *"God is everywhere."* If you asked further, *"Does that mean that God is here now with you?"* the person might look a little surprised, but he would answer, *"Yes."*

It is a sad fact that although we know that God is constantly with us, we seldom become aware of it except in times of crisis, like this woman. The greatest miracle in the world is one most of us hardly even notice, that is that God is with us, not just sometimes but every moment of our lives. Perhaps it is because it is such a wonderful thing that we are afraid to believe it, except in times of great stress. The only reason we have so many difficulties at all, is that we forget that God is right here for us to call on for advice, for help, and for guidance.

"Do I not fill heaven and earth, saith the Lord?" (Jeremiah 23:24)

❧ O God, help me to feel Thy Presence.

EVERYONE CAN DO SOMETHING

Christ chose not only the just to help Him, but He encouraged many a sinner to play a role in spreading His love. The more they did in this way, the better they became.

Startling as it may seem, even a pagan in darkest Africa or a Communist in the heart of America who learns even one of Christ's truths—and tries to spread that truth in the life stream of his land—is beginning to be, in a limited way at least, a Christopher or Christ-bearer, whether or not he realizes it.

The more one does for Christ, the closer he draws to Christ. You, in your own way, can be a bearer of that True Light *"which enlighteneth every man that cometh into this world."* The world itself can be a bit the better because you are in it.

Yes, you can be a partner with Him Who said: "I am the Way, and the Truth, and the Life." (John 14:6)

⋙ O God, help me to draw others to Thee, not keep them away.

FORGIVE AND FORGET

Forty-two years before Christ was born, there lived a man named Publilius Syrus who said: *"The remedy for wrongs is to forget them."*

Although it is reasonably easy to forget the wrongs we do to others, it seems to be so difficult to forget the wrongs that others do to us. We are inclined to magnify our grievances, to nurse and nurture them in our minds until they grow to alarming proportions. Before we realize it, our real or imagined hurts have become the main point in our thinking, and we are torn by the resentments that we have allowed to possess us.

Our Lord knew that hate and anger destroy the soul. His constant teaching was that we learn to love and forgive even as we expect our Heavenly Father to love and forgive us. To forgive someone truly is to put away all thought of the wrong that has been done, and to love them as before. Then we are really keeping God's Commandments, and our souls will be at peace.

"And when they were come to the place which is called Calvary, they crucified him there: and the robbers, one on the right hand and one on the left. And Jesus said, 'Father, forgive them for they know not what they do.'" (Luke 23:33-34)

&ᴥ O Holy Spirit, give us forgiving hearts.

LIFT UP YOUR HEART

You have probably heard many times the expression *"the pause that refreshes."* But have you ever thought of applying it to yourself in a spiritual way?

This is all you have to do. Take a few moments out each day to lift up your heart and mind to God.

In less than a minute you can, in your own way, make up a prayer that will contain the four essentials of the perfect prayer:

1) *Adoration*—Find any words you like to tell your Maker that you know He is the beginning and end of all life, the Author of our liberty here, the Fulfillment of our joy for all eternity.

2) *Thanksgiving*—Express gratitude for your many blessings—faith, health, education, and for the talents, few or many, entrusted to you.

3) *Petition*—Ask to be His instrument in reaching as many persons as possible during your lifetime with the peace of Heaven for which all men on earth so ardently yearn.

4) *Contrition*—Express regret for any mistakes you have made in lack of love for God and your fellowman.

If you make this a daily habit you will find that it truly is *"the pause that refreshes."* You will develop within yourself a strength that will give new meaning and purpose to the most menial tasks.

"I am the Way, and the Truth, and the Life." (John 14:6)

⋇ Help me, O Lord of Hosts, to be ever mindful that because Thou art always near, I have nothing to fear.

99

A GREAT DAY COMING

A woman who had just passed her sixtieth birthday had practically convinced herself that she was much younger than she looked.

Starting off early one Spring day, in all her finery—complete with a chic hat that she felt sure made her look years younger—she set out on a round that would take her to the beauty parlor, to the Ritz for lunch, and shopping and theatre for the afternoon.

Stepping spryly out of a taxi-cab, and full of zest for the big day ahead of her, she complimented the cab driver for the cautious manner in which he made his way through traffic. Highly pleased he thought he was returning the compliment when he said: *"Thanks, lady, I know how to handle old people like you!"*

That chance remark quickly subdued her. For the first time she felt every one of her sixty years. But it did more. It made her pause and think that she should be getting ready for eternity and not act only as if she had nothing to do but live on here forever.

"I am the resurrection and the life. He that believeth in me, although he be dead shall live." (John 11:25)

⋑ O God, help me to be ever conscious that I am but a pilgrim in this life.

LEAVING IT TO GEORGE

A poll was recently taken in New York State to determine what percentage of the adult population would favor their sons entering the field of politics. Only 28 per-cent said a definite "*yes.*" Six per-cent were of no opinion, and 66 per-cent were flatly against it.

Here are two of the main reasons given by those who said they would not want their sons in politics: "*There's too much graft and corruption in politics,*" and "*It's too hard for a politician to be honest.*"

By discouraging young people with high ideals from entering the field of government, parents may be playing into the hands of those who would wreck our country through the help of corrupt, inefficient or apathetic workers.

Until more people, fired with love of God and country, take up the responsibility of seeing to it that all men are provided with good government, a change for the better cannot come.

"*As the judge of the people is himself, so also are his ministers: and what manner of man the ruler of a city is, such also are they that dwell within.*" (Ecclesiasticus 10:2)

⊷§ Heavenly Father, give us the grace to be laborers for Thee, instead of laborers only for ourselves.

PENNY WISE

A woman in Iowa fumbling in her purse dropped a coin which rolled under her car. Unable to find it, she moved the car. In doing so she lost control of the car, and it rammed a parking meter, swiped the side of a building, and lurched half a block down the sidewalk. The damage amounted to $102. It was later discovered that the lost coin was a penny.

Not many of us would admit to being as "penny wise" and "pound foolish" as this woman. Probably most of us have a reasonably sound sense of values when it comes to money. But how many of us are as wise when it comes to our lives?

If we will permit ourselves true honesty, we might have to admit that we have often chased after the lesser things, and lost sight completely of the greater values. Often the cost of the trifling things has been far too dear in the toll they have taken on our time, our talents, and our energies. Let us make it a daily habit to ask God's help in seeing clearly what is worthwhile, and His grace to follow it.

"Seek ye therefore first the kingdom of God, and his justice, and all these things shall be added to you." (Matthew 6:33)

❧ O God, help me to serve Thee according to Thy will.

NOT WITHOUT CRITICISM

The CHICAGO TIMES, ninety-odd years ago, had this to say about the address that Lincoln delivered at Gettysburg:

"The cheek of every American must tingle with shame as he reads the silly, flat, and dishwatery utterances of the man who has to be pointed out to intelligent foreigners as the President of the United States."

Everyone who has ever risen to the level of greatness has found himself in for criticism.

You will probably find that the greater the service, the greater the criticism. There is no crown without a cross, but just as Lincoln was eventually recognized as being one of our greatest Presidents, so will the children of light find that their reward is sure, though it be late in coming.

"Blessed are ye when they shall revile you, and persecute you, and speak all that is evil against you, untruly, for my sake: Be glad and rejoice, for your reward is very great in heaven. For so they persecuted the prophets that were before you." (Matthew 5:11)

➳ Holy Spirit, let all I do and think and say be so filled with Thee, that it will not matter what others say about me.

HOME AGAIN

A patrolman in St. Petersburg, Florida, recently received a complaint that a dog was chasing chickens.

The officer caught the dog and hauled it out to the city pound. The dog warden blinked and looked again. His face slowly turned a bright red. *"Why, that's my dog,"* he stammered.

It is easy enough when things go wrong to find blame in others. Somehow or other, seldom do we look for blame in ourselves, and are always rather surprised when we find that we are in some measure responsible. For instance most people would be surprised if they were accused of having a share in the blame for the world's unrest. Yet the world is in the state it is today because the majority of the world's citizens have failed to accept their share of the responsibility to do their bit to bring God's love and peace into the world, to overcome and replace evil.

"So we being many are one body in Christ, and every one members one of another." (Romans 12:5)

ê O Christ, help us to love one another in word and in deed.

HE GAVE HIS ALL

Shortly before the Korean truce was signed Doctor Francis Hammond of Alexandria, Virginia, went out with his Marine Hospital patrol during the savage fighting for western front outposts. He never came back.

Bleeding badly from wounds, the doctor stayed on his feet aiding casualties until a Communist shell killed him. Witnesses told of the selflessness displayed by the doctor through the long terrible battle.

To sacrifice one's life for love of others is the greatest act of which man is capable, for by it one reflects the love of God that sacrificed His only begotten Son for men.

We may not all be called upon to sacrifice our lives on fields of battle as was this brave doctor. But we are all called upon to sacrifice our lives in some way for love of God.

To give of one's self—one's physical, material, intellectual or spiritual resources—so that others may benefit from them is no small sacrifice in the sight of God.

"Greater love than this no man hath, that a man lay down his life for his friends." (John 15:13)

⋙ Heavenly Father, grant that I may love Thee so greatly that I may be willing to sacrifice everything for Thee.

TOO EASY

In Redding, California, a thief rifled a store and left this note for the storekeeper: *"Get a new lock; this one is too easy."*

It is usually true that when thieves break in we have made it too easy for them to enter. This is also true when evil invades our lives, our communities, our nation, or the world.

Evil in one form or another usually enters in small inconspicuous ways and works unnoticed. It can grow to alarming proportions before we are aware of it. Homes are disrupted; communities and cities find themselves under the dominance of corrupt politics; wars destroy men and nations—all because no one prevented the small beginnings of evil.

We may smile amusedly at the old copy-book adage, *"A stitch in time saves nine,"* but if we would keep a better check on every smallest possible inlet for evil we would be able to avert most of the world's misery.

"Watch ye, therefore, praying at all times, that you may be accounted worthy to escape all these things that are to come, and to stand before the Son of man." (Luke 21:36)

～ O Lord, help me to be alert at all times to keep evil out.

MOUNTAINS OUT OF MOLEHILLS

Composer-pianist Leopold Godowsky once granted an audition to a young woman who was aspiring to be a concert-pianist. Her doting father accompanied her. When she had finished her rendition, the father, beaming with paternal pride, exclaimed to Godowsky: *"Isn't she brilliant? Did you ever see such technique?"*

"It certainly is remarkable," agreed Godowsky. *"I've never before seen anyone play such simple pieces with such difficulty."*

Somehow a lot of people live their lives as this girl played the piano, with extreme difficulty. The trouble is that we too often do not want to follow God's rules. We are afraid of self-discipline, of the sacrifice involved in serving Him and our fellow man. Most of all, we lack the faith in God as a Heavenly Father Who is willing and able to supply all our needs from day to day.

Actually, there is no need for this. God is unchangeably good, and He loves each and every one of His children. He has given us a set of rules to live by, and if we follow them living would be a very simple thing indeed.

"And how could any thing endure, if thou wouldst not? or be preserved, if not called by thee." (Wisdom 11:26)

ᴈ Heavenly Father, let me live each day according to Thy will.

HE DIDN'T KNOW WHEN TO STOP

Recently in New York a 42-year-old convicted pickpocket was shot to death by an unknown assailant. It was discovered that he had left an estate valued at $60,000.

One feels an odd sense of pity for this man who spent his lifetime making his fortune by such shoddy ways, only to die without ever having been able to enjoy any of it. Had he only known how to be satisfied with what he had he could have lived quite comfortably, and moreover he would have possibly been able to avoid his untimely death. The trouble with him was that he just couldn't get enough.

Greed is one of man's most insidious sins. All through history great men have been brought low because of an inordinate desire for too much.

When we love our neighbor as ourselves, and God more than all, we cannot possibly be greedy for we will ask no more than our share, nor would we ever deprive another of what is rightfully his.

"For the desire of money is the root of all evils; which some coveting have erred from the faith, and have entangled themselves in many sorrows." (1 Timothy 6:10)

&ss; O Lord, teach us to content ourselves with Thee.

THE PURPOSE OF LIFE

A 20-year-old woman in Tulsa, Oklahoma, was delivered prematurely of her girl baby to insure the baby's birth before the mother died of cancer. The risk that the delivery of the child would hasten her death did not cause her any hesitation. She wanted to know only that her child was safely born—that she had been an instrument in transmitting new life.

This woman knew that the main purpose of human life is to follow the pattern of Our Heavenly Father, in Whose image we are created, and transmit life.

We must in some way or other pass on the life which is Divinely given to us, whether it be physically, intellectually or spiritually. If we fail to do so, we partially die, in the real sense of the word, for life is continuous. If we dam it up within ourselves we become stagnant and dead. To give of oneself is to love, and to love is to live, for love is of God.

"A new commandment I give unto you: that you love one another, as I have loved you, that you also love one another." (John 13:34)

✒ O God, let me always give to others of the life You have given me.

TWO DEMOCRACIES

Arnold Lunn, the English author and lecturer, once wrote that there are two kinds of democracy. There is, as he put it, the democracy of the saint, which is based on compassion and humility, and says, *"You're as good as I am."* Opposed to that is the democracy of the sinner, which is based on envy and arrogance, and has as its slogan: *"I'm as good as you are."*

There is only a fine distinction in the wording, but a world of difference in the meanings. Real love reaches out to include others . . . making every effort to help them. When one's heart is full of the love of God, it just naturally overflows to others.

On the other hand those who are filled with self-seeking have no room for loving others, and therefore do not truly love God.

Those who are occupied with themselves to the exclusion of others are generally unhappy persons, for self-seeking brings a trail of unpleasant circumstances in its wake.

"Three things approved before God and men: The concord of brethren, and the love of neighbors, and man and wife that agree well together." (Ecclesiasticus 25:1-2)

⋙ Help me, O Lord, to love others so much that I do not love myself more than I should.

LOVE HAS ITS REWARDS

A woman in Beverly Hills, California, befriended a one-legged blue jay who was coming out second-best in competing for food with fellow jays in her front yard. She started feeding the bird, and before long it was coming around three times a day for meals.

One day the crippled jay bird got a chance to repay his friend's kindness. The woman was walking in her yard when suddenly the jay began fluttering violently around her, and chattering shrilly. She looked down and saw a rattlesnake in a clump of ivy at her feet. She killed the rattler with a shovel. *"That jay saved my life,"* she said later. *"Why, that rattler could have killed me."*

It should be reassuring to those who fail to see immediate returns from the good they do, to know that there is no kindness, however small, that is done with a pure spirit of charity that will not be rewarded. No good deed is ever lost, for God is infinitely just. The return may seem to be long in coming, but it is nonetheless certain.

"The blessing of God maketh swift haste to reward the just and in a swift hour his blessing beareth fruit." (Ecclesiasticus 11:24)

ᕗ O God, let me do kind deeds with a pure heart.

III

YOU MUST RETURN

In Jefferson City, Missouri, a man who had been a fugitive from justice for 34 years gave himself up to the authorities. He said that he had been so miserable all these years that he had been evading the law, that he wanted to finish out his prison term and *"get right with the Lord."* Recently he completed his term and was released on parole.

Although we may escape the just reward of evil-doing for a long time, the conscience that God has given us refuses to permit us to have complete personal peace until we have made all possible amends.

For 34 years this man lived with an uneasy conscience. Had he been able to bring himself to give himself up long before, he would have paid his debt to society and spared himself many unhappy years marred by feelings of guilt.

Although God will always in His goodness open the way to our salvation, it is left with us to accept it. God never forces Himself on anyone. But within each of us lies the spark of His Divinity that keeps urging us towards Him. When we followed the direction of God within us, we find peace and happiness.

"O that thou hadst harkened to my commandments: thy peace had been as a river, and thy justice as the waves of the sea." (Isaias 48:18)

≈§ Heavenly Father, give me grace in every trial to turn to Thee.

TRUTH IS LIGHT

In one of the prison camps of Korea, 50 U.S. captives were made to sit on the bare boards of a small barracks. A Communist propagandist denounced Americans as a barbarous race whose latest atrocity was the use of germ warfare. After the frenzied barrage of words he triumphantly produced the final touch. It was a small insect which he said was unspeakably deadly, and which was one of a batch of millions dropped by American planes.

He passed it around on a piece of paper. A GI in the front row picked it up, examined it carefully, and then to the teacher's horror, popped it into his mouth and swallowed it. He had ruined the whole possible effect of the teacher's lecture. The Reds waited tensely for something to happen to the soldier. Nothing did. Nor were there any more lectures on germ warfare.

Sometimes it takes drastic measures to disprove a lie. Always it takes courage to stand up for the truth. People who are afraid to defend the truth often do much harm by their silence, for their silence can be taken for assent. God's children must ever take positive and decisive action to manifest His truth.

"Stand therefore, having your loins girt about with truth, and having on the breastplate of justice." (Ephesians 6:14)

◄§ Holy Spirit, inspire me to be a messenger of Thy truth.

113

WHOM GOD HATH JOINED TOGETHER

In a small town in England there lived a couple who had never been apart even for one day in the 55 years of their married life. So deep was their love for each other that the broken-hearted husband who was 80, died on the day following the death of his wife who was 78. They were buried together in the little parish churchyard.

Obviously, these two had learned the secret of living happily together. A happy home is based on kindness and consideration for each other. It takes a lot of true charity to surmount the frictions that arise in the course of daily married life. Because of this, marriage should not be undertaken lightly or without due consideration. It should be preceded by much prayer and the wise counsel of those fitted to advise.

The habit of praying together should be carried through the years. To include God in a marriage is to insure its success. Couples who put this into practice, find that their lives together grow richer and fuller because of it.

"Nevertheless let every one of you in particular love his wife as himself, and let the wife fear her husband." (Ephesians 5:33)

⊸§ Heavenly Father, bless all marriages with Thy love.

POETIC JUSTICE

A woman patient was being discharged from a hospital where she had spent four months recuperating from a serious operation. On her way out she slipped and fell, breaking a leg. She had to be taken right back to the bed she had just vacated. When they undressed her for examination, it was discovered that she had six brand new hospital towels wrapped around her waist under her dress.

This woman learned rather sadly that *"your sins will always find you out."* One may never escape punishment for willful wrongdoing, although discovery may not always follow so immediately and dramatically as in her case. But sooner or later we inevitably reap what we sow.

The punishment we suffer as a result of our sins is not the vengeance of an angry God, but rather the lesson taught by a wise and loving Father, Who permits us to burn our fingers until we learn to stay away from the stove. When we learn this lesson we begin to understand that our suffering has been a blessing in disguise, for it opens the way to salvation.

"Is it my will that a sinner should die, saith the Lord God, and not that he should be converted from his ways and live?" (Ezechiel 18:23)

⁖ O Lord, help me to turn away from all my sins, and live only for Thee.

THE POWER OF SUGGESTION

It has been estimated that the United States Army saved $13,000,000 in 1952 as a result of suggestions submitted by servicemen and civilians. Of 57,517 suggestions submitted, 11,814 were accepted—13,000 more than the previous year. Civilians were awarded bonuses for their suggestions that were accepted.

A lot of people are aware that there is a great deal that needs to be done if our world is to be saved from its present state of chaos, and be made a better place in which to live. Yet they feel individually too small to do much by themselves. They ask, *"What can I do? I am only one person."*

Yet just as the Army saved $13,000,000 in one year by the thoughtful suggestions of individuals, many important changes can be made in the world by the individual efforts of those who love God. Even one word of suggestion to a friend . . . to a youngster deciding upon a career . . . to a school board . . . to a political group . . . may mean the far-reaching effect of a single influence for good.

"Exhort your hearts, and confirm you in every good work and word." (II Thessalonians 2:16)

⋘ Holy Spirit, inspire us to find more ways to work Thy will.

MUCH ADO ABOUT NOTHING

In a small town a garbage collector was making his rounds when some rubbish fell from an overstuffed can and landed on one side of a path that lay between two houses. The housewife who lived on the side of which the garbage had fallen, decided that her neighbor must have been to blame. Annoyed, she took a broom and swept the garbage over to the other side. Her neighbor, equally annoyed when she found it there, rushed out with her broom and swept it back. Back and forth the garbage went while the two women stormed at each other.

Finally one of them struck the other with her broom, and from there on it was a fight to the finish. Hauled into court with many bodily bruises, they were both fined for disturbing the peace.

Often, as in this instance, great conflicts can develop with serious results because of some small disagreement, which could easily enough have been settled at the outset had both parties stopped to gently reason it out.

The settling of a dispute can be easy enough if we remember to use kindness and restraint. It takes two to make a quarrel, and it is most difficult to become angry with one who answers quietly and kindly. Our lives would be much happier if we would always deal kindly with others.

"A mild answer breaketh wrath: but a harsh word stirreth up fury." (Proverbs 15:1)

&§ O Lord, help me to be kind in word and in deed.

LIP SERVICE

The *Montreal Star* caused its readers to smile when it printed this love-letter from an ardent swain: *"Dearest Betty, I would swim the mighty ocean for one glance from your dear eyes. I would walk through a wall of flame for one touch of your tiny hands. I would leap the widest stream in the world for a word from your lovely lips. As always, your Frank. P.S. I'll be over on Friday night if my toothache is better."*

Somehow our actions always speak more loudly than our words. Our most fervent avowals mean nothing if they are not substantiated by actions that prove them. For instance, people listen with tongue in cheek to the person who is always protesting his love of God, and yet whose actions prove just the opposite. There are those who exclaim constantly, "I love everybody!" and yet their love takes no visible form.

If we love God and our fellow men truly, it is seldom necessary to talk about it. Our lives, filled with daily acts of loving service, will speak in clear beautiful tones, far better than any words we can say.

"So let your light shine before men, that they may see your good works and glorify your Father who is in heaven." (Matthew 5:16)

⋖ O Father, let my acts glorify Thee.

A TIME TO PLAY

The American people spent almost 12 billion dollars during one year on all forms of recreation. According to figures released by the U. S. Department of Commerce, this included every type of amusement from dog racing and dance halls to the legitimate theatre, opera, book clubs, etc. However the receipts from entertainments of this last type were far less than any other.

It is necessary that people balance work with play. One becomes dull and one-sided when one doesn't allow a certain amount of time for relaxation and mental change. However the opposite extreme is even worse. The person who is wholly pleasure-seeking grows shallow and trifling. Man is a union of mind, body and soul, and to be healthy and contributive he must develop each side of his nature to its highest potential.

Most important of the three is the spiritual side of man, for it is the one that shall endure through eternity. Spiritual development is not a passive thing. Rather it is the continuous expression of love for God by active service. The man who does things for love of God is the man who grows closest in the knowledge of His Eternal Presence.

"All things have their season, and in their times all things pass under heaven." (Ecclesiastes 3:1)

&ς O Lord, help me to balance my life according to Thy will.

EACH ONE COUNTS

You've probably at some time or other watched a diesel-powered locomotive in operation, and been fascinated by its tremendous power. It has been estimated that between 150,000 and 200,000 parts, supplied by some 2200 manufacturers, go to produce a single diesel-powered locomotive. Each part is so important that the locomotive may not operate if one is missing.

Just as a locomotive is made of many, many parts, each one having a different function, and each one important —so God's plan for the world includes each one of us. We are the parts that go to make up the whole.

If we fail to do what is given us to do, we are failing our part in God's plan. The reason that there is so much unrest in the world is that so many of the parts aren't functioning as they should. If all of God's children could see themselves as important parts of a whole, and function accordingly, then like the locomotive we would have power!

"I am the vine; you the branches: He that abideth in me and I in him, the same beareth much fruit: for without me you can do nothing." (John 15:5)

&ξ O God, help me to see clearly what Thou wouldst have me do, and give me grace sufficient to do it.

IN A RUT

In Duluth, Minnesota, a burglar broke into the same service station three times in seventeen days, entering each time through the same window, and using the same tools to pry open the cash register.

You may find it incredible that the owners of this service station could have so failed to take the necessary precautions after the first burglary that it could happen again and again. Yet some of us, like them, go through life making the same mistakes over and over. Somehow, people seem to take a long time to profit from their mistakes; that is, all but the evil-doers. They have too much at stake to make the same mistakes more than once. As Jesus put it, *"The children of this world are wiser in their generation than the children of light."*

We who love God have repeatedly made the mistake of not being alert enough to see that those who hate Him do not have their way. If wars are ever to be prevented those who love peace must maintain an eternal vigilance against the enemies of peace.

"When a strong man armed keepeth his court, those things are in peace which he possesseth." (Luke 11:21)

᪒§ O Lord, keep us watchful against Thy enemies.

LOVE THY NEIGHBOR

A mother once asked her little girl if she knew what conscience was. *"Yes,"* replied the child. *"Conscience is something in me that tells me when Johnnie is doing wrong."*

The child probably didn't realize what she was saying, but she spoke with the attitude most of us have towards our neighbors. It is too difficult for us to face up to our own faults, but so easy to see the faults in others. We can always tell what's wrong with someone else, but we give little credit to what is right.

Perhaps one of our biggest faults is lack of charity. Charity in our day has taken on a new meaning. More and more it is used in terms of giving money. But real charity is more than that—love of the poor, the rich; the attractive, the unattractive; the good and the sinner; in short, love of all mankind.

"And if I should distribute all my goods to feed the poor, and if I should deliver my body to be burned, and have not charity, it profiteth me nothing." (Corinthians 13:3)

O, My Jesus, help me to develop a love for all men because they are made in Thy image.

ONE-SIDED HONESTY

Not long ago, in a gathering of businessmen, one man was holding forth on the horrifying increase in graft and corruption in government. He made a long vehement speech deploring the fact that there had been too many proofs of the acceptance of bribes by men in high places. The others, somewhat tired by his arguments, finally managed to veer the conversation into another channel. Someone remarked ruefully that he had received a traffic ticket that morning for speeding. *"Really?"* said our talkative friend. *"I know a man who can fix any traffic ticket."*

It is next to impossible to expect honesty in government while a lack of respect for it is shown in the home, in schools, in business, and in all walks of everyday life.

Those of us who love God should strive in every way to develop for ourselves, and engender in others that sense of integrity that will reflect in all our dealings, and will keep America strong.

". . . You cannot serve God and mammon." (Matthew 6:24)

◆§ O Lord, help me to serve You honestly.

YOU CAN'T ESCAPE

Recently a San Francisco physician was sued for $175,000 damages for injuries allegedly suffered by a man at his birth 21 years ago. The doctor was charged with failure to exercise due care and skill during the delivery, which resulted in partial paralysis of the child.

Many people think that because they do something they know is wrong, and seem to get away with it for a long time, they have completely escaped punishment. They forget that God sees and remembers our every act, and rewards us accordingly.

The sad thing about this sort of thinking is that once they have *"gotten away"* with wrong-doing, instead of seeking forgiveness and trying to make whatever amends possible, they usually begin to develop a pattern of errors. When finally they are made to suffer for it, the punishment is very great and takes them completely by surprise.

God is not only merciful, He is also just. We are told that we must *"reap what we sow."* And though our reward be slow in coming, it is nonetheless sure.

"For the Lord knoweth the way of the just: and the way of the wicked shall perish." (Psalms 1:6)

❧ O Lord, help me to remember that Thou rememberest everything I do.

MORE NEEDED

A woman in California put a want-ad in the paper, for a gardener to tend her rather fine garden. Interviewing the first applicant, she asked, *"Are you a good gardener?"* The man answered enthusiastically, *"I just love flowers!"*

"Yes," said the woman. *"That is good, but can you garden?"* She found that the man had no experience at all.

Our Lord often told his disciples that more than wishful thinking is needed to be a follower of Christ. Mere knowledge without application is of little value. A man may read and hear about God for years, but until he actually begins to apply the principles that will bring him into intimate contact with his Maker, he can not be said to know God.

This also applies to our relations with others. Love acts the part. When we truly love others we do all that is in our power to help them. To love is to do. Those who want to do their part to bring God's love and peace into the world, must be willing to work hard to bring this about.

"But be ye doers of the word and not hearers only, deceiving your own selves." (James 1:22)

⊸§ O Lord, help me to put my love into action.

THINK BIG!

Daniel H. Burnham once wrote: *"Make no little plans: They have no magic to stir men's blood, and probably themselves will not be realized. Make big plans, aim high in hope and work, remembering that a noble, logical diagram once recorded will never die, but long after we are gone will be a living thing asserting itself with ever increasing insistency."*

If there ever was a time when there was need for men of large vision and bold constructive action, it is now. If our world is to become a better place in which to live, then we must have men who will conceive and carry out a plan for spreading God's love and peace throughout the world.

The followers of Christ have a special obligation to live their Christianity in a global sense. We need to learn to look beyond the small circles of our individual lives, and realize that they are not islands unto themselves but part of a much larger world.

"Blessed are the peacemakers: for they shall be called the children of God." (Matthew 5:9)

⋙ Heavenly Father, use me I pray to help in the coming of Thy kingdom.

KINDNESS PAYS

In Tacoma, Wash., a gunman attempted a hold-up of a grocery store that was owned by two elderly women. One of the sisters pleaded gently with the robber. She told him her sister had a very bad heart, and that the shock of losing all their money might kill her. She appealed to the man's better nature and he responded. He apologized, asked to shake hands with them, and then walked out the front door.

This woman knew that kindness is a key to many locked doors. If she had not thought that there was a streak of decency in the gunman, and tried to uncover it by speaking to him gently, she and her sister would probably have lost what they had worked so hard for.

Jesus was always teaching his disciples to practice kindness in their dealings with their fellowmen. There is much wisdom in the time-worn saying, *"We win more flies with honey than with vinegar."*

"But I say to you: Love your enemies; do good to them that hate you; and pray for them that persecute and calumniate you." (Matthew 5:44)

◄§ O Heavenly Father, help us to deal kindly with all men.

YOU AND THE SICK

Until recently doctors have made a blood count—measuring the ratio of red blood cells—by a laborious method that usually takes an hour.

But now a new method is designed to take its place. An instrument called an electrohemograph, developed by Dr. A. F. Goodwin of Gloversville, N.Y., is now able to measure the size and quantity of 25,000 to 50,000 cells in about 45 seconds. It enables doctors to tell immediately what kind of anemia is affecting the patient, if any, and also whether therapy is being effective.

God has put a power in the hands of each of us that can in some way benefit others. You may not discover any new scientific cure for blood disease but there are countless ways in which you can bring relief to those who are broken in body as well as spirit.

You can show your sympathy for the sick by performing some corporal work of mercy—by visiting them, by writing to them or by fulfilling for them some obligation that their illness prevents them from attending to. In aiding even one sick person, you are helping Christ Himself.

"As long as you did it to one of these my least brethren, you did it to me." (Matthew 25:40)

ぉ Let me never overlook any opportunity to help one of Thy sick, O Lord.

THE WAY TO PROGRESS

George Washington Carver, the celebrated Negro chemurgist, once said: *"I discover nothing in my laboratory. If I come here of myself I am lost. But I can do all things through Christ. I am God's servant His agent, for here God and I are alone. I am just the instrument through which He speaks and I would be able to do more if I were to stay in closer touch with Him. With my prayers I mix my labors, and sometimes God is pleased with the results."*

Through the ages, men who have made a lasting contribution to the general welfare of humanity have realized that their powers came from God alone, and have turned to Him for inspiration and succor.

The realization that one is an instrument through which God works, gives one a sense of true freedom, for it bears the knowledge that working with God one has almost unlimited possibilities to work for Him, right here on earth. Another result will be to give me the confidence to branch out and do bigger things to spread God's kingdom on earth.

"Unless the Lord build the house, they labor in vain that build it. Unless the Lord keepeth the city, he watcheth in vain that keepeth it." (Psalm 126:1)

O Lord, help me to realize that all my powers come from Thee.

A LITTLE KNOWLEDGE

There is a story told of a young college student in France who was on his way home for a vacation. On the train he was seated opposite an elderly man who was devoutly saying his rosary.

The youth spoke to him and said that he was silly to believe in God and prayer. He scoffed and claimed that as a science student, he could prove that all things came from nature, that there was no God. He asked the man for his name and address and promised to send him literature that would enlighten his poor, uninformed mind.

The old man silently put his hand into his coat pocket, took out his card, and handed it to the student. The youth took the card, and read with some dismay the name: *"Louis Pasteur, Professor of Science."*

Unfortunately, there are others, like this lad, who having a surface knowledge of science, begin to think that science holds all the answers to the mysteries of the universe. They fail to see that although science progressively is able to explain the *"hows,"* it has never managed to explain the *"whys."*

It is indicative that those who have delved deeply into science, like Louis Pasteur, are led by their knowledge to understand how much greater are the things they do not know than the things they do.

"Then the Lord answered Job out of a whirlwind, and said: Where wast thou when I laid the foundations of the earth? tell me if thou hast understanding." (Job 38:1,2 and 4)

&ε O Lord, let me never forget that Thou art the Creator of all.

TRUTH MARCHES ON

Julia Ward Howe was visiting in Washington, D.C., in December, 1861. Signs of war were everywhere. The railroads were guarded by soldiers, and the streets were crowded with men in uniform singing war songs, among them the stirring tune, *"John Brown's Body."*

After hearing the song, Mrs. Howe found herself mentally composing new words for the tune—words that would lift the minds and hearts of the soldiers to God, words that would remind them that God's truth is ever *"marching on."* Her song turned out to be our great *"Battle Hymn of the Republic."*

This is a song that has come down to us through the years, intact in its own inner beauty, and has lost none of its appeal for the American people. This is because it is written in the spirit of freedom and inspires men to the knowledge that God's truth goes *"marching on."* It is this faith in God's truth that founded our nation. If we are to endure, we must remain on the side of truth, so that we may rest under the shadow of God's protection.

"What shall we then say to these things? If God be for us, who is against us?" (Romans 8:31)

⊷ O God, keep this nation in knowledge of Thy truth.

IN THEIR OWN BACKYARD

Police in an Illinois city were instructed to start enforcing regulations governing newly installed parking meters. Among the first cars tagged were those of the police chief, the city attorney, and the city inspector!

It would seem that this city government needed to have begun its reforms in its own backyard. Of course such regulations are necessary, but it is a common failing for us to be greatly aware of failings in others, and yet completely unseeing when it comes to our own. It is strangely easy for us to be critical of others, and yet enormously difficult to appraise ourselves honestly.

Criticism of others boomerangs by returning us an equal measure of judgment from God. Jesus warned against it when He told His disciples, *"Judge not, and you shall not be judged. Condemn not, and you shall not be condemned. Forgive and you shall be forgiven."*

When we learn to think kindly of everyone, seeing the good rather than the bad in them, we will be much more able to grow in grace and purity. It will not be difficult to refrain from judging others, if we have real love for God; for when we love God, we love all His creatures.

"And why seest thou the mote in thy brother's eye: but the beam that is in thy own eye thou considerest not?" (Luke 6:41)

❧ Holy Spirit, teach us to think of others as we wish to be thought of.

132

HE MAKES OTHERS HAPPY

Recently a man sent a letter to a Buffalo paper expressing his appreciation of a certain bus driver. He said that he had never seen a driver so *"courteous, cheerful and obliging"* as the one to whom he had reference. He said that he had noticed the contagious effect the driver's continual good humor had on the passengers—it made them cheerful and friendly too.

"On inquiring," he wrote, *"I found that this driver does extraordinary courtesies for his patrons. For instance, one rainy morning an old lady getting on the bus upset her pocketbook and some money rolled out the door on the street. Out went the driver in the pouring rain and picked it all up."*

Everybody is in a position to do something to change the world for the better. One thing everyone can do is to exert our influence for good simply by cultivating a cheerful, kindly disposition.

We never are able to estimate the far-reaching effect of our good will upon others. But we do know that our Father in heaven sees the chain reaction of our smiles and our kindnesses and they are never in vain. A cheerful *"Good morning"* or a *"God bless you"* to those who are in need of help is the sowing of a blessing that is sure to return.

"Behold thou hast taught many, and thou hast strengthened the weary hands." (Job 4:3)

⇜§ O Lord, help us to be cheerful and kindly.

AN ACCURATE MAP

Here are some interesting facts about the maps of our country that are now in use. Today, 460 years after Columbus, thousands of square miles in the U. S. are not accurately mapped. Contour maps showing the hills and valleys in an area, including roads and railroads, are virtually useless in planning new pipelines, irrigation and reclamation projects, and—most important—military defense.

As fast as it can, the U. S. Geological Survey is trying to rectify the situation by revisions of badly-scaled areas. In all, only a very small portion of the country is mapped in a manner that meets the established standard.

It takes a country hundreds of years to develop a reasonably accurate map of its territories. The bigger the country, of course, the harder the map, and the longer it takes.

It is the same with human life when we rely entirely on our own intelligence and wisdom. But God has given us one map that we may rely on completely. God gives us the life of His Son to show us the way to eternal life. If we follow Him, we cannot fail to get to Heaven.

"Jesus saith to him: I am the way, and the truth, and the life. No man cometh to the Father, but by me." (John 14:6)

◆§ O Lord, let me always follow Thee.

FOR WANT OF A DIME

Recently in Philadelphia $2,000 was lost for want of a dime. The cash, and $8,000 in antiques and furnishings was destroyed when fire wrecked the second floor of an historic suburban inn. There is a firehouse located right across the highway from the inn, but it is not manned at night. The owner of the inn told police that no one had a dime in change with which to phone for volunteer firemen.

Success of big projects often hinges as much on the little things as on the big. Just as a great loss was suffered in this instance because of the lack of ten cents, so many important losses are suffered for the want of a seemingly unimportant factor.

God made each of us with a definite purpose in view. Though we tend to play ourselves down as unimportant, we each have a definite role in bringing His kingdom into being. When we fail to do what God expects of us individually, we are failing our share in His great work.

If we neglect to use the talents and abilities that God has given us, we may let slip by opportunities which would make considerable changes for the better in a world that is in sad need of them.

"Thy kingdom come. Thy will be done on earth as it is in Heaven."

✦

✎§ O Lord, help me to do Thy will for me.

THE HEART OF A CHILD

An eight year old boy in Columbus, Ohio, climbed out on a fire escape, a large towel spread cape-like around his shoulders and hanging down his back. He poised himself like a bird and took off.

In the hospital with 2 broken wrists he explained tearfully, *"I thought the air would get under my towel and float me down like it does Superman. I suppose Superman may be able to fly, but little boys can't."*

This child's adventure should vividly point out to adult minds how very impressionable a child is apt to be. The line between reality and make-believe is very thin in childhood. In the very early years it hardly exists at all.

What a child thinks and dreams about is determined by the outside influences; the instruction given by parents and teachers, the books given him to read, the pictures he sees, the radio or television programs he listens to. These are all real experiences to him.

Therefore it is up to us to see that our childrens' thoughts and dreams are directed to the finer, better ideals, for how one thinks and acts as a child, determines how one will think and act as a man or woman.

What a challenge and a privilege this presents to those who are responsible before God for the quality of our children's growth!

"And it is better to die without children than to leave ungodly children." (Ecclesiasticus 16:4)

⊷§ O Lord, teach us how to teach our children.

DEAD OR ALIVE?

Recently in Texarkana, Texas, a man who had been away for some time, returned home to discover that he had been "dead" for three weeks.

It appears that an unidentified man answering to the same description, had been killed by a freight train, and our friend's grief-stricken family had claimed the body and buried it. Although it was a happy case of mistaken identity, when a friend explained his *"death"* and the subsequent funeral to him, the alive "dead man" collapsed in fright.

Perhaps most of us would react as this man did, were we suddenly confronted with evidence that we were "dead." Surely our own death is a solemn thing to contemplate. Yet it should not be so awesome as to paralyze us with fright. Strangely, although we know that death is inevitable, we rarely ever seem to regard it as an imminent possibility.

No one may predict the time of his own death with certainty, so the only way in which we may be sure to be prepared for it when it comes is to live each day as though it were our last.

Our daily lives should be lived so well and fully that whenever God calls us, we may go without fear, knowing that we have done our best.

"Amen, amen I say to you: if any man keep my word, he shall not see death for ever." (John 8:51)

∽§ O Lord, preserve us this and every day until our death.

A BEAN IN A KITCHEN

There was a freak accident in the kitchen of an Atlanta, Georgia, housewife recently. A butterbean clogged the safety valve of her steam pressure cooker. The cooker exploded and blew the lid through the kitchen ceiling. The housewife was hurled to the floor on her face and bruised. The hot water heater, 12 feet from the stove, hopped off its moorings. Bottles on the shelf flew in all directions, food was sprayed all over the kitchen walls, and a stove leg punched a hole in the floor.

We are apt to think that small things are of little consequence. But little things are of tremendous importance. A single defect in character is enough to destroy a soul.

It is true that God knows our weaknesses, but it is equally true that He expects us to work to overcome them. If we do not strive to conquer all that is undesirable in our natures, one fault may develop to so great an extent that we may one day find our lower nature completely out of control. Saint Augustine once said, *"This is the very perfection of a man, to find out his own imperfection."* Once we discover our imperfections then we can try to eliminate them.

"I am the Almighty God: walk before me, and be perfect." (Genesis 17:1)

&ᇰ O Lord, enable me to reach perfection.

NOT ENOUGH

A well-to-do businessman was approached by a woman who was selling tickets for a charity concert. Tired of the constant demands made upon him, the man spoke politely but firmly, *"I'm sorry,"* he said, *"but I won't be able to attend the concert. It's for a worthy cause, however, and I assure you that I shall be with you in spirit."*

"Fine," the woman answered brightly, but with equal firmness. *"Where would your spirit like to sit? The tickets are one and two dollars."*

She won her argument. *"I'll take a $2 one,"* the man said meekly.

Certainly as children of God, trying to do His will by serving others, we are often tempted to believe that the time has come when we deserve a well-earned rest from all the effort and responsibilities this entails.

Yet if we truly love God, we will realize that as long as we live, there can never come a time when we have done enough. God never sits down and says that He has done enough for us. He continues to send His blessings, and to follow in His footsteps, we must keep on serving others.

"And unto whomsoever much is given, of him much is required." (Luke 12:48)

❧ O Lord, help me to persevere in serving Thee.

139

ELIMINATE THE NEGATIVE

Not too long ago in Cushing, Oklahoma, a well-dressed man entered a hardware store and asked for a pair of pliers. The store-keeper obliged. The man opened his mouth, fastened the pliers onto a tooth, gave three yanks and out came the tooth. He quietly replaced the pliers, and smiled at the customers and the staff who were watching him with mouths agape. *"That tooth was killing me,"* he explained.

Although hardly any of us would be willing to take the drastic measures this man did to rid himself of that which was causing him pain, we must admit that he had the right objective. The only thing to do when something is wrong is to get rid of the source of the trouble.

There are many things in our lives, besides teeth, that if left unattended, may be *"killing us."* One serious defect can eventually destroy an otherwise sound character. One weakness in our social structure can be enough to demoralize our entire nation.

There is a great deal that we can do as individuals to weed out those negative elements in our personal lives and in our community, and supplant them with love and truth and justice. If each individual took this as his or her personal responsibility, soon we would be able to bring about peace and freedom for the world.

"And if thy right eye scandalize thee, pluck it out and cast it from thee. For it is expedient for thee that one of thy members should perish, rather than thy whole body be cast into hell." (Matthew 5:29)

&§ O Lord, help us to cast out evil.

ROAD TO ETERNITY

Some unknown author penned these pointed lines:

> "I sought my soul,
> But my soul I could not see.
> I sought my God,
> But my God eluded me.
> I sought my brother,
> And I found all three."

From the beginning of recorded time, man has had an instinctive awareness of the existence of God and of his own immortal soul. It is necessary that man live by faith, for faith is the way to his progress.

Our Lord came to earth to show men that the most effective way to know is to obey His simple Commandments—to love Him with all our heart and mind and strength, and to prove our love by loving all His children as our brothers.

When we love all men with the same love that we love ourselves, then we are pleasing to Him, and He dwells with us, leading, protecting and directing. Then we discover our true selves as children of The Most High, and we gain a certainty that study alone will not give.

"Dearly beloved, let us love one another, for charity is of God." (I John 4:7)

ৎ§ O God, help me to obey Thy commandments.

THERE'S ALWAYS ROOM

Some one once stated that *"Every noble activity makes room for itself."*

Many persons fail to develop their possible talents in any field because they lack the self-confidence that helps people to achieve. Often the reason is that they think that the competition is too keen. *"After all,"* they reason, *"I am only one person out of the two and one half billion in the world. How can I expect to be of any great service to mankind?"*

What these people forget, is that every person who has ever achieved anything worthy of note has been also "just one person." God never makes any mistakes. Although He has millions of earthly children, He has created a place for each one of us. No one can take it from us. No one can fill our niche, or do our job in exactly the same way that we can.

All we have to do is to find out what it is that God wants us to do, and then do it. Each one of us should strive to our utmost to develop along the lines where our natural talents and inclinations lie.

We will find that God will help us all the more as we help ourselves. There is room for everyone, but the higher our goals and the motives and ideals that lie behind them the greater the achievement. The greatest room is at the top.

"Covet earnestly the best gifts." (Corinthians 12:31)

⤳ O Lord, please use me for Thy service.

TOO MANY COOKS

A young man and his bride were living temporarily with his mother and sister. One day he brought home a new pair of trousers that were somewhat too long for him. He asked his wife to shorten them by two inches. She was busy at the time, so he asked his mother and then his sister to do it for him. They were also too busy.

That night at different intervals his wife, his mother and his sister each remembered his request. When the young man awoke the next day, his bride told him that she had shortened his trousers as he had asked. Pleasantly surprised, he put them on, to discover to his consternation that his mother and sister had also attended to the same little service. The trousers barely covered his knees.

One of the most essential factors in getting things successfully done is co-operation. When more than one person is engaged in any common undertaking it is necessary that each one definitely understands his or her role, and works in harmony rather than in conflict with the other.

Many people look upon life as a form of competition instead of as team-work. They fail to understand that the universe is created by an infinitely wise God, with no left-over parts. There is a definite role and calling for each of us if we will but find it.

"Because we are members of his body, of his flesh and of his bones." (Ephesians 5:30)

⋙ O Holy Spirit, teach us to cooperate with each other.

THE STILL SMALL VOICE

Mrs. McGuire of Hillside, New Jersey, was cleaning her upstairs bedroom. Through the windows came the frantic cries of a child and the equally frantic barks of a dog. Mrs. McGuire thought of her own two children, but she could hear them peacefully playing down stairs. For some reason or other she left the house and started to trace the cries—right down to the railroad tracks close by.

There was the child on the tracks of an onrushing train, and the faithful dog barking violently. Mrs. McGuire grabbed the child, and with the dog beside her, jumped clear of the train just in time.

Speaking of the episode later, Mrs. McGuire said she did all this by a *"mother's instinct."*

We say that mothers are possessed of a God-given instinct to be able to sense and prevent danger to their children. This instinct is the result of an intense unselfish love.

As our physical capacity for self-protection grows and we leave the shelter of our parents' care, our greatest dangers are spiritual ones. To protect us God gives us what we call our consciences, or the *"still small voice"* within. If we learn to recognize this as God within us watching and caring for us, we will listen to the *"voice"* and heed its warnings and directions.

"And thou shalt be the obedient son of the Most High, and he will have mercy on thee more than a mother." (Ecclesiasticus 4:11)

⚜ O Lord, teach me to trust in Your protection.

THE NICK OF TIME

A man in Los Angeles was driving along a road that wound around the top of an 800-foot cliff when his engine began to give him trouble. As he got out to see what was the matter he failed to secure the brake properly and the car started down the hill. Running alongside frantically, he grabbed the wheel and tried to stop it. Suddenly his sleeve caught in the gear shift. The very instant it plunged over the cliff he was able to tear himself loose —just in time to save his life.

It is true that it is always *"better late than never."* But somehow, we are not always willing to take this attitude in our human relationships, we are often apt to list certain physical, mental and spiritual ills as "incurable" and dismiss them as such.

One of the things for which the medical profession deserves lasting credit is the fact that even when a physician personally believes a case to be hopeless, he never ceases to treat it. The ethical standards of his profession obligate him to take the attitude that *"while there is life there is hope."*

It would be a wonderful thing if we could feel the same way when it comes to spiritual ills. The life within us is the spirit of God. As long as life endures we have a chance for salvation, no matter how lost or depraved a soul may seem. Our love for God should prompt us to do all in our power to help and redeem such souls to the last.

"As I live, saith the Lord God, I desire not the death of the wicked, but that the wicked turn from his way and live." (Ezechiel 33:11)

O Lord, help us to bring more souls to Thee.

REWARD OF HONESTY

A New York cab driver discovered that two teen-age girls —visitors from Venezuela—had dropped a purse containing $280 in his cab when he drove them from the airport to Manhattan. He took the money to the Venezuelan Consulate, driving eleven miles out of his way. He was thanked and given a $30 reward for his honesty.

Several days later he received a letter from the American Consulate in Venezuela telling him that his deed of honesty had been reported in the Venezuelan newspapers, and had served to make the people of that country more favorably inclined towards ours. Still later this driver was awarded a gift of $100 by the president of the New York Convention and Visitors Bureau for doing his part to strengthen international relations by setting an example of courtesy and kindliness.

In the minds of those who love God, there is never any doubt as to which course to take when it means the difference between right and wrong. We are sure that this man didn't foresee that by following the dictates of his conscience, he would do a service for his country and bring himself the approval and the admiration of his fellow citizens. This is the exciting thing about working for God. When we serve Him because we love Him, He blesses our service, and we never know the far-reaching effects for good that even our smallest actions may have.

"You are my friends, if you do the things that I command you." (John 15:14)

◄§ O Lord, may all my service be done for love of Thee.

146

BASEBALL VERSUS GEOGRAPHY

It was a hot afternoon in May and the boys were much more interested in the current baseball games than they were in school-work.

After giving a lesson in geography, a teacher began to ask questions of her pupils to see how much they had learned.

"Now, who can tell me where Cleveland is?" she asked.

A boy who hadn't been paying much attention raised his hand. He said confidently, *"Cleveland is playing in New York."*

This youngster was so interested in baseball that Cleveland to him was a baseball team, not a city.

God has a design for each of His children here on earth. To find and fulfill that design is the way for man to make his earthly life rich, abundant, and satisfying. When we work to develop our talents to their utmost we find that God, true to His promises, increases those we already have.

"Well done, thou good servant, because thou hast been faithful in a little, thou shalt have power over ten cities." (Luke 19:17)

&3 Heavenly Father, give me grace to see Thy will for me here on earth, and to use all the talents Thou hast given me to do it.

TRIUMPH OF LOVE

An 11-year-old boy in Kentucky is alive today because he has learned the power of love. Last year he was told by the doctors that he would not have much longer to live. Suffering from several serious ailments, and sad and fearful at his approaching death, he sent out a public plea: *"Won't somebody please write to me?"*

His request brought letters of encouragement and gifts from all over the world. He received almost 300,000 pieces of mail. Recently he was pronounced well enough to return to school. He gave his reason for getting well very simply, *"Too many people love me for me to die."*

Human beings have a great many desires. But the strongest of these is the desire to be loved. This is one example of the great healing power of love. It is heartening that when there is an instance such as this, people never fail to respond. It is proof of the innate goodness of mankind.

Yet, while most of us know that to be loved one must give love, it is usually only at a time like this that we give of the great store of love within us. This is strange, because life provides us daily opportunities to show our love for God's children. We do not need to wait for a case of unusual need. To show loving kindness to all those with whom we come in contact, is to fulfill God's commandments.

"This is my commandment, that you love one another as I have loved you." (John 15:12)

⊷ O Lord, fill our hearts with love.

148

KNOW THYSELF

There is an inscription over the door of an ancient temple at Delphi that reads, *"Know thyself."* It is believed to have been written more than 600 years before the birth of Christ. It is a bit of ancient wisdom that has been handed down through the years.

In contrast to this, a very wise philosopher was once asked what he thought was the most difficult thing for man to do. His answer was, *"To know one's self."*

When we stop to consider it, self-knowledge is at once the most important and the most difficult thing for man to achieve. Until a man is aware of his inclinations, his abilities, and his limitations he is not in a position to make much progress of any kind. How few of us live life to its fullest! How very few ever attain even a fraction of the greatness that we could, simply because we do not know ourselves!

The first step to self-knowledge is a recognition of ourselves as creatures of God. As His children we are capable of an ever-growing goodness, wisdom, and creativity. Each of us has the seeds of these qualities within us. When we discover that they are there then we may confidently begin to develop them.

"Lo, the kingdom of God is within you." (Luke 17:21)

◄§ Holy Spirit, help us to know ourselves as Thy children.

YOU CAN'T TAKE IT WITH YOU

Recently, at the Jamaica racetrack, a man placed a $2 bet. It was his lucky day. One by one he picked them, and won. His excitement and his elation mounted as his winnings soared. By three o'clock he had won $79.80 *"in the money."* Finally his luck gave out—at 3:15 he collapsed of a heart attack and died.

Many people spend their lifetimes chiefly in the pursuit of the material things this world has to offer. Their lives seem to be rather futile when the time of their death arrives, for then they must leave all that they have gained to be used by others.

Real satisfaction in life can only be had by choosing those goals which will better prepare us for the life everlasting. Those who choose to pursue wisdom, virtue, charity, service, are those who gain for themselves the rewards that death itself cannot take away from them.

"Lay not up for yourselves treasures on earth: where rust and moth consume, and where thieves break through and steal." (Matthew 6:19)

✍ O God, let me seek those things that are of Thee.

THAT REALLY COUNTS

One of the most hallowed spots in America is the Tomb of the Unknown Soldier. It is located in the National Cemetery in Arlington, Virginia, just a few minutes across the Potomac from Washington, D.C. This unusual memorial is a tribute for all those fallen in battle who could not be identified.

Inscribed on the tomb we find the acknowledgment of God's divine power in these eloquent words:

"Here lies in honored glory, an American soldier, known but to God."

One of the most consoling thoughts for each of us is to be constantly aware that God does know, no matter who else forgets. He is interested in every one of our thoughts, words and deeds. He hears every prayer, and knows even our least desires.

Those whom you strive to help may never know what you have tried to do for them until they stand before the judgment seat of God. But God knows, and that is what counts above all else.

"As long as you did it unto one of these my least brethren you did it to me." (Matthew 25:40)

⊷§ Give me strength, O God, to lose in this world that I may gain in the next.

LAST CHANCE

As a young man, Irvin Cobb came to New York City in search of his first job in the newspaper business. He went from one newspaper to another, but he was politely put on the waiting list of each one without even being granted an interview with the editors.

In desperation one day, he sat down and wrote each editor a letter, stating his qualifications, and telling them in no uncertain terms that this was their last chance to hire him. He wrote, *"Either you give me a job now, or you will kick yourself for having missed this golden opportunity. I am now accepting offers on a 'first come, first served' basis."* To his surprise, this last bit of daring worked! By return mail, he was swamped with offers.

Those who love and serve God will find that there are times when only strong measures bring about the desired results. Our Lord often taught that we should be fearless and bold in His service. When He found His disciples fishing near the shore and catching nothing, He said to them, *"Launch out into the deep."* And when we stop to consider it, it is only in the *"deep"* that the big fish are caught.

To stay timidly by the shore is to catch nothing of any great worth. The Christian way of life is an adventurous one, for the person with love of God and men in his heart must be willing to stand boldly and live daringly for the truth.

"So speak ye, and so do, as being judged by the law of liberty." (James 2:12)

⇜ O Lord, make us bold in serving Thee.

THE HARD WAY

In Hibbing, Minnesota, a burglar broke into a store, and proceeded to try to crack the safe. Anticipating a difficult job, he took along a sledge hammer, a screw driver, a claw hammer, a pipe wrench, and a blow torch.

This well-equipped safe-cracker worked very hard at it and finally was able to knock the hinges off the safe door. But still the door remained closed—he couldn't pry it loose. Before he could complete the job, a disturbance of some kind frightened him away. He departed quickly leaving behind his collection of tools.

The next day, the store owners found the evidence of the attempted burglary. They were disturbed by the damage done to the safe, but more amused at the great lengths to which the would-be thief had gone. They said that the safe contained no money, and moreover, if the burglar had but turned the safe handle, he would have found it unlocked.

Many of us are like this burglar. We overlook the obvious. We often clutter up the simplest tasks with a lot of meaningless details. We have a tendency to expend an enormous amount of time and energy in worrying about incidentals. This form of mental hammering, of course, never accomplishes much.

Someone has observed that *"worry is interest paid on trouble."* God's children should learn to substitute work and prayer for worry.

"Sufficient for the day is the evil thereof." (Matthew 6:34)

O Lord, help us to turn to Thee in all our problems.

THE PRICE OF SELFISHNESS

Four years ago, a woman juror voted to convict a man on trial for a $900 burglary although she considered him innocent. Recently, she petitioned that he be granted clemency. She said that she had voted for his conviction because, *"Ten of the twelve jurors thought him guilty, and some of them were impatient to attend a festival."* The conscience-stricken woman added, *"Had it not been Friday, I would not have given in. I was foolish to have done it."*

Few realize what a serious responsibility is involved in jury duty. Certainly attendance at a festival is a poor excuse for failing to see that justice is done to a fellow citizen whose future hangs in the balance.

While all of us feel entitled to the freedoms which our form of government grants us, we are not equally willing to serve it in return.

Those who are called to serve on juries should put themselves in place of the one on trial. How would it be for them, if the qualified people all tried to run out of serving as jurors? Or if they were too occupied with other things to see that justice was done?

"In carefulness not slothful, in spirit fervent, serving the Lord." (Romans 12:2)

✦ O Lord, help us to be faithful in doing our duty.

END OF AN ARGUMENT

A 65-year-old man was pronounced dead not long ago. But even before making funeral arrangements for him, his three sons began to argue about how his possessions were to be divided among them. The squabbling ended abruptly when the "dead" man unexpectedly revived. Angered by their lack of concern for him, he promptly disinherited all three.

There is an old Latin proverb that reads, *"Avarice is the mother of cruelty."* And certainly of all sins this is the one that seems to have a special power to curdle the milk of human kindness.

At a time like this, these three young men should normally have been saddened by the loss of their father. They should have been praying for the repose of his precious soul. Instead, their inordinate desire for his goods overshadowed the love that they should have had for him and for each other.

Avarice is one of the most insidious sins. It can harden any of us. We can resist beginnings by placing right emphasis on true values. Security is a good thing. But over-anxiety for it quickly puts a price tag on nearly everything.

The more we love God and our fellow man, the less danger there is of being caught in the quicksands of avarice.

"The desire of money is the root of all evils." (I Timothy 4:10)

∓ O Lord, keep us from selfishness.

A VOICE WAS HEARD

A man in the mid-west was recently selected to represent his local as a delegate at a widely publicized labor convention. He felt that as an individual, he could do little to help.

The convention was not long under way before a well-thought-out and carefully executed resolution was about to be passed which would have been detrimental to both labor and management. While most of the assembled delegates acted unaware of what was going on, this one delegate became alarmed at the implications of the resolution. At the last minute, he rose from his seat and addressed the chair. He was recognized, but became tongue-tied with fear; standing before 1600 gathered delegates, but he managed to stammer, *"I'm sorry, Mr. Chairman, but this whole thing doesn't seem honest to me."*

His simple statement was like an electric shock to the gathering. Immediately the passive majority awakened as if from a deep sleep. A heated discussion began, and the destructive resolution was voted down.

Most of us fail to realize the great power that we have in making our voices heard. Sometimes a word spoken in defense of truth and justice is enough to change the course of one or more lives for the better.

"Now you are clean by reason of the word, which I have spoken to you." (John 15:3)

&O Holy Spirit, inspire us to speak Thy truth when we should.

156

THEY TOOK HIS WALLET

A boy in St. Louis who had been playing with four other companions on the banks of the Mississippi fell into the river. Without any thought for his own safety, a man standing nearby threw off his shirt and plunged into the water to rescue the drowning lad.

His instinctive faith in human nature received a bad jolt when he returned with the rescued boy to find that the other boys had taken the wallet from his shirt pocket and made off with the $50 in it.

To make matters a little worse, the boy who owed his life to this man, took off after his companions as soon as he reached the shore. He did not even bother to say "Thank you."

There is an old Arab proverb that reads, *"Do no good— and you will suffer no ingratitude."* Those who try to serve God by serving their fellows often feel frustrated when they get nothing but unkindness and ingratitude in return. But we should not become bitter towards all, because a few turn out to be ungrateful.

We should always remember in doing a service for others that we are doing it because of our love for God. True love does not give because it expects to receive in return. Love gives because that is its very nature.

"What shall I render to the Lord, for all the things that he hath rendered to me?" (Psalms 115:12)

⋐ O Lord, let me not be bogged down by ingratitudes.

REACHING FOR THE WORLD

A 19-year-old English boy arrived in New York recently to visit some of the 4,000 friends he made in the United States as an amateur radio operator. Although he had not seen even one of his thousands of friends in America, he had spoken with each and all of them over the air waves.

Upon his arrival in this country, the young man, Robert W. Ainge, of Oakhanger, England, was met by one of his friends from Orange, N.J., whom he contacted many times through radio.

Invitations to visit them have been extended to Mr. Ainge by 69 other radio acquaintances around the country. All of them are anxious to develop the friendship that was started by the enterprise of this one individual.

You may not be able to reach into the lives of thousands of others over the earth through radio as this resourceful young Englishman has done. But if you show as much imagination and take as much trouble in reaching out with love to all mankind as he, you are bound to accomplish more good than you dream of. All you need do is use God's ways—prayer and work for love of Him.

"Seek, and you shall find: knock, and it shall be opened to you." (Matthew 7:7)

⋙ O Lord of Hosts, grant me the grace to reach as many persons as possible with Thy love before I die.

158

EVIL WILL OUT

A man in Tokyo began to have great pain and swelling in his left arm. He couldn't figure out why. But it became so painful that he had to go to a hospital.

Upon examining the arm, doctors became convinced that some foreign element was lodged in it. Probing, they discovered a Russian bullet that had been there since the man had been wounded in the Russo-Japanese War. That was more than fifty years ago—in 1904!

Defects of character like those of the body show up sooner or later, if allowed to take root. Many of us are lulled into complacency because evil lies hidden for a time.

For many years now seeds of evil have been quietly planted and are taking root in our nation. They have lain there for a long time, taking root, and slowly but surely spreading like a cancer that may eventually destroy us.

Those who hate God have been gradually spreading the idea that His Commandments have no real truth or meaning. If those who love God do not work speedily to undo the damage already done, we may find ourselves suddenly the victims of great disaster.

"Take heed, watch and pray. For ye know not when the time is." (Mark 13:33)

&ξ O Lord, help us to be watchful to avoid evil.

A CLEVER DECEPTION

Recently in a city in Europe, outside a heavily guarded munitions factory, a worker was stopped on his way home. He was pushing a wheelbarrow which was filled with straw. As he passed through the gates he was halted. *"What have you there?"* the guard asked. *"Only a wheelbarrow of straw,"* the man replied. Suspicious, the guard made a thorough search of the wheelbarrow. He could find nothing. A little puzzled, he let the man go on his way.

His curiosity mounted as day after day the man carted away a wheelbarrow of straw. But never was he able to find any traces of any goods being removed from the factory. Only many months later it was discovered that the man was stealing wheelbarrows.

The guard in this case was fooled for so long by the very simplicity of the theft. It is strange that usually we expect evil-doers to work in very clever and ingenious ways.

If they can use ordinary means to destroy, it should be much easier for us to use them for the benefit of all.

"Then the devil cometh, and taketh the word out of their heart, lest believeing they should be saved." (Luke 8:12)

&§ O Heavenly Father, enlighten us that we may see on all sides countless opportunities to do good.

THE TIME IS NOW

A man was trying to persuade his friend to visit a fortune-teller with him. The second man declined saying that looking too far into the future often prevents us from observing what is happening right under our noses.

Then he added: *"If you'll get your mind off that fortune-teller for a moment, you will see that you are about to fall into that open manhole right in front of you."*

A most important step in successful living is learning that the only time we may ever act in is NOW. The present is a rare moment. There is little we can do about the past, even if God forgives our mistakes.

Then the future is a sealed book until it becomes the present. One effective way to shape the future is to act here and now. If we live each day to its fullest, giving our best possible service to God and man the future will take care of itself.

Time and time again, Jesus advised his disciples not to be overly concerned for the future. He taught them to pray, *"Give us this day our daily bread,"* knowing that if we trust Him, our Heavenly Father will provide for our every need as it arises.

"Be not therefore solicitous for tomorrow; for the morrow will be solicitous for itself. Sufficient for the day is the evil thereof." (Matthew 6:34)

⟞§ O God, help me every day of my life to trust in Thee.

THROUGH SHARK-INFESTED WATERS

Ever since he was a child, a 22-year-old Japanese dreamed of one day coming to America. He had heard of the wonders of the strong, brave, free country in which we live. He wanted to see it for himself. Somehow he never seemed to be able to obtain either the money or the visa on which to come.

He finally determined that *"where there is a will there's a way."* So recently he stowed away on a liner headed for Hawaii which he felt was the first stepping-stone to the United States

Ten miles off the shores of Hawaii, he feared he was to be discovered. He jumped overboard. For 8 hours he swam the remaining distance through the shark-infested waters. Finally he was washed ashore, completely exhausted from shock and exposure. Hawaiian fishermen picked him up and took him to the hospital for treatment.

Upon recovery, he was whisked off to jail, charged with illegal entry into U.S. territory. But he isn't discouraged, *"I've been dreaming of America for ten years,"* he told the authorities.

Newspapers are full of examples that prove beyond question that the average individual is endowed by God with a tremendous amount of imagination and daring— even though it is often misplaced.

Once a person wants the right thing strongly enough he shows the same resourcefulness for good.

"But he that shall persevere to the end, he shall be saved." (Matthew 24:13)

⋙ Heavenly Father, help us to be daring for good.

ALL GOD'S CHILDREN

A substitute teacher was assigned to take over the fifth grade in a school in the desert of Southern California. She found it a most unruly class. One boy in particular was forever making fun of those with different racial and cultural backgrounds.

One day she singled him out when he was picking on an underdog. *"Paul,"* she said, *"you shouldn't speak to Bob like that. He's your brother."*

Paul, of course, objected strenuously to that. He told her emphatically that Bob was not his brother. Speaking gently but firmly the teacher explained to him that if he wanted to be a good American, he had to look upon Bob as his brother, for the Declaration of Independence stated that God was the Creator of all, and therefore the Father of all, which made all men brothers. The whole class was impressed by this simple explanation. They wondered why they had not been taught it before. They began to see something in each other they never saw before. As a result an unruly class quickly changed into a most friendly one.

If we are ever to have a better understanding between races and nations, we must begin early to teach those concepts of the Fatherhood of God and the brotherhood of man on which our nation was founded.

"Have we not all one father? hath not one God created us?" (Malachias 2:10)

&§ O Holy Spirit, teach us to see our brother in each and every human being.

163

HE KNEW WHAT TO DO

An 11-year-old Boy Scout in Tucson, Arizona, recently flunked a simple test of following the right directions while on a hiking trip in the mountains.

Night fell, and the boy had not returned. A party of 100 searchers began looking for him. His parents were frantic with fear. Desperation mounted as morning came and there was still no sign of him.

But there was one person who was quite unafraid—the boy himself. When he was certain that he had missed the trail, and so was apparently lost, he refused to grow panicky. He checked the location of the sun with his watch as he had been taught to do. When he was sure of his direction, he began the trek home. It was a fifteen-mile journey, but he traveled with confidence because he knew where he was going. He arrived home safely the following afternoon.

God has given us numerous signs to guide us along the way of life. If we ever stray from the path that leads to heaven, He is always near and anxious to lead us out of our difficulties.

"For though I should walk in the midst of the shadow of death, I will fear no evils, for thou art with me." (Psalm 22:4)

❧ O Lord, help me always to follow Thy divine guidance.

164

MAN ABOVE ALL

Some geologists were excavating in Sardinia, an island in the Mediterranean, when they came upon the skeletons of two giant men. The geologists estimated that these men died about 4,000 years ago. The skeletons were over eight feet tall, and were discovered surrounded by weapons, which indicates that these men must have been warriors.

For centuries man has dug the earth to try to learn more and more about his ancestors. This lively curiosity has added considerably to our progress. It has enabled us to build upon the knowledge and skills developed by ancient civilizations. But more than that, it has given us a larger sense of man's importance in the world.

As far as scientists can estimate, the universe is billions of years old. During this time many revolutionary changes have taken place in the structure of the earth, and in plant and animal life. But of all the creatures that have ever inhabited the earth, mankind is the only one to whom God has given dominion. He has given him the power literally to possess the earth but only as a temporary trust and preparation for the perfect and everlasting peace of eternity.

"What is man that thou art mindful of him . . . Thou hast made him a little less than the angels, thou hast crowned him with glory and honour." (Psalms 8:5, 6)

&ς O Lord God, keep me ever mindful of the privilege and responsibility that is mine in being the noblest of Thy creatures.

KEEP DRILLING!

Last year more oil was found in the United States than the country used. It was the year of the greatest oil search in history. Known fields were expanded. New wildcat areas were explored.

But to reach this goal large sums of money were spent drilling no less than 17,714 dry holes that brought in nothing. Great risks had to be taken because even under favorable conditions the odds of finding a successful oil well are 8 to 1: eight dry holes for every one that produces.

Many persons become discouraged too quickly. They don't realize that to achieve success in this world or the next, one must be willing to fail and fail again without ever giving up. *The only real failure lies in quitting.*

There have been times in the lives of practically every man or woman who has made his mark before God when he felt he was getting nowhere. But he knew that in his relentless pursuit, he, like the oil-drillers, had to expect "*8 dry holes*" for the one that made the effort worth while.

God expects us to push on in the face of difficulties and seeming failure. It is the test of how much we love and trust Him.

"*No man putting his hand to the plough, and looking back, is fit for the kingdom of God.*" (Luke 9:62)

ᴇᔞ O Lord, teach me to work diligently for Thee, and to wait patiently for my reward.

166

ALL OR NOTHING

It was a sunny day on the coast of Scotland. There was a fresh breeze that lightened the heart of the fishermen. Surely, it was a fine day for a catch.

"Sail far out to sea, my men," the skipper yelled. *" 'Tis a fine haul, we'll make today!"*

The crew obeyed. The skipper was right. Forty miles off shore they sighted a school of cod. Excitedly they let down their nets. Hundreds of fish swarmed into them. In no time at all the nets were filled to bursting. They had caught about 30,000 pounds of fish. It was too big a catch to land on their boat. The skipper decided to take a chance—to tow the huge prize back to the harbor.

For twelve hours the small skiff laboriously towed its heavy load towards the shore, 40 miles away. The men gave a sigh of relief when at last they crossed the harbor bar. The sigh changed suddenly to a wail. Just at that moment the net broke and 30,000 pounds of cod swam swiftly back to the ocean.

Getting well-intentioned persons to overdo is one way the Devil often employs to get them off the right track. Yes, strive hard in these critical times to bring back the love and truth of Christ into the thick of things. But don't bite off more than you can safely chew—or you may lose everything you have gained.

"I must work the works of him that sent me, whilst it is day: the night cometh, when no man can work." (John 9:4)

⁓§ Lord, help me to know my full powers but also my limitations.

167

A DARING YOUNG MAN

A daring young man from Frankfurt, Germany, recently announced his intention to ride a motorcycle on a tightrope stretched above the gorge just below the Niagara Falls. This 24-year-old adventurer is convinced that his experience in the past will aid him. Two years ago he rode his motorcycle over a tightrope suspended from two peaks in the Bavarian Alps.

Few will ever have any reason to be as daring. But too often we go to the other extreme. We become so cautious that we lead dull, monotonous, sterile lives. We don't fully live. Merely existing, we scarcely touch the tremendous power for good that God has entrusted to even the least individual.

You can be daring in your own way—and still keep your feet on the ground. You can dare to stir up others, kindly and tactfully, to fulfil their moral and civic responsibilities. You can dare to take a stand for good when it's not the popular thing to do, to tell the truth about others when they are accused unjustly.

Yes, with God's help, there are a thousand ways in which you can show imagination and enterprise, without ever trying to ride a motorcycle over Niagara or the Alps.

"A wise man is strong: and a knowing man stout and valiant." (Proverbs 24:5)

⁖ O Lord, let us be daring in Thy service.

AVOID EXTREMES

One sunny morning, a Chicago motorist was stopped on the highway and given a ticket for speeding. Shrugging philosophically, he continued on his way.

A quarter-hour later he was stopped again for speeding, and given another ticket. Deciding to take no chances, he grimly slowed down to about 15 miles per hour, confident that he would be more than safe.

Imagine his surprise when a third officer pulled him off to the side of the road. Ready for fight, he glared at the officer and demanded to know why he had been stopped. The officer replied, *"Bud, there's not a car on this road that can get past you. You've slowed traffic on this highway down to a crawl!"*

In our own personal lives we often go from one extreme to the other. We are led by our emotions more than by reason. As a result, we lose that moderation and sense of proportion which gives balance to our lives. We forget that the laws of God and man are not made to hurt us, but to help us.

"Moderation in all things" guarantees much peace and happiness in this life and is a sure road to heaven. But to be moderate is not to be mediocre. It is only to put first things first, to see things in the long run, for after all, a steady "40 miles an hour," will usually get you there quicker and safer—and no traffic tickets along the way!

"Blessed is the man that findeth wisdom and is rich in prudence." (Proverbs 3:13)

◄§ O Lord, give me that sense of balance that both Thou and my fellowmen expect of me.

169

ENCOURAGE THE YOUNG

The University of Buffalo Placement Bureau was surprised and a little amused recently, when two 10-year-old boys walked into the office and applied for a job they had read about in the paper.

The boys had seen a want-ad requesting a university student to pose as a space man at a children's carnival. The applicant, the ad stated, had to be at least twenty years old. But figuring that 10 and 10 make 20, the two youngsters had decided to apply for this very exciting job.

They were very disappointed when the Bureau Director explained that their proposal did not fill the requirements. *"But,"* he told them kindly, *"if you'll come back in ten years, we'll see what we can do."*

Encourage in every way the idealism that God has implanted in every young person. Treat it with care. Nurture and guide along paths that can have far-reaching effects. Many a young person, for instance, has the makings of a devoted teacher, a loyal public servant, or a television script writer who in the years ahead could exert a great influence for good on millions. If you cannot say anything to stimulate, be sure not to ridicule, belittle or otherwise chill the first signs of the creative spark that the Creator has entrusted to the young.

"Suffer the little children to come unto me, and forbid them not. For of such is the kingdom of God." (Mark 10:14)

~§ O Lord, remind me to encourage, not discourage those who want to do things to help others.

GOD BLESSES THOSE WHO TRY

A short time ago in Atlanta, Georgia, an eight year old boy choked on a piece of chewing gum. A neighbor got him into his truck, and the two speeded down the highway, heading for the hospital. En route, the neighbor glanced at the boy. He was frightened. The youngster had turned a sickly blue color, and had stopped breathing. He went even faster.

In his hurry, he went through a red light and had crashed into an automobile. Both the truck and the automobile were badly wrecked. Fearing for the worst, the driver looked to the back of the truck. What a surprise he got! The impact of the crash had saved the boy's life, dislodging the gum in his throat.

So often we see some good resulting from seeming disaster. As in this case—the collision, instead of killing, saved a life. If only we can remember that our present misfortune may ultimately prove to be our good fortune—our lives can be happier, our paths smoother.

This does not mean acting recklessly to be sure. But if, in trying to do good for love of God, you make unintentional mistakes, don't be disheartened. Some good is bound to result.

"Who hath delivered, and doth deliver us out of so great dangers: in Whom we trust that He will yet also deliver us." (II Corinthians 1:10)

⇒ O God, help me to be so generous in serving Thee that some good may even come from my mistakes.

171

THE PRICE WE MUST PAY

It takes about a ton of ore to produce a small ball of gold, the size of a button, weighing only a fraction of an ounce, and worth about $14.

The extraction of gold from the earth is a slow, hard, complicated process. It has to be blasted out of solid rock, taken with great difficulty from the depths of a mine, crushed, washed, blended with mercury, heated in a furnace and soaked with cyanide, before it can finally be sold at the United States Mint in the form of gold bricks.

Discovering and developing the good, the true and the beautiful that God has deposited in you and every other human being is like extracting gold from the earth. It takes vision, diligence and patience.

To fulfill the purpose of our existence means constantly exercising the will to be creative, to be selfless, to be wise, to be good. But the attainment of the kingdom of heaven is worth all the lifetime of effort it takes to attain it. It is the pure gold of the spirit.

"Be thou faithful unto death: and I will give thee the crown of life." (Apocalypse 2:10)

⋙ Holy Spirit, inspire me to keep ever striving to fulfill the reason for which I was born.

THE PRICE OF ANGER

In a recent golf tournament in Oklahoma City one contestant found himself a loser in the first round. He had lost his ball in the deep rough, and had searched for it for fifteen minutes instead of the five allowed by the rules.

When he was penalized by the chairman of the rules committee, he became so angry that he slammed his driver against the ground and broke it. As a club may only be replaced when damaged in the normal course of play, he was not permitted to use another.

Through losing his temper, he lost not only a valuable club, but the golf match as well. To lose control is often to lose control of everything, of one's mind, heart and soul. In a moment of passion we may do something which we may regret the rest of our lives.

It is not necessary for anyone to be a slave to any harmful emotion. One of man's noblest assets is the God-given ability to control himself.

The best way to master our emotions is to fill our hearts with God's love. We will find our love for each other increasing so much that anger will be well nigh impossible.

"Revenge not yourselves, my dearly beloved, but give place to wrath." (Romans 12:19)

᷎ O God, help us to master ourselves.

AN INVESTMENT FOR ETERNITY

Twenty years ago a Philadelphia coal dealer invested $300 in some stock. The investment prospered and is now worth $1,000 which he will receive when and if he is found.

The big problem is to find him. No one seems to be able to locate him.

Perhaps over the years this coal dealer forgot that he set aside this sum. At any rate, we are sure that if he is found, he will be greatly surprised to find that his original investment has more than trebled.

Whenever we do something for love of God, we are making an investment that will last for eternity, even though we may not be aware of it. Very often people are disappointed because they spend a lifetime doing good for His sake, and they don't seem to be appreciated.

Some are even tempted to think that God has forgotten them. But God never forgets what we do for His sake. He had promised to reward all our endeavors—even to the handing of a cup of cold water to one who is thirsty.

The Supreme Judge of the world sees and remembers all we do, and though we may not be rewarded here, our reward will be even greater in eternity with Him. We can't lose!

"The Lord is the portion of my inheritance and of my cup: it is thou that wilt restore my inheritance to me." (Psalms 15:5)

~§ O Lord, help us to take the long view in all that we do for Thee and others.

174

ADVENTURE IN THE RIGHT DIRECTION

A fifteen-year-old boy in Port Chester, N.Y., was recently turned over to the Juvenile Court for setting fire to two lumber yards and causing damages estimated at $275,000.

When asked why he did it, the teen-ager replied that he threw lighted matches on the dry grass in the yards because he wanted to see the fire engines come to put out the blaze.

The yearning for adventure is common to all human beings. It is especially evident in young people for they have not yet lost the fearlessness of danger that steadily diminishes in adults.

Love of adventure is not evil in itself. It is only made so when it is directed into wrong channels. In fact, it is this same God-given urge that is responsible for most of the world's progress.

It is not necessary for youngsters to become vandals in order to find excitement. We live in a world that needs those who are willing to leave the beaten paths and blaze new ways of adopting the changeless truths to our changing times.

"Instruct thy son, and labour about him, lest his lewd behavior be an offence to thee." (Ecclesiasticus 30:13)

᷒ᔆ O God, give us wisdom to channel in the right direction the spirit of adventure Thou has placed in the young.

LEARN FROM MISTAKES

A famous playwright met some friends just after the first performance of his new play which had been given a chilly reception by the first-night audience.

"How did your play go tonight?" one of them asked.

"Oh," he answered, *"the play was a great success, but the audience was a failure."*

It is natural for most of us to avoid admitting we may be wrong in our approach. We tend to blame others. We lose much if we do.

If we take an honest appraisal of why and how we make mistakes and then proceed to use what we have learned to prevent future ones we gain much.

If we are to do effective work in the service of God, we must learn how to shoulder our responsibilities, and how honestly and fearlessly to face up to our mistakes and failures when we make them, and then to do all we can to right them. From every criticism, each of us can learn something, especially if it does not stop us, but helps to purify our intentions and stimulate us to greater courage.

"Who can say: My heart is clean, I am pure from sin?" (Proverbs 20:9)

O Lord, teach us to see ourselves as Thou dost see us.

A COSTLY OVERSIGHT

A radio store owner in Oakland, Calif., was recently taught a sharp lesson. To stimulate trade he had sponsored a contest, offering a television set as a prize to the winner. The contestants merely had to guess the correct four-numbered combination to his store's safe. It did not occur to the store owner to set a limit on the number of entries. And this was where he made his big mistake.

An ingenious, if somewhat roguish contestant was the only one to submit the winning number. He took the prize by using this single loophole. He submitted 10,000 numbers, starting with 1000 and ending with 9999 covering every possible combination that could open the safe.

The incensed store owner went to the police with his problem. But they assured him that the man had won fairly since he had overlooked placing any limit on the number of entries.

In these critical times when so much is at stake none of us can afford to be negligent even in the slightest detail. Those who would enslave and destroy all mankind are ever alert. They shrewdly watch for even the slightest oversight on the part of those who should be devoted to love of God and country.

"Be ye therefore wise as serpents and simple as doves." (Matthew 10:16)

ᴥ§ Keep me keen and ever-watchful, O Lord, where the welfare of all men is at stake.

HONESTY BRINGS PEACE OF MIND

A psychiatrist in Long Beach, Calif., listened quietly as the nervous woman before him poured out her tale. Her body shook nervously as she told him the reason for her five years of steadily increasing mental suffering. Scarcely had she finished her account when the doctor got up, held out her coat for her, and said gently, *"We are going to the police."*

At the police station, the psychiatrist did the explaining. Five years ago his patient had found a wallet containing $35. She knew that she should return it to the owner, whose name and address were on the identification card, but she couldn't bring herself to return the money.

The whole thing had preyed so on her mind, that she was in danger of a nervous breakdown.

Dishonesty, even on a small scale, can warp a person's life. It is one more proof that the laws of God cannot be trifled with. On the other hand, devotion to truth and honesty brings great peace of mind.

"Therefore let us follow after the things that are of peace; and keep the things that are of edification, one towards another." (Romans 14:19)

&O Supreme Judge, keep me ever mindful that one day at Thy high tribunal I must render an account of all my thoughts, words and deeds.

NIP IN THE BUD

Two women in Hamilton, Ohio, have been neighbors for some time, but a deep-rooted ill-feeling between them recently brought them into court.

The woman who filed the complaint against her neighbor wrote three type-written pages, listing her grievances. She said that her neighbor deliberately poured hot grease on her rose and lilac bushes; that she shoved a burning tub so close to the plants that it scorched them; that she pushed the nozzle of a hose into the ground so that the flow of water would damage the foundation of her home; that she trampled down a fence and smeared crayon marks on her newly painted garage.

She felt that she had suffered enough at the hands of this unkind woman, and so she brought suit against her for $35,000.

Squabbles of this sort can usually be nipped in the bud if one "contestant" overcomes his or her natural tendency to fight back. Put into practice the divine recommendation of Christ to continue to be kind and patient with others. It not only helps you retain your calm, but in a most disarming way it gradually calms down the other person too.

"If therefore thou offer thy gift at the altar, and there thou remember that thy brother hath anything against thee; . . . go first to be reconciled to thy brother, and then coming thou shalt offer thy gift." (Matthew 5:23, 24)

O Lord, let me realize that I can start to bring peace to the world from my own little circle.

179

HABITS CAN BE GOOD OR EVIL

Back in 1905 the first telephone coin boxes were installed in San Francisco. This opened a new avenue for petty theft. One man found himself serving his first jail term for looting the coin boxes.

He was released in due time, but somehow he hadn't learned his lesson. He continued his petty thievery through the years.

Time and time again he was arrested. He spent many nights in jail and served two long prison terms. Recently, he was picked up and sent to jail again. He is now 89 years old. The charge—*looting telephone coin boxes!*

One of the greatest dangers of allowing seemingly small defects to develop in our lives is that they slowly but surely develop into lifelong habits that are difficult to uproot.

The more each of us takes it upon himself to devote our time and talents to seeking the well-being of others, the less we tend to cater to our own weaker instincts. Good habits in this direction are easily developed and make the path to heaven a comparatively easy one.

"Make unto you friends of the mammon of iniquity; that when you shall fail, they may receive you into everlasting dwellings." (Luke 16:9)

≈§ O Lord, let me be so busy doing good for others that I will not have a chance to be caught in my own failings.

WHEN THINGS SEEM HOPELESS

Watching a parade in Springfield, Mass., a man leaned a little too far out a third story hotel window and lost his balance. As he started to fall his eye caught sight of a flagpole jutting out below his window. He grabbed for it and made it.

But the pole was frail. Hardly had he caught it, when it began to bend under his weight. He looked around quickly. Seeing a sign bracket directly beneath him he lunged for it. The sharp iron cut into his palms and, powerless, he felt himself losing his grip on the sign. Again he fell, this time about 10 feet. Once more his searching hands found a chain which supported the lower end of a sign. Fright and genuine physical peril had weakened him, however, and he knew his safety was only temporary.

By this time, spectators below were aware of his strange descent and had rushed upstairs, managing to haul him through a second-story window just in time.

In any situation or circumstance where everything seems hopeless, then is the time to remind ourselves that God is ever near and ready to help if only we will let Him. Look hard enough and you will always find "a flagpole, a sign, a chain" to protect you.

"And though in the sight of men they suffered torments, their hope is full of immortality . . . God hath tried them, and found them worthy of himself." (Wisdom 3:4, 5)

⇐§ Dear Lord, when misfortune is my lot, be near, and keep me safe.

FIND YOUR HAPPINESS IN OTHERS

In Korea in July of 1953, a 21-year-old young man died under enemy fire just one hour before an official halt was called to the shooting. He had been in the army only eight months.

Back home in New York, his mother received the shocking telegram with stunned disbelief. He had been her youngest son, and the news of his death was almost more than she could bear. For many months, she bore her silent grief in despairing numbness. Life seemed to have lost all meaning for her.

Then on Christmas morning, her doorbell rang, and a neighbor with a telegram in her hand said excitedly, "I ran over to tell you that my son is coming home." The bereaved mother looked at her neighbor's radiant face. "And suddenly I felt better," she told friends, who were amazed at the change in her attitude.

By rejoicing in the good fortune of others we can often lighten our own burdens. In fact, excessive sadness is frequently a form of possessive selfishness rather than real concern for others or resignation to the will of God. Entering into the joys and sorrows of others is the divine formula for getting out of our own sadness and depression.

"Blessed are they that mourn: for they shall be comforted." (Matthew 5:5)

⋙ Help me by love of others, O Lord, to overcome my own problems.

THE CHANCES MEN WILL TAKE

You would think steeplejacks have enough danger in their lives without looking for more of it. But four of them in Buffalo found climbing steeples tame work in comparison to an adventure on which they recently embarked.

With only $1000 each, they set off on a 12,000-mile expedition that was to take at least six months to complete.

They went first to Okefinokee Swamp in Georgia looking for a 12-foot alligator for the St. Louis Zoo.

From there they went to the Superstition Mountains in Arizona to hunt for the fabulous lost Dutchman gold mine which was covered up by a landslide in the last century.

After that they pushed their way into the Nicaraguan jungle to snare jaguars for the Buffalo Zoo.

They filmed 6-foot lizards in Panama and then started out for the Galapagos Islands in the Pacific to record the antics of giant turtles.

It is amazing to see to what lengths men will go, what chances they will take, for a small gain. If they would spend one tenth of the time and energy striving for the rewards that last for eternity we couldn't help having peace in this world.

"Fight the good fight of faith." (I Timothy 6:12)

ᴥᣠ O Lord, inspire me to be as daring for the rewards of eternity as others are for the fleeting gains of this life.

FEEL SORRY FOR YOURSELF?

A traveler strolled up to a fisherman. *"Having any luck?"*

"Pretty good," replied the angler. *"I haven't had a bite in three hours."*

"What's so good about that?" asked the amazed traveler.

"You see that guy over there? Well, he hasn't had a bite in six hours."

Many people spend a good part of their lives feeling sorry for themselves. They would help themselves and countless others by thanking God for His many blessings and showing a thoughtful concern for those who are less fortunate.

For example, you could do a little work in a hospital ward or an orphanage; spend some time with the mentally ill; visit war veterans who are largely forgotten by the general public for whom they fought so bravely.

Knowing and sympathizing with the troubles and heartaches of others can also be a powerful stimulant to those who live a safe, sheltered existence. It may encourage them to get into the mainstream of life and strive to correct in Christ's name some of the abuses that bring misery and death into the lives of many.

"As long as you did it to one of these my least brethren, you did it unto me." (Matthew 25:40)

⁊ Help me, dear Jesus, to show sympathy for others, not seek it for myself.

184

TAKING A STAND

On July 4, 1776, the Declaration of Independence, the basic document of our heritage of freedom, received its first signature by John Hancock, the delegate from Massachusetts.

Grasping the pen, he wrote his name in letters so sweeping that since that day *"putting your John Hancock"* on paper has become synonymous with making a signature. As he wrote it, he exclaimed: *"There! John Bull can read that without spectacles, and may double his reward of five hundred pounds for my head. That is my defiance!"*

Courage on the part of the least individual can have far-reaching results. Courage, too, is contagious. A brave stand by one person can inspire countless others to bring into play the force for God that He has entrusted to every one of us.

Now more than ever in our nation's history is a time for great courage, in ideals, purpose and action. We stand at a crossroads in history. Our hope for survival lies in bold action to uphold and strengthen those principles of freedom for all under God, on which our nation was founded.

"The Lord will give strength to his people: the Lord will bless his people with peace." (Psalms 28:10)

❧ O Lord, inspire us with reverence for Thee and courage in fighting for the rights of all.

DID THE SANDWICHES COUNT MORE?

The little boy's father was standing at the edge of a cliff admiring the scenery. In his hand was a small lunch box.

While the father was gazing in rapture at the sea below, his son approached him and shouted: *"Mother says it isn't safe here—and you are either to come away or else give me the sandwiches."*

In one way or another we all reveal the real purpose behind our thoughts, words and deeds. We may outwardly pretend to be deeply interested in others and yet be inwardly striving to further our own personal advantage regardless of the rights and well-being of others. But sooner or later one's selfishness betrays itself to others in some way.

In developing a love of others for the sake of God, the most important step to take is to build up within yourself—in your mind and heart—that inner strength of spirit that must be the foundation of all outward goodness.

"Out of the abundance of the heart, the mouth speaketh." (Matthew 12:34)

 O Divine Redeemer, teach me to develop by reflection and prayer that inner power that will give a true force to all that I say and do.

TRAPPED IN THE QUICKSANDS

A 12-year-old boy in Houston, Texas, was saved in the nick of time from almost certain death. This youngster, Bobby Vick, and another boy had been wading in an inlet. The water was only two or three inches deep but under it lay a lot of soft mud. Bobby had caught a crawfish and ventured a few feet further to release it.

Sooner than he realized, he had sunk to his knees in the soft mud. Sinking deeper and deeper, he pleaded with his companion to run for help. Soon two men hurried to the scene and quickly tied a rope around Bobby. They pulled him out just in time.

You read much these days about young people being caught in the *"quicksands"* of juvenile delinquency, immorality, narcotics, thievery and other evils that can suck them into deadly and dangerous habits much sooner than most think.

But don't be merely a bystander, standing on the banks and watching them sink. Do something positive and constructive to pull them out while there is still hope.

Few young people are bad at heart. But seeking normal, harmless adventure they can easily be tricked. There is something that you, personally and individually, can do to provide them with the wholesome entertainment that they seek and deserve.

"As long as you did it to one of these my least brethren, you did it to me." (Matthew 25:40)

↞§ O Lord, inspire me to work as hard to save the body and soul of youth as others do to debase them.

187

TWO POINTS OF VIEW

An art teacher we know claims that there are abundant opportunities under existing laws to mention God in classroom teaching.

She told us of an experience she had not long ago. A discussion in her class centered on Rodin's famous sculpture, *"The Thinker."* One of the students said: *"He is saying to himself: 'The cost of living is going up. Times are very bad.'"*

The teacher replied: *"No, I do not believe he is thinking of that. He is more likely thinking of eternity. He seems to say: 'Who put me here, and what am I here for?'"*

A full objective treatment of art cannot escape frequent reference to the things of God. The competent teacher who is interested in transmitting the full meaning of art will respect this fact and feel an obligation to transmit it to those who look to her for guidance.

The truth, the goodness and the beauty of God reflect themselves in a thousand ways.

Rather than spend too much time criticizing those who see the glum, seamy side of things, do what you can to draw attention to what is noble and inspiring. You will be surprised some day how many you will have helped.

"Whither shall I go from thy spirit? or whither shall I flee from thy face? If I ascend into heaven, thou art there: if I descend into hell, thou art present." (Psalms 138:7, 8)

ᅫ§ Grant, O divine Beauty, that I may constantly remind others that they may have Thee for time and eternity.

THIS ABOVE ALL

A woman in Chicago gave a very significant answer when she was asked why she spent most of her life working for others less fortunate than herself. At first she said that she was only doing what God expected of any person blessed with a little extra of this world's goods and time to spare. She put it this way: *"I love people. I love everyone with whom I come in contact."*

In her own way, she imitates Christ in an all-embracing love that includes all and excludes none.

The greater your love for everyone without exception, the more good you are bound to do in life. There is no substitute for love. You hurt nobody by loving them. There is no one so hostile or unfriendly who will not *"defrost"* at least a tiny bit as the result of an act or word of kindness. The more hateful one may be, the more love he needs.

Christ put His command to love others for love of God above all else. It is something that even the least person can do. And the more he strives to enrich the lives of others, the more he unconsciously enriches his own.

"This is my commandment, that you love one another, as I have loved you." (John 15:12)

✑ Allow me, O Savior, to carry Thy divine love to the millions who long for it.

DON'T LET THEM FOOL YOU

A fortuneteller surveyed a prosperous looking man who came into her shop. The man seemed to be a likely prospect. He was taken behind the dingy curtains.

"You will marry the girl you are taking out," he was told. The man smiled. Encouraged, the gypsy went on. She leaned forward earnestly. *"I see money for you—a lot of money—$10,000 that should come to you. But you will not receive this money until a curse hanging over you has been removed."*

The man looked at her sharply. *"How can I have this curse removed?"* he asked.

The gypsy waved her hand dramatically. *"It is simple,"* she said. *"For $5 I could easily break the curse."*

The fortuneteller was quite happy with such easy pickings. But her joy was short-lived. The man suddenly produced a police badge, and hauled her off to the station.

When she stood before the judge, she had her own future read without benefit of crystal ball or any other medium. She was told to leave town within two weeks, or she would be put in jail. She was glad to go, especially after learning that the detective was already happily married.

"Seek ye therefore first the kingdom of God and his justice, and all these things shall be added unto you." (Matthew 6:33)

⊷§ O God, keep me from being swayed or duped by the catchy half-truths of those who would lead me away from Thee.

WHAT ONE BUS DRIVER CAN DO

It was a crowded bus that I boarded on 8th Avenue in New York City. But different than others, most passengers on this bus seemed to have a pleasant, relaxed look.

It didn't take long to discover why. One person was responsible for it—the bus driver. He went out of his way to be kind and considerate to every person that got on and off.

Sitting a few seats behind him, I watched this unusual driver cheerfully adapt himself to the whims of the endless stream of passengers that made him their target in one way or another.

There were countless excuses for him to get impatient. But for him, each person was an individual who deserved to be treated with consideration. No bill was too large for him to change. No question was asked that exasperated him. He took a moment to help old ladies down to the curb.

Yes, the world is a bit better because that one bus driver is in it. It can be because you are, too. You can be an important instrument in bringing a little of Christ's love into a world that needs and wants it so much.

"So let your light shine before men, that they may see your good works, and glorify your Father who is in heaven." (Matthew 5:16)

✎ O Jesus, allow me to reach as many persons as possible with the love and peace for which all men yearn.

LOTS FOR LITTLE

A 22-year-old business man in Somerville, Mass., paid a premium of $60 on an insurance policy—and 3 months later collected $62,336!

This is how it happened. He and a friend of his took out a partnership insurance which would cover the life of each partner. One month later, the other man was killed, and as a consequence—all for the price of $60—the remaining partner will receive $24,970 outright, and an additional $37,366 at the rate of $208 a month for the next fifteen years! The John Hancock Insurance Co. said it was one of the largest amounts ever paid for that type of policy.

We seldom advert to the fact that Almighty God makes a far greater return to the slightest investment we make on our own initiative in the lasting values of heaven.

Over and over again in the Gospels, Christ reminds us in a hundred different ways that we can lay up huge treasures for eternity if in this life we give of ourselves in working for the best interests of others.

"Lay up to yourselves treasures in heaven: where neither the rust nor moth doth consume, and where thieves do not break through, nor steal." (Matthew 6:20)

⟡ O Judge of the world, instill in me the wisdom of investing for eternity.

THEY STOPPED THE WRONG MAN

It was the noon hour in downtown Philadelphia, and the man was hungry. Through the plate-glass window of a restaurant he could see the fragrant hot food being served to the noonday customers. He had started through the door when he was suddenly snatched back onto the sidewalk.

Two clean-shaven young men in business suits firmly propelled their indignant victim to the side and produced police badges for his inspection.

"Now, where do you work, Buster?" one of them demanded.

"At the police station," the man answered with a twinkle in his eye.

"Oh, a wise guy, huh?" the questioner growled.

"No," replied the man, still calmly. *"I'm the magistrate of this precinct,"* and he produced his identification to prove it.

The two youthful policemen in plain clothes were more than confused. They had mistaken the magistrate for a certain bookie that had been ordered arrested.

In the pursuit of duty, we should be valiant and courageous. But we must likewise take great care not to jump to conclusions that are unfair to others.

"With what judgment you judge, you shall be judged."
(Matthew 7:2)

≈§ Holy Spirit, help me to treat others as I wish to be treated myself.

GETTING THERE IS HALF THE FUN

You may have seen the full page advertisement that a trans-Atlantic steamship line ran in several magazines recently. It was topped with these words in big, bold letters: *"Getting there is half the fun!"*

There was something alluring about the way this reminder stressed that a sea trip could do magic things. *"Evenings brilliant with gaiety, dancing, social activities,"* it went on to say and then continued the rosy picture with *"days of continuous pleasure and relaxation in the wonderful, healthful sea air! Whether you cross to Europe or cruise to glamorous ports, the problems of the world fade away and peace and happiness move in . . ."*

No question about it, a sea trip even on a freighter can be stimulating and invigorating. But sooner or later like it or not, the gay traveler finds himself very much back in the *"problems of the world."*

Look around you and note the peace of mind and soul in those who are patiently and persistently trying to sail the stormy seas of life to the port of Heaven. They find a certain fun in life. Everything has a meaning. They know why they are here and where they are going.

They have actually begun their heaven on earth. Yes, in one sense, too, they show that they are getting a real joy in just trying to get to heaven—that *"getting there is half the fun."*

"Fear not little flock, for it has pleased your Father to give you a kingdom." (Luke 12:32)

⋘ O Jesus, help millions to realize the real fun in life is knowing Thee.

STUMBLING INTO TROUBLE

A construction worker in Baltimore suffered a painful, costly accident not long ago. A piece of equipment fell on him and broke both his arms and legs. He was laid up for months.

When he went back to work, he was determined to be particularly careful. He kept his eyes riveted above him whenever any heavy object had to be passed over his head.

One day recently a piece of steel was being swung above him. As usual the worker fastened his eyes on it, so as to jump to safety if it happened to fall in his direction. While he was most cautious about danger from above, he neglected to observe trouble right under his nose. He didn't see the eight-inch hole in the ground before him. He walked right into it, and broke his leg.

In the busy, complicated, modern life that confronts practically all of us, we have difficulty in avoiding trouble of one kind or another even when we make a special effort to lead normal, sensible lives.

But if we stray away from God's law and the moral principles that are essential to peace, we stumble into trouble that hurts not only ourselves but the numerous others who are affected by the way we act.

"And lead us not into temptation. But deliver us from evil." (Matthew 6:13)

⊷ Grant, O Lord, that I may avoid evil by doing good.

EVERY LIFE IS IMPORTANT

Five floors above 106th Street in New York, a policeman had to talk and act fast to save a man's life. The man had dashed to the roof of a building and was threatening to leap. Neighbors called the police, and when they arrived the man was poised on the roof's edge, ready to jump.

One of the patrolmen crept, inch by inch, to the edge of the roof, meanwhile engrossing the man in conversation. But his words had no effect. As the policeman drew near, the would-be suicide cried, *"Don't come any closer or I'll grab you by the hand, and take you with me!"*

But the policeman kept coming, and finally reached out to take his hand. True to his word, the would-be suicide grabbed him, and attempted to drag him over the parapet. But the patrolman was the stronger, and he pulled him away from the roof's edge to safety.

Life is cheap in many lands. Little or no effort is made to save the lives of others who are endangered. In the United States we instinctively think and act differently because our concept of the individual is rooted in the divine truth that even the least individual is important because he is made in God's image. Do all you can to revive that concept of man and to restore it to all phases of American life.

"As long as you did it to one of these my least brethren, you did it to me." (Matthew 25:40)

&⸸ O God, help me to see Thy likeness in those who stray furthest from Thee.

196

HE SPOKE UP

Two hundred and fifty thousand spectators lined the Lake Washington Course Gold Cup boat races, and hundreds of thousands more were looking at them on television when one of the boats crashed, killing the driver and co-driver.

Immediately Bill O'Mara, reporting this sports classic on TV, fell to his knees and said to his vast audience: *"I know only one thing I can do now for those men. Won't you join me in saying the Lord's Prayer for them?"*

The television audience saw the kneeling figure of the popular sports announcer. They heard his voice leading them in prayer for the souls of the men who had just been killed.

The TV station received many calls regarding this dramatic incident. Practically all praised O'Mara's good deed.

Most people believe in God. But all too often we tend to keep silent about it and to regard worship of God as a private, even secretive, affair rather than as a great gift to be shared with others.

Perhaps if—as this reporter—we had the courage to be open in our beliefs, many others would have their faith strengthened.

"Everyone that shall confess me before men, I will also confess him before my Father who is in heaven." (Matthew 10:32)

⸫ O Saviour of the world, give me the zeal to do all in my power to bring Thee to a world that needs Thee so much.

TAKE RESPONSIBILITY—DON'T RUN AWAY FROM IT

A study made not long ago revealed that most young Americans look for jobs that pay a lot of money, require little work, and provide long vacations.

From a natural point of view, that is understandable. But there is a hidden danger in taking the line of least resistance. It quickly develops a reluctance to take responsibility. God expects each of us to carry our share of the load in the home, work, school, government, trade unions and in fashioning the trends of the day. If we run away, it simply means that the part that God expects each of us to play in bringing peace to the world is not played!

Worse still, shirking our responsibilities is playing right into the hands of those who are dedicated to corruption, disloyalty, subversion or any other form of evil that undermines our institutions and leaves them open to those whose goal is to enslave all mankind. Seldom if ever do you find the apostles of evil evading responsibility. They are ever alert to take up every bit that the average good person abandons.

Do what you can to spread a better understanding of the importance of each taking responsibility instead of running away from it. You will be doing a work of God if you do!

"I must work the works of him that sent me, whilst it is day: the night cometh, when no man can work." (John 9:4)

⋙ Let me know my duty, O Holy Spirit, and give me the wisdom and strength to fulfill my obligations rather than evade them.

HE GAVE 273 PINTS OF BLOOD

A Cherokee Indian, Chief Running Horse, recently donated his 273rd pint of blood to the Red Cross.

It was back in 1928 that he started sharing his blood with others. For some time he was giving a pint or more per week. When questioned he said that he suffered no ill effects from giving away so much blood. *"I never miss it,"* he claimed. Chief Running Horse is strong and hardy, and loves outdoor life. His blood replenishes itself with amazing rapidity.

If you single out some person who is as generous, as the Indian was, in sharing the mental and spiritual troubles of others, you will probably find that they are none the worse for it either. In fact, in most instances they gain greater interior strength for themselves the more they give of themselves.

Notice likewise that those who live for themselves and carefully avoid giving of themselves—physically, mentally or spiritually—for the sake of others begin to deteriorate and shrivel up long before their time.

God hides a special reward for those who dare to do His will. They find that by enriching the lives of others, they enrich their own even more.

"He who loses his life shall find it . . ." (Matthew 10:39)

O Lord, let me continue without ceasing to give of myself to others.

FOR GOOD OR FOR EVIL

In an address at the eighth annual convention of the Radio-Television News Directors Association in Washington, D. C., Mr. Harold E. Fellows, the president of the Association, called on radio-TV newsmen to do all they could to weed out the undesirable influences from their ranks.

"A few among our own profession have as little sense of responsibility and integrity and as little direct respect for the truth as an habitual murderer has for human life," he said.

"One of the purposes to which such a professional society as yours should be devoted is that of digging out of the profession the malcontents and ne'er-do-wells, the liars and libelers, the irresponsible and the unjust."

Then he added, *"No medium in the history of mankind can tell a bigger lie than radio. We have seen it converted to that purpose, at the expense of world peace, within our time. Nor could any medium, by the same token, tell a bigger truth."*

There is something that you can do to encourage more with high ideals and competence to take up careers in the fields that shape, for better or for worse, the thought of mankind.

"Lift up your eyes and see the countries, for they are white already to harvest." (John 4:35)

✤ Grant, O Lord, that those in positions of influence are ever conscious of their responsibility.

IN THE CLUTCHES OF AVARICE

The change agent in a New York subway station was suddenly tensely alert. There he was again, the nattily dressed little old man that he had been looking for.

He would usually appear during the rush hour, glance furtively in the direction of the agent's cage, and then quickly pull the turn-stile towards him in the direction used for exits and skip through for a free ride.

But this time a transit patrolman was nearby. Quietly he spoke to the police officer waiting for his man to move. The elderly man now became suspicious. For two hours he just hung around. Even after the patrolman seemed to have left, he waited. Finally, he was convinced that both the agent and the patrolman had given up. But when he pulled the turnstile towards him, the patrolman who had been hiding was waiting for him.

The police discovered that this man had $1197 in cash, and $10,027 in bank deposits. And yet he took great trouble and risks to save 15¢ carfare by sneaking into the subway.

One of the best ways to keep far from the dangers of avarice is to devote your time, thought, prayers and money aiding others less fortunate than yourself.

"For the desire of money is the root of all evil." (I Timothy 6:9)

 O Divine Savior, grant me that generosity of soul that is sure protection against avarice.

LET NO DISASTER STOP YOU

A forty-five minute blaze in mid-town New York swept away the life work of sculptor Jacques Lipschitz.

"It's awful, just awful, part of my life is gone," the old sculptor moaned. But in the very same breath he caught himself. The greatness of his soul rose above the tragedy of the moment and he bravely and cheerfully said: *"I shall simply have to start all over again."*

You should never forget that, no matter what disaster may befall you, you have it within yourself to rise above your misfortune.

You have a bit of greatness that you may never have discovered. It is a gift of God to you *personally*. It is one tiny part of His Almighty power that He has entrusted to you and to nobody else.

Don't wait for misfortune to bring out the hidden greatness that is yours. One of the best ways to find it and strengthen it is to see Christ in every human being, and yearn to help each and all, even the worst.

"He that shall persevere unto the end shall be saved." (Matthew 10:22)

⇜ O Lord, grant me the vision and courage to push ahead through every difficulty.

A TEEN-AGER ON THE JOB

Shirley Lentz, a 17-year-old baby sitter, recently saved the lives of four small children and kept their home from burning down.

While waiting for the parents of the little ones to return, Shirley sensed that something was wrong. Smelling smoke, she flew to the kitchen. Her first reaction was one of helpless terror. One entire wall was ablaze.

Rushing into the children's bedroom, she quickly bundled them into their clothes and hurried them out of the house to a place of safety.

That wasn't enough for Shirley. Devotion to duty spurred her on to another daring act. There was a home to be saved. She was the only one who could make even an attempt to put out the fire.

Returning quickly into the burning house, she started to fight the flames with water. Her singlehanded fight was far from in vain. Firemen arrived just in time. Said one of them, *"In another ten minutes the house would have been gone."*

There is a tremendous potential for good in every teenager. Put youthful enthusiasm and resourcefulness to work in the right direction, and you will considerably lessen its trend towards evil.

"Rejoice therefore, in thy youth and let thy heart be in that which is good in the days of thy youth." (Ecclesiasticus X 11)

 O Divine Savior, help me to help others to help themselves.

SHARKS ARE COWARDS

Deep-sea divers have recently discovered that man-eating sharks are big cowards at heart. They have found that the shark is only provoked to attack when one tries to run away from it. That explains why swimmers, frightened at the sight of a shark fin cutting through the surface of the water, are frequently bitten when they try to hurry away in the opposite direction.

On the other hand, if one swims towards it, as if to attack, any variety of shark will usually turn tail and flee.

Some divers carry small gas guns which shoot a stream of bubbles. This strange phenomenon puzzles the sharks and they leave in a hurry.

As a display of courage will surprise and frighten away a shark, so will it take the wind out of the sails of those bent on graft, corruption, immorality, subversion and nearly every other kind of evil. They know in their hearts that they are wrong. That's one big reason why they are cowards at heart.

Speak up when trouble is brewing that may have an effect on everybody. God blesses in a special way those who make their voices heard for truth. If you take it upon yourself to resist beginnings of evil, you may prevent endless trouble for yourself and countless others.

"But God is faithful, who will strengthen and keep you from evil." (II Thessalonians 3:3)

&§ O Holy Spirit, let me show persevering courage where divine truth is at stake.

THEIR STRENGTH OUR WEAKNESS

The president of the AFL Hotel and Restaurant Workers Union, Hugo Ernst, recently called upon the rank and file of the 400,000-member union to assume their individual responsibility to help make their union more efficient, cooperative and honest.

Mr. Ernst pointed out that any breach of faith on the part of the union leaders is directly traceable to some failure on the part of the membership. Inertia or indifference on the part of the membership leaves the way open for corrupt leadership. He said that the membership has the power to control the union not only through union rules and constitutions, but especially by an active interest and participation that sees to it that principles are put into practices.

It seldom occurs to the average person that defects in the running of government, schools, labor relations the world over are largely due to the neglect of millions like himself.

If you are conscientious about your own obligations, especially since they affect the welfare of others, you will shoulder your own share of the responsibilities. It is between you and God how you put your convictions into practice. But it is important that you do it without delay.

"He that loveth not knoweth not God: for God is charity." (I John 4:7–8)

◦§ Help me to remember, O Lord, that neglect to fulfill my obligations can harm countless others.

PEACE STARTS WITH YOU

A woman in Ann Arbor, Michigan rushed into the traffic bureau, with three parking tickets. The police clerk was busy at the time and she showed great impatience as she waited for him.

The clerk looked at her in surprise. *"What's your hurry, lady?"* he asked when he got to her.

"My car is parked in a 'no parking' zone, and I have to hurry and move it before I get another ticket," she answered as she hurried towards the street, after paying her fines.

One reason why the world is in such a dither today is that too many people fail to realize that lasting peace cannot come to humanity until enough people take it upon themselves to bring law and order right into their own lives.

For one person to continue to show disregard for authority, honesty and God's laws seems of little consequence. But when tens of millions of individuals start thinking and acting that way, then we are all just a couple of jumps ahead of chaos.

What can you do about it? More than you think. Figure out what is necessary for peace in the world and then start applying the conclusions to your own life. Next step: be a committee of one in sharing this reminder with others.

"Let peace be thy strength." (Psalms 121:7)

❧ Let me relearn, O Lord, that the peace of the world begins at my own doorstep.

MAKING A BAD SITUATION MUCH WORSE

A man in Pittsburgh, was in a big hurry. He had many appointments to keep that day. It was late, and he rushed out of the hotel down to the nearest restaurant to get something to eat before he went about his evening schedule.

After a hurried meal, he walked briskly up the street, and then suddenly stopped short. He had forgotten his hat!

Turning back towards the restaurant, he found to his dismay that it was closed. With a sudden surge of desperation, he took a brick and smashed the two plate glass windows till he had made a hole large enough to enter. After a long search, he finally decided that the hat wasn't there. Disappointed, he made his way back out through the broken windows right into the arms of a waiting policeman.

Hauled into court, he was charged $380 for damages. Rather a high price for any hat. It was only then that he discovered that the offending hat was left in the hotel, not in the restaurant!

Resorting to violence usually means jumping from the frying pan into the fire. If you are dominated by the love and truth of Christ, you will more easily exercise the self-control expected of you.

"In your patience you shall possess your souls . . ."
(Luke 21:19)

⇛ Help me, O my Redeemer, to show self-restraint in all that I do.

EVEN WHEN THE CUSTOMER IS WRONG

A clerk in a St. Louis department store gave one of her confreres a simple formula for remaining serene under all circumstances.

The second clerk, frequently exasperated by the unreasonable demands of customers, asked her friend how she managed to remain so calm and pleasant even when those on the other side of the counter showed a lack of consideration.

With a smile the first clerk replied: *"There is a bit of good in the most annoying customer. Try to find it and work on it. You'd be surprised how this disarms even the most disagreeable of them. Then too, it saves wear and tear on one's self—makes selling much more interesting."*

To be upset by those who are rude—or to be rude in return accomplishes nothing. In fact, you take a loss. Nothing burns up energy so fast as resentment and bitterness. You hurt no one more than yourself by returning meanness for meanness.

By being kind and considerate to those in your own home, at work or any other place even when they get on your nerves will help you to reach out to the bigger world to countless others who need the warmth and love that God sends them through you.

"The patient man is better than the valiant." (Proverbs 16:22)

 Let me show a loving patience, O Lord, towards those who ordinarily annoy me.

208

YOUR IMAGINATION CAN PLAY TRICKS

A group of doctors recently made tests to determine if a certain drug, tolserol, would help relieve anxiety and tension, or whether these symptoms were purely mental. Thirty-one test patients were given pills which looked exactly alike. But there was a difference—some of them were the new drug, the others were made of sugar. Code numbers held the secret as to which were which.

The patients believed that they were all taking the new drug. The results were interesting. About one-third reported that they felt better from either kind of pill. More than fifty per-cent experienced no change. But 10 to 20 per-cent said they felt worse. Some who had been taking sugar pills let their imagination get the best of them. They reported that they suffered palpitations, nausea and diarrhea as a result of the supposed medicine. One got a bad skin rash.

Because of our weakened nature, we often tend to put obstacles in our own way, to see the worst side of others, to complain rather than do something constructive. One way to bring out the best that is in you and at the same time overcome your failing is deliberately and bravely to start playing the role of a Christ-bearer or Christopher and working for the best interests of others.

"A fearful heart in the imagination of a fool shall not resist against the violence of fear." (Ecclesiasticus 22:22)

❧ O God, let me be so busy finding the good in others that I will have no time to be critical of them.

THE POWER OF YOUNGSTERS

Educators have discovered that the average child between the ages of 4 and 6, can learn to speak several
languages simultaneously, without interfering with his
native tongue. They have found further, that after the
age of six, the child is not as apt in the learning of
foreign languages as before.

For a long time now, our schools have followed the
theory that foreign languages are not to be taught until
the child has reached the high school level. Usually, the
courses are short basic ones, and the high school gradu-
ate seldom has more than a scant unworkable knowledge
of any other than his native tongue.

Don't underestimate either the capacity of youngsters,
even 6 years old, to show great vision for the future.
God has hidden great power in each of them. More than
a few have had their first dreams of dedicating their
lives to the service of others in religion, in medicine, in
journalism and other worthwhile careers at a tender age.
Many others would start thinking of a lifetime of use-
fulness if given a word of encouragement. Show a kindly,
thoughtful interest in the young people. They can be
the hope of the future if they are directed in the way
of Christ.

*"Suffer the little children and forbid them not to come
to me: for the kingdom of heaven is for such."* (Matthew 19:14)

⚬ Bless O Lord, all the young people and inspire them
to dedicate themselves to peace.

THE MISSING $10,000

A 74-year-old man walked up to the Traveler's Aid department in the Union Station in St. Louis, Missouri and told the directress, somewhat apologetically, that he was stranded, without money, and that he wanted to get back to his home in Arkansas.

The man's appearance belied his being penniless. *"Don't you have any money at all?"* the directress asked curiously. *"Oh, yes,"* the man answered. *"I have $10,-000."*

"Ten thousand dollars!" the woman exclaimed. *"And you're asking for help!"*

"Well, you see," the man exclaimed sadly *"The other day I put it in a bank for safe keeping. But now I can't remember which bank it was. I've been doing a lot of travelling. And I'm not even sure what town I deposited it in."*

You can do a great service to countless people if you take it upon yourself to help those who are stranded spiritually.

More and more human beings are baffled and frustrated by the delusions of modern life. They have forgotten where they came from, why they are here and where they are going. If you make an honest, persevering attempt to aid others in this way, God will show you many openings.

"He saith to him: Feed my lambs." (John 21:15)

Allow me, O Lord, to be Thy instrument in helping those who have lost their way to reach their heavenly home.

PLAYS ACCORDION FOR 75 HOURS

In Lausanne, Switzerland, an accordion player decided recently to break a world's record. Sitting down in a café at 8 o'clock one night, he started his unique marathon. With only a 15 minute break every three hours for meals, and a 20 minute break in the morning to wash, this brave man kept playing his accordion night and day for more than three successive days.

On the fourth day at 11 A.M.—75 hours later—the would-be champion dropped his tired accordion, claiming that he had broken all records. One wonders how an individual can go through such an ordeal for any sort of a title.

Regardless of what many may think of this sort of enterprise it is just one more proof that there is enormous power stored up in every individual. Once he sets his mind on any goal that is humanly possible he will endure anything to achieve it.

Many who devote such extraordinary energy and devotion to the pursuit of dubious honors the world over might accomplish great things for God and humanity if they decided to direct that power into channels that would be of lasting benefit to all.

"And the unprofitable servant, cast ye out into exterior darkness." (Matthew 25:30)

Help me, O Lord, to discover the talent that you have entrusted to me and to put it to use in the way that Thou wouldst have me do.

PEACE STARTS WITH YOU

Some time ago, the Safety Council of Worcester County, Mass., used to offer a weekly award to drivers who observed the safety rules and exhibited courtesy on the roads.

But eventually it was found necessary to discontinue this practice. The chairman of the council gave this as the reason: *"It is too difficult to find a courteous driver every week."*

Most of us keep wondering why we don't have peace in the world. Yet we overlook the fact that we can start right with ourselves in changing the world for the better.

There are a lot of things most of us cannot do. But it is within the grasp of one and all without exception to be courteous. A kind word or act takes only a moment whether you are at home, in the office, at the ball game, or driving in traffic.

But before there is any outward expression of courtesy there must be an inner love of people glowing in your heart and soul. Yes, the peace of the world begins in your very heart. If you fill it with the true love of God and others, it is bound to overflow in everything you do.

"And as you would that men should do to you, do you also to them in like manner." (Luke 7:31)

⌁ Let me learn to be courteous to all who cross my path, O Lord, so that I may be better prepared to bring peace to all men.

213

HOW MUCH IS A BILLION?

When things are numbered in terms of billions we rarely have an adequate conception of what these numbers mean. The following estimate gives us some understanding of how great a billion really is.

If a person had started in business in the year 1 A.D. with a capital of one billion dollars, and had managed his business so poorly that he would have lost $1,000 each day, by the year 1960 he would still have sufficient capital left from the original billion to continue in business, and lose $1,000 per day for nearly an additional 800 years.

If it is difficult to comprehend what a billion dollars amount to, it is well nigh impossible for the human mind to grasp the meaning of eternity. A billion years is only the beginning of the life hereafter which God has prepared for those that love and serve Him in this life.

The longest life is short compared to the endless years of eternity. Every hour of every day offers us countless opportunities to prepare for it.

"Eye hath not seen, nor ear heard, neither hath it entered into the heart of man, what things God hath prepared for them that love him." (I Corinthians 2:9)

∽§ Grant that I may so live, O my God, that I may merit to be with Thee for all eternity.

TIGER IN THE HOUSE

Not long ago, in Sydney, Australia, a little girl woke up in bed, and called out to her father: *"Daddy, quick, help me. Stop this big dog licking my face. He's on my bed."*

The father went to the child's room and stopped in horror. A tiger was on the bed licking the face of his 7-year-old daughter who was cowering under the covers, while her 3-year-old sister slept undisturbed beside her.

Quietly the father took his 22-calibre rifle and went into action. Taking careful aim he fired, and the bullet went through the tiger's nose and jaw.

Like a flash the tiger dashed through the door into the street. The animal, which had escaped from a nearby circus, was found dying from loss of blood.

Modern dangers that threaten young people are not as easy to detect and correct as a tiger licking a child's face. For the last few decades, there has been a world-wide conspiracy to teach children that they are not made in the image of God, but are merely another kind of animal. The debasing and brutalizing effect of this is beginning to show up in delinquency, crime, immorality and irreligion on a scale never known before.

You can do something to correct this dangerous trend by taking steps to see that a recognition of God and the moral law is restored to all phases of education.

"Suffer the little children to come unto me, and forbid them not. For of such is the kingdom of God." (Mark 10:14)

&§ Grant, O Lord, that I may work as hard to spiritualize youth as others are striving to brutalize them.

HE LEFT A HALF MILLION

When an 84-year-old man died in Brooklyn not long ago he was found to be so poor that he had to be buried in potter's field.

After his death, investigators were amazed to find that his dilapidated house was literally filled with junk which he had been gathering for years as he prowled the streets.

While they were in the midst of their search, the investigators stumbled on a much bigger surprise. They discovered that the *"poverty-stricken"* deceased had left $500,000 in a safe deposit vault.

What a terrible plight must all be in who when they stand before the Judgment Seat of God have nothing to show but a life of selfishness that has already been a torture in itself.

Pause occasionally and observe what punishment those take upon themselves who are driven by selfishness, pride or avarice. The goals they set for themselves are usually far more exacting than the sacrifice that Christ Crucified proposes to those who would win peace without end in preference to the fleeting and questionable rewards of this life.

"Lay not up to yourselves treasures on earth: where the rust and moth consume, and where thieves break through, and steal." (Matthew 6:19)

Let me never be so preoccupied by the flimsy attractions of the world, O Lord, that I miss eternal joys.

GARAGE BURNS UNDETECTED IN SMOG

The smog was so heavy in London recently that a garage burned to the ground without being seen. It was one more reminder of deathly danger in the air that has defied all efforts to offset it.

Authorities worried by 4000 deaths in one year as a result of the thick, smothering fog warned both householders and factories to stoke their fires and use smokeless fuels as much as possible.

"Please try to cut down on your emissions of smoke in order not to make the atmosphere thicker than it is," was the directive broadcasted by B.B.C.

Atmosphere of another kind is having a choking, deadly effect on modern life. The thick fog of pagan thought, carrying in it hidden and poisonous fumes, is taking a far greater toll in souls than most imagine.

Do all in your power to check the added trouble that may come from mistakes on your part or from the thought-forming channels that influence the destiny of millions.

Better still, pray and work to freshen up the atmosphere by bringing into the market-place the life-giving truth and joy of Christ that He intended for all men without exception.

"The path of the just, as a shining light, goeth forwards and increaseth even to perfect day." (Proverbs 4:18)

 O Lord, make me an instrument of Thy love and peace.

A COSTLY SHORT CUT

A man in Peoria, Ill., was anxious to avoid the necessity of buying new license plates for his car. So he set about finding some way in which to outwit the State.

One night he made his way to a junk yard and removed the plates from a wrecked auto. These he put on his own car. They were fairly new plates and in good condition, so he felt quite safe.

But he had underestimated the police system in his city. It wasn't long before he was hauled into the Police Court. He discovered too late that he had been penny wise and pound foolish. His fine was $76.50. New license plates would have cost him only $5.25!

Taking the law into our own hands seldom results in anything more than multiplying confusion and harm. Following orderly processes takes a bit longer, but it is God's way of doing things and it avoids plenty of trouble for time and eternity.

Those who complain of corruption, graft and underhandedness in offices of high standing seldom notice their own lapses in this direction. Never forget, for instance, that there is a briber behind everyone taking a bribe!

"If you love me, keep my commandments." (John 14:15)

⋙ Give me the wisdom to know Thy will, O Lord, and the courage to put it into practice.

FOR THOSE WHO SUFFER

Recently, a dentist in St. Louis, came up with a new idea to help remove some of the fear of dentists from the minds of children who came to his office.

Instead of the conventional white attire, he dresses in pastel colors, usually in soft yellows and greens. His two women assistants wear blue, and his office is decorated in pastel hues.

The dentist gave as his reason for this the fact that children seem to associate the usual sterile white with doctors in general and the shots that they receive periodically at school and at home. Usually, at the first sight of the dental office children burst into tears. This dentist reports that the change in the color scheme has worked wonders to alleviate this fear.

You may not be able to bring complete relief to countless persons afflicted in body or soul, gripped by passion, wasting away in concentration camps, or whose minds, hearts and souls are being tortured or poisoned by hatred and error. But the fact that you cannot do everything does not mean that you cannot do something.

Be it no more than a kind word, a brief prayer or a thoughtful act that you offer in Christ's Name, it can count for all eternity.

"As long as you did it to one of these my least brethren, you did it to me." (Matthew 25:40)

․§ Help me, O Lord, to seize every opportunity to relieve the suffering of others.

A LIFE FOR FIFTY CENTS

In a café on Broadway in New York City, a 19-year-old marine became involved in an argument with his companions about a check amounting to 50¢.

One word led to another, and pretty soon a fist-fight started. The police were not able to discover immediately how it happened. But whether he was thrown or fell, this young Marine went smashing through the plate glass door of the restaurant.

He was rushed to a hospital, but he died within an hour. Because of 50¢ a young life had been snuffed out.

It doesn't require very deep study to discover that most of the trouble that wracks the world today had its origin in seemingly minor difficulties that could have easily been solved if caught in time.

It is within your power to better rather than worsen problems and difficulties in which you may happen to be involved.

But do more than that. Reach out as far as you can in bringing the peace and truth of Christ to others. One day when you stand before the judgment seat of God, you may be surprised and delighted at all the good you have accomplished in this way.

"Blessed are the peace-makers: for they shall be called the children of God." (Matthew 5:9)

&§ O Lord, grant me the grace to draw people together through Thy love.

THE FINAL ACCOUNTING

A judgment of $12,000,000, one of the largest against a single individual, was recently decided against a 78-year-old man who had nearly finished his career in apparent glory.

It was a great blow to this businessman who was considered a great success in the eyes of the world. Financially he had all he wanted. He had arrived socially. His wife was numbered among the best dressed women in America.

Then almost overnight all this glittering success disappeared. He became an object of public shame. It was discovered that over a period of twenty years he had taken $12,000,000 of stockholders' money.

Sooner or later each and every one of us will have to answer before the Supreme Judge for every detail of our lives. We will report in detail on how we have respected the rights of others. An eternity of peace will await us if we have loved God above all things and our neighbor as ourselves.

"Give an account of thy stewardship: for now thou canst be steward no longer." (Luke 16:2)

⧉ O God, keep reminding me to be as thoughtful of the rights of others as I am of my own.

GREAT PROVOCATION

A man in Atlanta, Ga., recently reached the end of the proverbial rope of patience.

His neighbor in the apartment immediately below him had acquired a new television set, and kept it on full blast, so that night after night the man upstairs, his wife and baby were kept awake by the noise. Far into the night the man paced the floor to the blatant TV sounds and the screams of his restless child.

One night he had had enough. He took his 22-calibre rifle and went down to demand that his neighbor be more considerate. When the neighbor refused to open the door, he fired a bullet into the door. His frightened adversary phoned for the police.

While it is often difficult to restrain one's self when others show disregard for the rights of others, little is gained by *"shooting your way through."* Stubborn people seldom soften when methods are used that merely make them more stubborn.

It is easier to say than to put into practice, but there is something Christlike about being able to disagree without getting disagreeable. Even if you don't gain your end, at least you don't make a bad situation worse.

"And let every man be swift to hear, but slow to speak, and slow to anger." (James 1:19)

&ſ Teach me to mix much kindness with firmness when I must take a stand, O Lord.

A COSTLY DIVE

A 52-year-old Miami lawyer lost his life recently while attempting to break a diving record in the choppy blue waters of the Gulf Stream. A close friend had begged him not to attempt the hazardous venture especially in rough weather, but he persisted, saying he couldn't resist a challenge.

The lawyer's ambition was to break the diving record set by a Frenchman who descended to 396 feet but came up dead. The Miamian achieved his objective by plunging to a depth of 410 feet. But it meant little to him personally. He likewise died in the attempt.

Carried to an extreme, a laudable ambition can become a vice. Nothing can suck one into endless trouble and even death more completely than excessive pride. It can blind us if we throw caution to the winds and madly pursue our vain dreams.

The best protection against succumbing to this alluring vice is to practice the opposite—to seek the glory of God and the well-being of others.

"Never suffer pride to reign in thy mind, or in thy words: for from it all perdition took its beginning." (Tobias 4:14)

⊷§ Lord, teach me that humility of heart which will keep me from vain dreams and harmful pursuits.

223

ONE AIRLINE STEWARDESS' DEVOTION

The plane was taking off as scheduled from Idlewild International Airport in New York. The 33-year-old Philadelphia stewardess, Anne Louise Krause, made her usual check of the 27 passengers.

"Fasten your safety belts, please," she cautioned. Everything seemed to be the normal routine. It promised to be a pleasant flight. The weather was good.

Instead of making the usual swift ascent, the plane was bumping along the ground. In a matter of seconds there was a tremendous explosion.

The stewardess was thrown to the floor. She quickly regained her balance, realizing her first duty was to help the passengers to safety. Quietly, calmly, she spoke to them . . . reassuring them . . . telling them what to do. The screams subsided. The flames licked her neck and face and hands, the heat was almost unbearable, but she ignored it. One by one she helped them out the emergency door. When all were out, she got out herself, and kept the passengers together until help arrived.

You may never be called to show the heroism displayed by this stewardess. But in your individual way you can bring into play the same devotion and courage in caring for the temporal and eternal welfare of others. Many need the sympathetic leadership that you, personally and individually, can give them.

"Do ye manfully, and let your heart be strengthened, all ye that hope in the Lord." (Psalms 30:25)

🍃 Inspire me, O Lord, with daring and devotion in everything that concerns the eternal destiny of my fellowman.

THROUGH 500 KILLINGS

After 28 years as official photographer for the department of homicide investigation in New York County, a 61-year-old man recently retired. All these years, it has been his job to cover the picture end of homicides. Dozens of times he has had to hide in a truck or auto and take motion pictures of racketeers or hoodlums in action.

Often he risked his life to secure pictures of anything that the prosecutors thought might be used as evidence in a case.

During the 28 years of his career, this man covered more than 500 homicide cases with his camera. He estimated that in this time he took more than 100,000 pictures. He's retiring now because he says that he has had enough. Five hundred killings are quite a lot for one man.

Most persons would get tired of dealing with death far more quickly than this photographer. That is understandable. God has so constituted each of us that we find much more interest and stimulation in creating new life, sustaining weakened life, and in reclaiming and rehabilitating broken life—physical, spiritual and mental.

The more you do to restore the way, the truth and the life of Christ to all phases of private and public life, the less need there will be for homicide photographers.

"I am come that they may have life, and have it more abundantly." (John 10:10)

⋙ O Jesus, let me spend myself in bringing Thy life to as many as I can before I die.

225

UNDER A FREIGHT TRAIN

Christine Ragen, 18 months old, and her brother, Pat, aged 3, lived just fifty yards away from the railroad tracks in Townsend, Mont. But they didn't mind this at all. In fact they rather liked it. Whenever they heard the whistle of an approaching train, they would run outside to see it as it roared by.

But their mother was not so happy about the site of their home. Time and time again she warned them to stay far away from the tracks. But small children forget quickly.

She was very busy about the house on the day that the whistle sounded to herald the train. Suddenly she heard the screams of her small son. Her heart almost stopped as she ran out and saw a 50-car freight train halted in front of her door. The engineer was emerging from under it with the limp body of her daughter in his arms.

But relief flooded her when she found that the child was all right. She had run towards the train and fallen between the rails. The big locomotive and six cars had roared over her before the train could be brought to a halt. But miraculously, she had escaped uninjured.

When there is solicitude for those who are in danger, God often rewards this generosity with a special care.

Do your part in bringing the peace of Christ to all men.

"For he hath given his angels charge over thee; to keep thee in all thy ways." (Psalm 90:11)

◄§ Enable me, O Jesus, to be alert in helping those who cannot help themselves.

GOD NEVER FORGETS

Last winter a young woman in Vernon, N.Y., went into a store to buy a pair of gloves for her twin brother. Since they wore the same size gloves she tried several pair to see if they would fit.

Eventually she chose something else as a gift and left. Later she discovered that she had lost her ring. She was very disturbed at the loss. But not knowing where it could have occurred, she finally gave up the search.

A year later, her brother went shopping for a pair of gloves. He went into the same store that his sister had visited and tried on a pair. There in the finger of one of them was his sister's ring!

One great consolation we can have at all times is that nothing is ever lost as far as God is concerned.

You may have completely forgotten some good deed that you performed five or ten years ago—or even during the past few months. But it is registered in heaven in records that never fail.

The time is short for all of us on earth. We are here for only one purpose—to love our Maker above all things and our neighbor as ourselves. Every thought, word and action of love on your part will count for all eternity. Not one of them will ever be lost!

"And whosoever shall give to drink to one of these little ones a cup of cold water . . . he shall not lose his reward." (Matthew 10:42)

⊷ O Lord, I can never thank Thee enough for loving me even when I forget Thee.

GOOD IN THE WORST

Two New York policemen making their rounds late one night noticed two teen-age boys hurrying along rather furtively at an intersection. The boys spotted them at the same time, and began to run. Suspicions aroused, the policemen chased after them.

When the boys were caught, they would give no reason for their sudden flight. The policemen searched them, and found $61.25 in the pockets of one. After questioning, the boys admitted that they had just robbed a restaurant that had closed for the night. The policemen had the boys lead them to the place.

When they reached it they were all in for a surprise. Through the plate glass window, they saw another young man searching through the cash register. The policemen called to him to climb out over the transom. Caught redhanded, there was nothing for him to do but obey. But when he reached the sidewalk, he made an angry protest. *"That place has been robbed,"* he said. *"There isn't a nickel left."*

It's a bit of a paradox to have a thief complain about thievery, but still there's an element of hope in that contradiction. A sense of truth and justice lingers in even the worst. Build on that, with God's help, and you may turn many a sinner into a saint.

"Why seest thou the mote that is in thy brother's eye; and seest not the beam that is in thy own eye?" (Matthew 7:3)

◆§ Give me the wisdom and patience, O Jesus, to see the element of good in those who flaunt Thy law.

OLD PHOTO WINS HALF MILLION

A 67-year-old St. Louis, Mo., widow, Mrs. Della McKeon, who was forced by illness to quit her job 23 years ago, was recently notified that she would receive $479,730 of a three-and-a-half-million dollar will.

After a lengthy search, it was finally concluded that she was the missing heir. A faded photograph discovered in a distant relative's album in Pittsburgh first established her identity. Fortunately Mrs. McKeon had also kept a copy of the same photograph herself even though it had been taken 50 years ago when she was 17. This matching photo was the missing link that confirmed her right to share in the estate.

Mrs. McKeon, who has been living for the past few years in a two-room apartment with her son could hardly believe that it was true that she was to receive such a large inheritance.

Not one person in a hundred thousand can expect to meet with the good fortune of this widow. But it is a consoling thought to know that you will be remembered by Almighty God without having to go to the bother of furnishing any photographs or other evidence.

When you stand before the Judgment Seat you will be surprised and delighted to see that the slightest service you have rendered to others in Christ's Name will be rewarded for all eternity.

"That eye hath not seen, nor ear heard, neither hath it entered into the heart of man, what things God hath prepared for them that love him." (I Corinthians 2:9)

❧ Let me keep ever conscious, O Lord, that Thy reward is everlasting.

DEATH FOR DISOBEDIENCE

A man lay restless in an oxygen tent in a hospital in New Rochelle, N.Y. When admitted the night before, because of a heart attack, he was too ill to care about anything.

But feeling better the next morning, he desperately wanted a cigaret. But smoking was not permitted in his ward. As added precaution a big *"No Smoking"* sign was painted on the side of his oxygen tent. Despite these warnings, he decided to take a chance. No one would know the difference. He'd just have a puff or two. He took the pack of cigarets that they had left lying on the table beside him.

He never got even one puff. The very attempt to light his cigaret ignited a flash flame that swept over his body and burned him to death.

In many different ways God has revealed the law of life that He expects us to follow if we would make this life a fitting preparation for that life without end that begins when we have run our course on earth. At the same time, in deference to the free will He has given each of us, He leaves us at liberty to choose good or evil. Do all you can to remind others of the importance for eternity of the decisions they make each day.

"But I say unto you, that every idle word that men shall speak, they shall render an account for it in the day of judgment." (Matthew 12:36)

❧ O my God, let me use to advantage Thy gift of free will—not abuse it.

13-YEAR-OLD BOY LANDS PLANE SAFELY

Tony Hammond, a 13-year-old schoolboy, who never had any experience piloting a plane, surprised terrified spectators by landing a runaway private plane in Rocky Mount, N.C., not long ago.

It happened that Tony was sitting at the controls of the Piper Cub, while the pilot, William Gaither, was outside, twirling the propellor to start the engine. To his surprise, the engine suddenly started and the plane, with the throttle stuck, raced down the runway and into the air.

Even more amazed and horrified than young Tony was Richard Floyd, who had been sitting in the stationed plane and suddenly found himself on his first plane ride with a teen-ager at the controls who had no formal instruction.

Tony put to quick use the few principles he had learned out of textbooks about piloting a plane. For a quarter of an hour, he circled the airport. Then he decided to dare a landing. He pointed the nose towards the airfield and in a matter of moments had landed the plane safe and sound.

Teen-agers have a tremendous amount of resourcefulness within them. God has put that power there. He leaves it to each to discover for himself, with the help of others who should guide him.

"Rejoice therefore, O young man, in thy youth, and let thy heart be in that which is good in the days of thy youth." (Ecclesiastes 11:9)

O Lord, help me to help young people to use their power for good.

231

ENTERPRISE FOR EVIL

Recently, a 25-year-old kitchen-worker in London was arrested on the following charges: turning in 118 false fire alarms; sending 200 taxis on false errands; stealing approximately 300 letters; forging withdrawals on a stolen bank book; and stealing money from fellow porters.

The police said that beside these charges there were 130 more minor misdemeanors laid to his door, including desertion from the army on four different occasions.

This young man shows a strange display of enterprise. It requires considerable resourcefulness to follow through with even one of these misdeeds. It is certainly eloquent proof of the power possessed by one individual, even when it is used for mischief. God allots to each of us a generous supply of imagination to help us apply the power which He has also entrusted to every individual. In His extraordinary generosity, He then allows us to use it as we choose—for good or evil.

Those bent on evil, the headlines show, are certainly putting their imagination to work. What about you? Never forget Christ's warning:

"I would thou wert hot or cold. But because thou art lukewarm and neither hot nor cold I will begin to vomit thee out of my mouth." (Apocalypse 3:15, 16)

◄§ Inspire me, O God, to show as much enterprise for peace as the evil do to spread trouble and confusion.

SHE THREW THE BURGLAR OUT

A young woman who runs a shop in Philadelphia recently was the victim of an attempted hold-up—the third in two years. The first bandit had made away with $300. And the second, less fortunate than the first, had absconded with $38.

This time when a bold looking burglar entered the shop, and demanded *"her money or her life,"* the young woman was too angry to consider her danger. She had had enough!

She flew around the counter to the surprise of everyone, including the bandit. Furiously grabbing him with both hands, and with all the weight of her 124 pounds, she threw him out into the street. Returning to her openmouthed customers she then phoned the police.

Much of our present-day trouble would be cleared up in short order if enough individuals would take it upon themselves to be as quick and daring in meeting evil as this young lady was.

Those who are dedicated to lawlessness and crime are usually cowards at heart. Their bravery is more apparent than real. Nobody is more taken off guard than the followers of the Devil when they see the followers of Christ showing a little spirit and daring.

"Be ye therefore wise as serpents and simple as doves." (Matthew 10:16)

⮑ Help me, O Lord, to never cringe in the face of evil.

DON'T LET GEORGE DO IT

Two deputy sheriffs were out scouting around in Knoxville, Tenn., when they came across a man fast asleep on the railroad tracks, his head on one rail and his feet on the other.

In puzzled dismay, they woke him up. *"What in the world are you doing here? Do you want to be killed?"*

The man looked at them sleepily. *"What time is it?"* he asked.

"Why, it's four o'clock," they answered.

"Well then," the man said. *"I ain't got a thing to worry about. The engineer who runs the next train always stops for me."*

This tramp took a lot for granted. And in this way he resembles many today. A large number of people are beginning to act like this knight of the road in one way or another: we take a lot for granted.

Dodging responsibility whenever we can, and taking the *"let George do it"* attitude about our private, family, business and public obligations seems to do little harm at first. But it is dangerous business.

One person who fails to register and vote, for instance, may not wreck a country. But nevertheless he is helping to do just that. A nation is weakened, however slightly, by even one individual neglecting to carry his share of the load in protecting the God-given freedom of all.

"Lord what wilt thou have me to do?" (Acts 9:6)

⊷§ O Lord, keep me ever mindful that by even one sin of omission I can do much harm.

AS SIMPLE AS THAT

A small boy in Ironton, Ohio, recently told his parents that he couldn't see the blackboard in his classroom and this was the reason for his doing so poorly at school.

The parents were naturally quite concerned, so they took the child to an eye specialist. After many tests the doctor was certain that there was nothing wrong with the boy's eyes.

"Why can't you see the blackboard, Johnny?" the doctor finally asked in bewilderment.

"Because a big boy is sitting in front of me!" he exclaimed.

Despite the best of intentions, many tend to overlook the obvious when looking for the heart of the trouble that afflicts either the individual or society.

More often than not we can find right under our very noses a bit of trouble that we can clear up and thus contribute at least one step towards peace. God expects each of us to be alert and observant.

"Watch ye therefore, because ye know not what hour your Lord will come." (Matthew 24:42)

❧ O Lord Jesus, let me not miss the opportunities right in front of me.

KOREAN VETERAN DIES FOR A RECRUIT

Not long ago, Sgt. Leonard Moran, a 22-year-old Korean war veteran from South Boston, Mass., gave his life at Fort Dix, N.J., to protect a recruit from an exploding hand grenade.

Sgt. Moran was instructing the new private in a trench on the grenade range. The private, following his instructions had attempted to throw the hand grenade out of the trench to a specified target. The unpinned grenade hit the parapet, and rolled back into the trench. An explosion was imminent.

The sergeant, without thought for himself, threw his body between the recruit and the blast. He died within a few hours. His pupil incurred minor injuries.

In times of emergency, the nobility and greatness that God has implanted in all men often bursts forth in deeds of great heroism.

The aim of the Christophers is to stimulate millions to apply this inborn greatness on a day-to-day basis to the solution of the many problems that vex the modern world.

Instead of sitting idly by until the shooting begins, you can do much right now to show an apostolic zeal in integrating the Christian principles of peace to the spheres of influence that affect the destiny of everybody. If you act in time, you may help save millions dying for peace.

"Greater love than this no man hath that he lay down his life for his friends." (John 15:13)

&⸸ Help me, O Jesus, to be willing to suffer much in bringing peace to all men.

236

WATCH WHERE YOU BUILD

A man in Knoxville, Tenn., set out to put up a house. He secured a good architect, and the building got underway. All went well, and in due time the owner was delighted to find himself the owner of a beautiful home.

He was all prepared to move in when the City authorities arrived with some bad news. The house belonged to him, they told him, but the ground under it did not. The deeds that he possessed gave him the ownership of Lot 17, whereas he had built his dwelling on Lot 175. His dilemma was happily solved however, when they permitted him to purchase the lot on which his house stood.

This man was fortunate to have his mistake rectified so quickly and so agreeably. The solution is not such an easy one for those who build their lives on the weak foundation of a false philosophy.

It is a powerful experience to go most of the way through life and then discover—when it is almost too late to make a new beginning—that one has built on the shifting sands of error and falsehood rather than on the solid foundation of God's truth.

Recall frequently the powerful reminder the Hebrew psalmist uttered centuries ago:

"Unless the Lord build the house they labor in vain who build it." (Psalms 126:1)

⤺ Show me the way and the truth, O Lord.

A LESSON FROM AN INDIAN

There's an old Indian who had lived fifty years in the woods, without ever once coming in contact with civilization.

One day, a reporter from a large city newspaper who was on a hunting trip became acquainted with the Indian, and decided that it would be interesting to bring him into the city, and watch his reactions to our modern way of life.

Acting on his impulse, the newsman spent the following week introducing the Indian to all the wonders of city life. He showed him the tall buildings, automobiles, airplanes, and the many inventions which facilitate our living.

Then he asked him what he felt was the greatest thing we have. The Indian walked over to the kitchen sink, turned on the faucet, and smilingly pointed to it as the water gushed out. *"This,"* he said.

It is easy to become such a slave to gadgets that they complicate life. Instead of allowing them to dominate and therefore depersonalize us, we should see that they are used to provide food and shelter for all instead of comfort only for the few.

"For whosoever shall give you to drink a cup of water in my name, because you belong to Christ, amen I say to you, he shall not lose his reward." (Mark 9:40)

❧ O Lord, help me to use all things for Thy glory and the good of all.

238

PEACE BEGINS WITH YOU

Thieves in Pittsburgh, Pa., recently made away with 500 chickens from a poultry farm.

The police began an immediate search for the culprits, and with a deeper concern than usual. These 500 chickens had recently been fed large quantities of arsenic to help develop the quality of their meat. While arsenic can be taken inwardly by fowls with no ill effects, it can be a deadly poison to human beings.

Those who disregard or flaunt the normal standards of law and order seldom give a thought to the far-reaching consequences that may bring serious harm to countless others—as well as to themselves.

The slightest dishonesty, the least falsehood, the smallest theft of possessions or time that rightfully belong to others are all little disorders that help to prevent law and order in the world. In their own way, when multiplied over and over again, they can be a real obstacle to that lasting peace which every person so ardently desires and yet which too few ardently promote in their own lives.

"Seek ye good, and not evil, that you may live." (Amos 5:14)

⤐ Help me, O Lord, to keep ever mindful that peace in the world begins at my front doorstep.

A BLIND MAN GOT A DRIVER'S LICENSE

A man in Rapid City, S.D., walked up to a window at the Motor Vehicles Bureau and handed the clerk 50 cents. In return he was handed a driving license.

The people in the Bureau turned in puzzled surprise as the man suddenly burst into hilarious laughter. *"What a gag! What a gag!"* he kept saying.

It was quite a while before they could learn from him the cause of his amusement. He and his wife had made the trip to the Court House on a wager. He had obtained his driver's license without any trouble. But he had been blind for nine years!

It is bad enough for an occasional person to fool state officials. But how much more serious is it when those who are intellectually or spiritually blind succeed in getting into positions where they wield great influence in shaping the lives of others. Unlike the blind man who was trying a gag, those afflicted with a far more serious type of blindness make it their business to impose their defects upon others.

Do all in your power to see that every sphere of influence is staffed by those who are both talented and endowed by a deep love of God and man.

"Can the blind lead the blind? Do they not both fall into the ditch?" (Luke 6:39)

&ξ O Lord, grant that I may see the truth and detect error.

THE POOR MAN HAD $17,000

Not long ago, in St. Petersburg, Fla., an 80-year-old man was hauled into court on charges of stealing 28 cents worth of meat. The judge asked why he had stolen food, and he replied that all the money he had in the world was $20. He said further that he had no relatives and no home —that he slept wherever he could find shelter.

The sheriff was inclined to be sympathetic until $96 was discovered in the old man's wallet. Suspicious, he had a more detailed search made of the man's person. Pinned to the worn underclothing were bills amounting to $17,000.

Avarice afflicts both rich and poor alike. Excessive attachment to money has a shriveling effect upon one and all who worship at the altar of Mammon. It can grow from small beginnings which can scarcely be detected, especially if one has his sights on the passing gains of this life rather than on the lasting rewards of eternity.

Those who allow avarice to creep into their lives seldom experience any peace of heart and soul. Possessed by their possessions the miserly hurt themselves; they go to the extreme of depriving themselves of the necessities of life.

One of the best ways to resist all trace of avarice is to share your time, your goods, your talent and your prayers with those less fortunate.

"Lay not up to yourselves treasures on earth: where the rust and moth consume, and where thieves break through, and steal." (Matthew 6:19)

◄§ O Lord, let me protect myself by helping others who are in need.

THE TAX DODGER RETURNED

Back in 1919 a man fled from Russia to this country to escape persecution and death. He settled in Philadelphia, and in the ensuing years he did very well for himself.

First he opened an auto repair shop, and eventually bought a thriving used car business. He made a great deal of money.

But unwilling to pay the government his taxes he misrepresented his income. Finally the government caught up with him and demanded the $95,000 in evaded taxes.

Rather than pay this amount, he fled to Europe. For four years he lived there, discovering too late the advantages of the American way of life. Finally, the hardship was too much for him, and he returned and gave himself up to the authorities. He said, *"No amount of money can compensate for the privilege of being an American."* He urged all citizens to pay their taxes without quibbling.

Those who dodge paying just taxes are dishonest to begin with. And besides, they damage the freedom that makes it possible for them to prosper. Those who evade their tax responsibilities merely shirk a burden that must be shouldered by others. If they feel taxes are unjust, they should do something to have them adjusted but should not leave it to others to foot their share.

"Render therefore to Caesar the things that are Caesar's; and to God, the things that are God's." (Matthew 22:21)

✑ Help me to carry my own share, O Lord, and not to leave it to others.

SERUM FROM U.S. SAVES AUSTRIAN BOY

An 8-year-old boy in Innsbruck, Austria, recently lay perilously close to death, suffering from hemophilia. A small wound can cause a victim of this affliction to bleed to death. The child had received a wound from which he would bleed to death. The only hope of saving him lay in a certain serum being administered in time.

The trouble was that this serum had to be obtained from the United States, some 4500 miles away. A call for the serum was sent out. All the doctors could do was wait and hope that it would arrive in time.

Despite bad flying weather the dangerous mercy flight began instantly. The precious serum was sent on its way from the State health laboratories at Lansing, Mich. The plane bearing it arrived on time, and two German drivers in a jeep sped over snow-covered Alpine roads to deliver the serum to the hospital. The combined efforts of many saved the life of an 8-year-old boy.

In sections of the world where the worth of every human being, proclaimed by Jesus Christ nearly 2000 years ago, has yet to be announced, there is little concern over the life or death of a youngster. Life becomes cheap when God is banished from all spheres of influence.

If you truly cherish your real significance as an individual, you will undergo much sacrifice to see that the truth that each and every person is made in God's image is recognized in every phase of life.

"As long as you did it to one of these my least brethren, you did it to me." (Matthew 25:40)

⌇ Help me, O Divine Savior, to champion Thy truth which makes possible my freedom.

BREAD ONCE A WEEK

A little girl was going through the *"why?"* period. A hundred times a day she asked her mother and father—*"Why, Mommy?" "Why, Daddy?"* The parents tried as best they could to satisfy their child's insatiable curiosity, but there seemed no end to the *"why(s)?"*

One day, as the family sat down to the evening meal, the little girl asked *"Daddy, why do we have to pray every day for our daily bread? Why can't we just ask once a week?"*

The father sighed, but his small son came to his rescue. He said *"You're a silly dilly, Mary. D'ya suppose we wanna eat stale bread?"*

The reply of Mary's brother, even if somewhat incomplete, helps us to see in ourselves a tendency to look for complete security with the least amount of effort.

Providence is generous to man and beast alike. But while God promised to *"feed the birds of the air,"* it does not mean that He will put the food in their nests.

The Lord wishes all of us to have the security that ensures the essentials of food, clothing and shelter. But He certainly didn't intend that we should be so preoccupied with security of body that we forget the security of soul which alone can assure that inner peace for which all men yearn.

"Man liveth not by bread alone, but by every word of God." (Luke 4:4)

&5 O God, let me show by thought, word and deed that I want Thy will to be done.

A LANDSLIDE THAT CAN BE STOPPED

Recently a landslide occurred on Mt. Boschi, a mountain in the Appenine chain near Modena, Italy, which was the largest that had occurred in the Appenines in 25 years.

A great mass of earth and rock and uprooted trees slowly began making its way down the mountain side, travelling at about a yard an hour and having a front two miles wide, destroying houses and property as it pushed everything before it.

Engineers, after having observed it, reported that nothing could be done to stop it. It had to be allowed to run its course, despite all the destruction it would cause.

With evil trends started by men the outlook is far more hopeful. No matter how harmful and destructive they may be, they can gradually be slowed down, stopped and a trend for the better started.

Less than 1% of mankind is responsible for the unusual wave of hatred, chaos and death that has been sweeping over the globe during the past few decades. Another 1% working just as hard for good could offset their march of death. You, personally and individually, can be one of that 1%!

"Be not overcome by evil, but overcome evil by good." (Romans 12:21)

&§ Inspire me, O Lord, to strive as hard for love as others work for hatred.

245

A LESSON FROM A SIX-YEAR-OLD

A six-year-old boy was downtown in a crowded New York shopping area with his mother one day, when he suddenly discovered that he was lost.

He wandered around for a little while looking for her. But although he saw many nice ladies with packages, not one of them was his mother.

He wanted very much to cry. But he was a big boy now, and he knew what to do if ever he got lost. He set his chin firmly and approached the big policeman on the corner.

"Yes, sonny?" the policeman said kindly. The little boy spoke with a brave nonchalance, *"Did you happen to see a lady going by without me?"* he asked.

This resourceful youngster was accidentally lost by his mother. But he was shrewd enough to know that he had a right to her attention, a fact that is often overlooked by parents who reason the other way around.

There would be far less juvenile delinquency today if those who undertake the great privilege of parenthood would recognize that they are God's agents in giving to the immature the care, guidance and devotion that rightfully belong to them.

"Suffer the little children, and forbid them not to come to me." (Matthew 19:14)

&§ How can I thank Thee enough, O Lord, for the privilege of transmitting to others the love Thou has sent them through me.

THE BLESSING OF HARDSHIP

The pearl, which is considered one of the most beautiful of jewels, is the one gem that is not mined from the earth, but which is grown in the shell of an oyster.

But the oyster does not make the pearl for the purpose of adorning the necks of women. It makes it only as a means of self-protection.

Sometimes, a hard, tiny object such as a grain of sand finds its way inside the shell, and irritates the soft sensitive flesh. The oyster has no way to rid itself of it.

As a protection the oyster begins to cover the object with a thick fluid from its own body. When this layer hardens, and the irritation begins again, another layer is added. This goes on for many years, until finally the oyster has produced a beautiful pearl.

Anyone who would be a Christopher or a Christ-bearer can learn an important lesson from the origin and development of the pearl. He can see a hidden blessing in every obstacle.

We may never know until we stand before the Judgment Seat of God how a little cross in our lives has prepared the way for a lasting crown.

"I have fought a good fight, I have finished my course, I have kept the faith. As to the rest, there is laid up for me a crown of justice, which the Lord the just judge will render me in that day." (II Timothy 4:7, 8)

Let me see, O Lord, some advantage in every hardship.

FORTY YEARS OF PLANNING

Not long ago in the blue Mediterranean off the Isle of Ponza, Italy, Professor August Piccard and his son, Jacques, risked their lives—descending nearly 2 miles into the ocean to successfully test a new type bathsphere designed by Prof. Piccard. This is 4,000 feet deeper than man has ever been able to go before. It was the fulfillment of a specific plan first formed nearly 40 years ago. The dive itself was the result of many months of preparation. The operating devices aboard the craft were so complex that life hung on a thread every second of the descent.

A very important man once had this to say about success and failure. *"Some persons work; others loaf. Some have minds open for new ideas; others have closed minds. Some are inquisitive, which leads them to invention and discovery; others lack imagination entirely. Some have great courage. A few are lucky.*

"However, there is one major idea which seems to dominate many great lives. It is the relentless determination to master some one occupation or profession."

Of course, this has been proved through all the ages. The men who have risen to greatness have been the men who have chosen one goal and followed it relentlessly.

The worth-while objectives take a long time and a great deal of effort to achieve. Those who work for God can't afford to spread themselves thin. They should choose the thing that God wants them to do and stick to it.

"Seest thou a man diligent in his business? He shall stand before kings." (Proverbs 22:29)

ᔕ O Lord, let me work diligently for Thee.

248

A PARALYZED BOY SAVED A HOME

A 16-year-old boy in Philadelphia was alone in his second story bedroom. It was a beautiful sunny day, and he could hear the laughing shouts of other boys in the neighborhood at play. He would have liked to be out with them. But he couldn't, because he was paralyzed. Everyone was out of the house and he was alone.

Suddenly, he grew very tense. There was an unmistakable smell of smoke coming from downstairs. There was no one to help. He had to do something! He dragged himself from the bed. He reached the dresser, but then he couldn't go any further.

His mind worked furiously. He took a bottle, and with all his strength threw it through the window, smashing it, and calling for help. The neighbors heard, and summoned the firemen. They arrived in time to put out the fire.

As the quick thinking of a paralyzed boy prevented a home from being destroyed by fire, so you—whoever you are and whatever your disabilities may be—can do something to change the dangerous trends of the world today.

If you have a sincere desire to make the world itself better for your being in it, and are looking for the opportunity to be of service, God will open the door for you in one way or another.

"Be ye wise as serpents and simple as doves." (Matthew 10:16)

∾§ To Thee, O my God, I render thanks for allowing me to play any part in bringing Thy love and peace to the world.

THE DEVOTION OF GRACIE THE MARE

There's a dispensary for sick animals in London, England, which gives a regular award to animals that have distinguished themselves by saving the life of people.

Last year the award was given to Gracie, a 20-year-old mare who for many years has assisted her master in delivering his wares by wagon.

One day, the vendor became very ill and collapsed unconscious. Noticing that she was receiving no orders, Gracie waited for awhile, and then took charge.

Making her way down the busiest street, she instinctively obeyed the road rules, even stopping at traffic lights, until she reached the warehouse from which she left every morning. Then she whinnied and snorted until help came for her beloved master.

Animals often show a remarkable sense of devotion. The Lord of all creation has endowed even the lowest forms of life with something of His truth, goodness and beauty. But to the human being He has been extraordinarily generous. No other creature has been so favored as man.

With the advantage of intelligence and will each of us is equipped in an outstanding manner to treat our fellow human beings with reverence, honor and devotion. In fact, our very salvation for all eternity rests on how much love we show for one another.

"Which of these was neighbor to him . . . he that showed mercy to him." (Luke 10:36, 37)

Let me grow, O Jesus, in devotion for Thee and all mankind.

250

THE FORGERY WAS ALMOST PERFECT

A young man who worked in a certain business concern envied his employer. For years he had harbored a secret resentment that he had to work so hard for what he considered a meagre salary, while his boss did, what he called, *"sitting back and reaping the harvest."*

Finally, he hit upon a scheme by which he felt that he could get even. He would make a perfect forgery of his employer's signature, relieving him of a large majority of his money; and thereafter, he would be the one, and his boss would know how it felt to be poor.

He practiced the employer's signature until he felt that the forgery was letter perfect. It was too. The bank-teller accepted the signature without trouble, but on a hunch he checked the man's account and found—insufficient funds.

Much of the world's trouble is based on misunderstandings. Most envy and jealousy originate in the mistaken notion that the best way to lessen one's own failure is to belittle or even destroy the success of others.

There are injustices in the world, but trying to cure them by more injustice only adds misery to trouble. In trying to correct abuses, make sure to stick to the laws of God regarding the rights of others. Everybody will gain in the long run.

"Treasures of wickedness shall profit nothing: but justice shall deliver from death." (Prov. 10:2)

O Lord, keep me ever aware that I must respect the rights of others while striving to solve my own difficulties.

A JOLT THAT WAS A BLESSING

Recently a mother in Denver had a violent fright. Her 18-month-old son accidentally swallowed a souvenir gold piece about the size of a half dollar. He was gasping for breath, and slowly turning blue.

Praying desperately, the mother called the police. They came quickly, and with red light and shrieking siren they rushed the mother and child to the nearest hospital. The mother was panic-stricken, fearing that they would not get there in time, for the child seemed to be nearly dead.

Suddenly, the speeding patrol car hit a sharp dip in the pavement, severely jolting the occupants. But the bounce was a blessing in disguise, for with it up came the coin from the child's throat.

It often takes a jolt of some kind to stir the average person out of the apathy into which he gradually slips when he prays and works only in terms of his own selfish advantage. A trend in this direction, if indulged in by too many, can lead to disaster.

So when obstacles, set-backs, misunderstandings and trouble of any sort suddenly appear, don't take too dim a view of them. They may be heaven-sent reminders to jolt you out of a great and imminent danger that could mean the death of your soul.

"... *Rather fear him that can destroy both soul and body in hell.*" (Matthew 10:28)

↪ Let me see, O Lord, a blessing in every cross.

SHE FOUND A THOUSAND DOLLAR BILL

Carol Schindler, a 13-year-old girl in New York City, was on her way to her dancing lesson recently when she happened to glance down, and there, to her surprise, lay something that was unmistakably a crisp new greenback.

The child was well acquainted with money of different denominations, yet this was one with which she was unfamiliar. She picked it up, and examined it carefully. It was a thousand dollar bill!

She was quite excited about her find. But it wasn't hers and she knew that whoever had lost it might be worried about it. So she brought it to the nearest police station.

Under New York law, money that remains unclaimed for 30 days goes to the finder. And after 30 days, Carol was given the $1,000.

Most of us go through life without once setting our eyes upon a thousand dollar bill. And there isn't one chance in a million of any of us spotting a stray one on the sidewalks of New York or Kokomo.

But there are opportunities galore that God has scattered on all sides for your happiness here and hereafter. Most of them are worth far more than a thousand dollars. And whether you are young or old, they are yours for the asking. But God wants you to discover them for yourself. So keep your eyes open!

"Seek, and you shall find; knock, and it shall be opened to you." (Matthew 7:7)

⇜ To Thee be praise, honor, glory and thanksgiving, O most blessed Trinity, for showering upon us so many opportunities for happiness.

253

HE SHOT THE BOILED CHICKEN

There's a man in Washington, D.C., who just can't stand boiled chicken. Whenever his wife would prepare it, he would plead with her in almost tearful tones to fix it some other way the next time. But unfortunately, his wife had a great fondness for boiled chicken, and over his protests she continued to serve it at regular intervals.

One day, the man returned home from a hard day's work to find a chicken boiling merrily on the kitchen stove. In a sudden rage, he took a .32 caliber pistol and shot twice through the boiling pot.

Hauled before the judge for illegally discharging a firearm, he tried to explain the reason for his action. The judge, unimpressed, imposed a fine of $100.

Many are tempted to *"shoot their way"* through various problems that confront them. If they don't do it literally with a gun, at least they attempt to ride roughshod over the rights of others.

While anyone can resort to violence, since it is a sign of weakness, only those who have the strength of character can restrain and discipline themselves in respecting the rights and wishes of others, as God wishes all of us to do. It is a real sign of advance in virtue when you are able to disagree without getting disagreeable.

"By this shall all men know that you are my disciples if have love one for another." (John 13:35)

❧ Grant me the grace, O Jesus, to be able to differ without hate.

254

YOU PAY THE PENALTY

On September 12, 1951, a pasenger train from New York to St. Louis was running thirty minutes late. The engineer, a veteran of 48 years service, was eager to make up the lost time.

He came to a signal approach block and instead of reducing his speed to 30 miles per hour as regulations required he sped on. He passed through a stop signal—beyond which was a stalled troop train. He applied the emergency brakes, but it was too late. The giant diesel ripped into the troop train, killing 33 service men.

We all suffer from the temptation sometimes to defy God's laws. We may even think that those who yield to the temptation seem to get on all right in the world. Perhaps they do—for a while. But sooner or later they must pay the penalty for their folly and disobedience. Make no mistake about it. You cannot defy God's laws and not pay the consequences.

Longfellow put it this way: *"Though the mills of God grind slowly, yet they grind exceeding small."*

"It is easier for heaven and earth to pass, than one tittle of the law to fall." (Luke 16:17)

⋙ O God of Justice, help me to honor Thee by keeping Thy commandments.

ACTIONS SPEAK LOUDER

The oldest of three daughters, a 9-year-old girl, was gay and affectionate. She climbed up into her mother's lap, and put her arm about her neck. *"Mother, I love you so much,"* she said. *"Do you know what I'm going to do when I grow up? I'm going to buy you the biggest car in all the world, and drive you everywhere."*

The second little girl was very like her sister. Climbing onto the other knee, she whispered breathlessly, *"I love you too. And when I grow up, I'm going to buy you a big, beautiful house with lots of servants, so you won't have to work any more."*

The mother smiled. *"How lovely!"* she said. She turned to the youngest, a quiet, thoughtful child who said nothing. *"And you, dear, don't you love me too?"*

"Yes, mother, you know I do," she answered simply. *"But I must go and finish washing the dishes now."*

The best test of true love is not what will be done in the vague, distant future, but rather in the here and now. It is easy to make big promises that are seldom translated into action. But it is something else again to put high-sounding phrases into practical application.

If you have a true love of people—rooted in a love of God, you will put yourself out to see that they are provided with good government, good education and good everything else!

"If you love me, keep my commandments." (John 14:15)

🙌 O Jesus, let me talk little and do much for the good of others.

256

THE DANGER OF BEING TOO GULLIBLE

There has been an alarming rise throughout the country in what is known as *"charity rackets."* Unscrupulous persons have found a lucrative enterprise in trading on the natural generosity of human nature.

Mr. Emerson Andrews, director of philanthropic research for the Russell Sage Foundation, testified on the subject before a joint state legislature in New York.

He said that many persons will give money in the name of charity, without making any effort to investigate whether or not the cause is legitimate.

For instance, a man who wanted to prove this collected a sizable sum from donors for the *"widow of the unknown soldier."* Only when he returned the money to them, did they realize how gullible they had been.

It is basically the generous trait in the average person that fakers of all sorts work on. They know that such people take it for granted that others are as well-intentioned and honest as they are themselves.

Putting unwarranted faith in the high-sounding but hollow claims of Communism, Nazism, and Fascism has brought disaster and even death to countless millions. You can do something to bring the Truth to those who may be caught off guard.

"By their fruits you shall know them." (Matthew 7:16)

◆ Strengthen me, O God, to help others from being too gullible.

257

NO IDENTIFICATION NEEDED

President Auriol of France was fishing one day on the River Seine. His police guards had left him alone to enjoy himself. While they were gone a game warden asked to see his fishing license. Unfortunately, he had left it at home.

"But it's quite all right," Mr. Auriol said. *"I'm the President of France."*

"Yes," said the warden. *"And I'm President Eisenhower. Come along."*

Luckily the guards returned just as the warden was taking the President of France to jail.

It's easy to imagine such an incident occurring here on earth. But of one thing you can be sure—you need no identification to be known to God. He sees everything you do and knows your every thought. Each of us is important in His eyes. He loves all and awaits the return of the greatest sinner.

This love can be a great comfort to us when misunderstanding and false judgment befall us in this life.

"In God have I hoped, I will not fear what man can do to me." (Psalms 55:11)

&O Lord, never let me forget that Thou lovest me despite my faults.

258

LOVE NEVER FAILS

A 71-year-old widow was robbed by her son of her life savings which amounted to several thousand dollars. The 43-year-old son took the money from his mother's safe deposit box, and bet the whole amount on a horse that lost.

The old mother refused to prosecute. She told the judge, *"He is my son and I love him. I haven't long to live, and I pray that God will be as forgiving of me as I am of my son."*

Of all earthly affections we possibly regard mother-love as the purest and the most enduring. Somehow other loves are apt to fail when the loved one inflicts hurt or disappointment in return for kindness. But a true mother never deserts her children, not even when they grieve and wound her deeply. She stands always ready to pardon and to assist.

Our limited human minds find it difficult to grasp the pure unbounded love of God of each one of us. But when we think about the depth of the love an earthly mother has for her children we can understand in small part the love of Our Heavenly Father that pardons our sins time without number and that remains constant through all eternity.

"And thou shalt be as the obedient son to the Most High, and He will have mercy on thee more than a mother." (Ecclesiasticus 4:11)

⊷§ Heavenly Father, I thank Thee for loving me so.

ONE AND ONE

We haven't been able to secure the exact figures telling how many kinds of wild flowers there are on the face of God's green earth. However we are sure that there must be many thousands of them—each one different.

A field of daisies is in itself a powerful sermon on the beauty and the love of our Heavenly Father. Yet have you ever stopped to think that one such field is comprised of millions and millions of individual flowers? Each one is important because it goes to make up the whole field of loveliness.

When we consider that there are more than 2 billion people in the world, we may as individuals begin to feel very small and unimportant indeed. Yet God has need of each one of us or He wouldn't have made us. We are each important to the world, because we each go to make up the world.

"And God created man to his own image." (Genesis 1:27)

⋙ O God, help me to know my worth as Thy child.

KEROSENE RUINED THE MILK

A truck loaded with ten thousand containers of milk was left standing in Brooklyn for a short period before taking off to distribute it to schools and hospitals.

For some strange reason pranksters took it upon themselves to pour kerosene over the containers, completely ruining the milk. Instead of being given to the sick and children, the milk was emptied into the sewer.

Few people would be so reckless and wasteful as to deliberately spoil such a large quantity of milk. But we may bring about as much harm in a less noticeable manner.

By failing to fulfill our responsibilities, by neglecting to assist others in need, by refusing to put to work the talents that God has entrusted to us, we may inadvertently be doing something that is more destructive than wantonly pouring kerosene on milk.

God has made you to be creative in body, in soul, and in mind. He expects you to use that power for His glory and for the good of others. In doing that, you help yourself more than would be possible in any other way.

"I am not come to destroy, but to fulfill." (Matthew 5:17)

⊷ Help me, O Jesus, to spend so much time in doing good that I have no time to spend in doing harm.

261

WORDS AND DEEDS

It was one Havana's hottest days when Jack Johnson, the great Negro heavyweight boxing champion, fought his championship bout in an open arena with Jess Willard back in 1915. A spectator at the ringside kept needling Johnson constantly. He criticized his style, his ancestry, his color, and finally his courage in the ring.

Johnson seemed oblivious to it for a long time, but finally he leaned over the ropes between rounds, smiled, and said: *"Man, you're down there talking. I'm up here fighting."*

The big reason that so often there have been glaring weaknesses in government is that far too many have stood on the sidelines and criticized it but done nothing at all to help remedy it. Anyone at all can sit back and find fault. It takes courage and effort to get out and do one's part.

Our chief defect as citizens is that many of us have put aside our duty. We think the job of government is for everyone else but ourselves.

If we are to have a better form of government, then it is left with each and every citizen to contribute his share of effort to see that good government is put into action.

"You are my friends if you do the things that I command you." (John 15:14)

◂§ O Lord, help me to do my part to make this a better world.

SHE DID SOMETHING

There's a seven-year-old girl in Detroit who can't swim but who recently saved her father from drowning. She was playing on the beach when her father, who was swimming near the shore, suffered a heart-attack and fell face downward in the shallow water. Without heeding the danger to herself, the child, screaming for help, waded out to him and held his head above water for five minutes until two policemen heard her shouts and came to the rescue. The father recovered.

In this emergency, there was no time for the child to learn to swim. Something had to be done immediately if her father's life was to be saved. She did it.

In our time we are faced with what definitely amounts to an emergency. Our nation—indeed our world—is threatened with destruction not only from without, but also by a moral disintegration from within. We cannot afford to rely only on long-time measures. There is need for immediate action on the part of each of us if we are to stave off disaster.

If, personally and individually, we each accept our responsibility to restore God's love and peace to the world, think what great changes for the better we could bring about.

"For it is God who worketh in you, both to will and to accomplish according to his will." (Philippians 2:13)

“O Lord, give me the vision to know Thy will.

A WINNER MUST WANT TO

A scout for the big leagues was once asked how he was able to spot baseball players who were big league material.

"It's simple enough," he answered. *"Give me a boy who can hit hard, throw hard, run hard and wants to play! We used to take that 'wanting to play' for granted, but we found out that lots of them had what we were looking for, but didn't want to play. Getting into the big leagues means hard work. A boy has to want to, if he's going to make it."*

Life is like baseball in that respect. To get into the big leagues we not only have to have all the necessary requirements, but we have to *"want to"* as well.

If you've ever wondered how it is that one man forges ahead, while another with seemingly equal possibilities flounders about at the bottom of the rung, look at it this way: God goes scouting for men of worth to serve Him, but He isn't going to force anybody to join up. To get into His *"big league,"* you first have to want to, and keep wanting to, even when you get temporarily *"struck out."* It's that spirit of constantly *"wanting to"* that makes major league material.

"And He said unto them: The harvest indeed is great, but the labourers are few. Pray ye therefore the Lord of the harvest that he send labourers into His harvest." (Luke 10:2)

⋙ Heavenly Father, enable me always to want to do Thy Holy will.

264

BLIND MAN'S BUFF

A high-school football player in Detroit was running with the ball when he knocked himself out by crashing head-first into a steel post. Later he explained, *"I run faster with my eyes shut."*

Perhaps, as this youngster thought, he could pick up more speed with his eyes shut. But certainly with closed eyes he couldn't see where he was going. Running with our eyes shut, instead of taking us where we really want to go will often find us knocked out completely by something we did not see because we did not look where we were going.

Many of us go through life with our eyes shut, oblivious to the need to see what happens around us daily, unheeding and uncaring of the welfare of others just so we get where we want to go.

To succeed in life one must not only diligently pursue a goal but also be concerned about others in doing so. Obstacles in the paths of others are also potential obstacles to ourselves. This, if for no other reason, makes it advisable for us to be concerned with the welfare of others as well as of our own.

"Open thou my eyes: and I will consider the wondrous things of thy law." (Psalms 118:18)

❧ O Holy Spirit, keep me aware of the needs of others every day I live.

END OF THE ROPE

A young French mountain-climber fell and dangled for three days over a precipice on Mt. Blanc, Europe's highest mountain. He was rescued just as the rope holding him was about to be cut through by jagged rocks. He said afterwards that through the long hours he kept saying to himself, *"Hang on, hang on."*

There are times in nearly everybody's life when one reaches the end of the rope, and hangs like the mountain climber in great peril of death, unable to help oneself. In times like these all we can do is to take hold of the rope of our faith in God and *"hang on."*

Sometimes God tests us so that we may have to hang on till the rope begins to fray. Even then, God will not fail to rescue His children who call upon Him. He will not come too late.

"O God, come to my assistance; O Lord, make haste to help me." (Psalms 69:2)

&§ Heavenly Father, help me to persevere.

THE GAME AND THE CANDLE

Four years ago an Englishman was swept off a small boat on which he was trying to cross the Atlantic. Undeterred by this misfortune, his wife left England in May 1952 on a 23-foot, five horsepower Diesel engine yacht in an attempt to accomplish the same feat.

Sailing via Spain, Casablanca, the Canary Islands, and the Virgin Islands the yacht was stalled for three weeks in mid-Atlantic and was buffeted by many storms. At one time the brave woman skipper sailed steadily for three days without sleep. One year after her departure from England, she brought her battered boat safely into port at Nassau in the Bahamas.

We cannot say if in the end this woman found the *"game worth the candle."* But the courage and endurance she exhibited merit admiration.

Were we, who seek to do God's will, to follow His plan for us with the same courage and endurance we would spread our influence for good far and wide and leave a lasting influence on those who follow in our footsteps. For in God's service, the *"game"* is always *"worth the candle."*

"Every excellent work shall be justified: and the worker thereof shall be honored therein." (Ecclesiasticus 14:21)

&§ O God, help me to work only for Thee.

SUNFLOWERS OR BEANS?

A man in Seattle, Wash., heard on the radio that sunflowers make fine beanpoles. Impressed by the idea he planted a sunflower with each hill of beans.

When the beans came up, they twined themselves around the sunflowers, just as the radio broadcast said they would. But the sunflowers grew so fast that they pulled the beans right out of the soil by the roots. Soon there were plenty of bright sunflowers, but no beans.

It is remarkable how often we plant *"sunflowers"* that we don't really want in our lives, and allow them to root up the *"beans."* In other words, do we not place so much reliance on *"means"* (the sunflower), that we lose sight of the end, or goal (the beans).

"And he that received the seed among thorns, is he that heareth the word, and the care of this world and the deceitfulness of riches choketh up the work, and he becometh fruitless." (Matthew 13:22)

✍ Heavenly Father, help me not to waste time on things that do not matter.

ANGRY PEOPLE IMPOSE ON OTHERS

There are many youngsters who profess a dislike for school. But, to our knowledge, there has never been one who has gone to as great lengths to prove it, as a certain 15-year-old boy in Needles, Calif.

Recently he went on a rampage against the offending school building. He broke the glass panes in several of the doors. He set fire to the books in the library. He set fire to the principal's desk. And then to be sure that his purpose couldn't be thwarted, he emptied the fire extinguishers. When the fires were well underway, he walked out of the building.

Later, he admitted to the police chief that he had done all this because he *"hated school."*

Those who give vent to their anger do great harm to others as well as to themselves. It is bad enough to lose control of one's self to such an extent as to act like a wild animal out of the jungle. But it is something else again when indulging in one's tantrums harms others.

Angry people usually show a complete disregard for the rights of others while insisting on the right to act as they like.

When you feel the slightest temptation to anger or impatience, nip it in the bud. Channel the energy you would have expended on it into some act of love of God or your fellow man.

"And let every man be swift to hear, but slow to speak, and slow to anger." (James 1:19)

✑ O God, help me to control myself by devoting my time and talent to Thy glory.

MORE THAN KNOWLEDGE NEEDED

In Raleigh, N.C., a highway patrolman nabbed a speeder through the use of an electric speed clock.

The motorist protested his innocence, but the officer explained to him that the speed clocks do not make mistakes.

"Oh, I know that," said the man, and to the patrolman's surprise he went on to describe in detail exactly how the speed clock operates.

"How do you happen to know so much about speed clocks?" the curious patrolman asked.

"Oh, I ought to," the man replied. *"You see I'm the assistant sales manager for the blankety, blank things!"*

Much is said these days about the *"right to know."* This is an important right. But too seldom does one hear about man's obligation to live up to the knowledge entrusted to him.

Some of the most brilliant scientists have conspired to brutalize, enslave and even destroy millions of innocent people. Their partially-developed minds, lacking the balancing force of a strong will, have become a menace to everybody rather than a benefit.

"I confess to thee, O Father, Lord of heaven and earth, because thou hast hid these things from the wise and prudent and hast revealed them to little ones." (Matthew 11:25)

⋙ Keep me ever conscious, O my God, that with every truth goes responsibility.

THE PRINCE WANTED TO BE A PLUMBER

You would hardly expect a prince to have an ambition to be a plumber, would you? Since an heir to a throne can look forward to someday becoming a king, there is little incentive for him to bother about ordinary labor and toil.

But 13-year-old Prince Ingolf of Denmark is strangely and refreshingly unimpressed with his princely state. Recently he expressed the wish to be a plumber instead of a king when he would grow up.

It is hardly possible that his wish will be granted. But his innocent ambition so touched the hearts of people all over the world, that he was officially made an honorary master plumber by the Associated Plumbing Contractors of Los Angeles, Calif.

Do what you can to stress the dignity of labor. In our day love of pleasure has been overemphasized. Many are getting farther and farther away from the very peace and happiness they seek by trying to dodge the share of work that should be their lot in the home, factory, school, shop, office or on the farm.

God wants us to have a fair measure of joy and pleasure in this life as a foretaste of everlasting peace to come. But He has planned that it should come as the result of labor —not from dodging it.

"In the sweat of thy face shalt thou eat bread." (Genesis 3:19)

◂§ Teach me, O Lord, to show greater respect for those who toil and labor.

AWOL ONE YEAR

Early in 1953 an Army private in Germany was granted leave to visit his home in Jersey City. While he was at home, his father became very ill so he applied through the Red Cross for an extension of leave. But when he received no word, he decided he'd better return to his unit. He went to his Port of Embarkation and requested transportation back to Germany. They sent him home to await further orders. A year passed, and no orders came. Frightened, the private wrote a local newspaper for help. They discovered that he was listed as a deserter by his outfit in Germany. The private surrendered and was sent to the stockade on Governor's Island while his case is being investigated.

Despite the best of efforts to *"follow the rules"* as this soldier tried to do, one can get into trouble. An oversight on the part of another, however unintentional, can bring about endless confusion.

Jesus Christ our Lord stressed that misunderstandings, difficulties and trouble of all kinds should be regarded as a matter of course for any and all who would volunteer to be His co-workers as Christ-bearers or Christophers. Here is the way He put it:

"If any man will come after me, let him . . . take up his cross daily, and follow me." (Luke 9:23)

◄§ Bestow upon me the grace, O Lord, to welcome trouble for Thy sake rather than dodge it.

272

CHILD WALKS 15 MILES TO FIND DOG

Seven-year-old Billy is usually a happy little boy. But recently something happened to make him very sad.

It was a Friday, right after he had had his lunch, that he discovered that his dog Spartan was lost. At first he was puzzled. Spartan usually waited for him for their after-lunch walk. Perhaps he had tired of waiting, and had started off without him.

Billy started walking in the direction they usually took, whistling for his friend as he went.

He walked a long way, but there was no sign of Spartan. Night fell and he was frightened, but he kept trudging hopefully on.

They found him in New York City, 15 miles away, drooping with fatigue still looking for his dog which, incidentally, had returned home, safe and sound.

The devotion of this youngster for his pet is a reminder of the great potential for good in every child. God Himself has put it there. He leaves it to parents, teachers and others who guide the young to discover, develop and apply both the talent and the bit of missionary implanted in every child. It is a great challenge as well as responsibility.

"A young man according to his way, even when he is old he will not depart from it." (Proverbs 22:6)

⋖§ Allow me to play a part, O Lord, in bringing out of the young the greatness that Thou hast hidden within them.

THE ASTRONOMER FELL INTO THE WELL

According to a fable, one night, as an astronomer was wandering on the outskirts of the city, and gazing at the stars, he fell into a well. For long hours he called and shouted for help.

Finally, one of the villagers came to see what was the matter. He peered into the well and saw the hapless astronomer struggling to get out.

"How did you ever manage to get in there?" he asked. The astronomer explained. The villager burst into uproarious laughter. *"My good man,"* he said. *"While you are trying to pry into the mystery of the heavens, you overlook the common objects that are under your feet!"*

Those who are blessed by God with talent, both spiritual and intellectual, often deprive themselves and everyone else of much happiness by failing to apply the truths entrusted to them for the problems of the day.

The one big aim of the Christopher movement is to encourage the millions in low station and high to come to grips with perils that confront all humanity in these perilous times. There is something that you, personally and individually, can do here and now to change the world for the better. God will bless your every try.

"In the sweat of thy face shalt thou eat bread till thou return to the earth." (Genesis 3:18)

◄§ Inspire me, O Lord, to enter into the problems that vex the world, rather than run away from them.

A TELEPHONE CALL AND A GUN

In South California two children became suddenly ill. Their father immediately went to the phone to call a doctor.

But when he picked up the phone voices were chattering away over the party line. Politely, he apologized for interrupting, and explained that he needed to call a doctor for his children.

But the neighbor refused to hang up. He kept right on talking. The infuriated father took his gun and stormed out to discover which party was holding up the line. When he had definitely ascertained which neighbor it was, he kicked down his front door and threatened to shoot him. Only the pleas of the man's wife stopped him.

It is easy to argue that a man like this should control his temper. It is going far beyond the bounds of what is fair and reasonable to threaten to *"shoot up everybody"* under any circumstances.

But a case like this is a reminder of how serious trouble can be caused by little acts of selfishness. A disregard of the ordinary rights of others—a failure to treat others with the same consideration that you expect of them is so often the tiny spark that ignites the big blaze of hatred and destruction. Jesus Christ gave a standard that all can follow:

"All things therefore whatsoever you would that men should do to you, do you also to them." (Matthew 7:12)

&§ O Lord, remind me to think of the rights of others while striving for my own wants.

HE DROVE INTO THE RIVER

A fifty-year-old man in Nashville, Tenn., drove his truck off a ferry dock. Of course, what he had wanted to do was to drive his truck onto the ferry to get across the river. But he arrived at a time when the ferry was at the other side.

Luckily, some people were standing by when the accident happened, and they fished him out of the water.

"*What happened?*" they asked when the man revived. "*Couldn't you see that the ferry wasn't there?*"

"*Oh, yes!*" the man replied. "*I saw that. But you see, I just wasn't paying attention.*"

There is more than a little consolation in the fact that much, if not most, of the trouble that afflicts our world today is the result of neglect or stupidity. Very little of it originates in downright malice, even though those who are bent on evil are quick to take advantage of even the slightest weakness or mistake on the part of the negligent.

It takes time and patience to change people from the "*debit*" to the "*asset*" side, but this is the very work the Redeemer of all came on earth to do. You can be a real Christopher or Christ-bearer by playing your own role in this way.

"*And we beseech you . . . rebuke the unquiet, comfort the feeble-minded, support the weak, be patient towards all men.*" (I Thessalonians 5:14)

Help me, O Lord, to find the good in the worst of men and to build on that.

A 52-YEAR-OLD CASE OF CONSCIENCE

Fifty-two years ago Great Britain was engaged in fighting the Boer War. A 20-year-old British soldier suddenly found himself sick and tired of the whole thing. He ran away to the United States and became a citizen without even waiting for discharge papers.

He settled in New York and proceeded for the next fifty years to live the life of the average American citizen. But through the years he was plagued by pangs of conscience for his cowardly desertion.

Not long ago, this 72-year-old man sought to make some amends for his early wrongdoing. He wrote to Queen Elizabeth at Buckingham Palace, explaining the situation, and seeking her official pardon.

The War Office sounded a merciful note when it stated: *"There must be a graceful way out, and doubtless it will be found."*

Too seldom do we think of the mercies of the Lord. Holy Scriptures abound with examples of God's forgiveness for man when he is truly repentant.

You can render a great service to those who are depressed, frustrated and often bitter because of past mistakes. In your own tactful way, you can remind them that no one is beyond redemption in the eyes of Christ. He has provided ways and means that anyone can follow in seeking His pardon for even the most heinous crime.

"Be ye therefore merciful, as your Heavenly Father also is Merciful." (Luke 6:36)

⊷ Have mercy on me, O Lord, and forgive my iniquities.

LEST WE DESTROY OURSELVES

A young man in Grass Valley, Calif., built the gallows which hung him!

He was chosen as the director of an amateur theatre group. The scene called for a gallows, which he personally constructed. He placed a large mirror before it so that he could make sketches and designs for costumes.

When everything was done, he put his sketchbook close by, stepped up on the box, and slipped his head into the noose to see the effect.

He had arranged a break-away slip-knot as precaution against accident. But because the rope was new and rough, the knot failed as he stepped from the box to the floor. He strangled to death with his toes just above the floor!

In the hurry and bustle of modern life, with its extraordinary devotion to material advantages, there is an increasing danger that the very things that man concocts for his pleasure or service may destroy him.

Atomic energy, for instance, if properly used can serve as one of man's greatest servants. Or it can be the worst scourge of mankind.

"For the desire of money is the root of all evil; which some coveting, have erred from the faith, and have entangled themselves in many sorrows." (I Timothy 6:9, 10)

⋙ Let me use every opportunity, O Jesus, to help and not hurt myself and others.

A PIGEON FLIES 7000 MILES

Paris is 7000 miles from Saigon, Indo-China. By any standards it would make a long, difficult trip. To go by air can well be considered a technical marvel, especially when one considers all that is involved.

And yet, this marvel of human ingenuity is dwarfed into insignificance when we hear of how a homing pigeon was carried in a covered cage from France to Indo-China, a place where it had never been before; and how immediately upon release it took to the air and twenty-four days later arrived in Paris safe and sound.

God has endowed you with a far greater power for finding your way *"back home"* than He has entrusted to the homing pigeon. You have come from the hand of God —from heaven—and He wants you to find your way back there. He offers you countless aids of mind, heart and soul, His constant grace, plus all the revealed Truth that He has bidden His church to offer you throughout your entire journey of life.

Keep ever in mind where you came from, why you are here and where you should go and you will do an even better job than that homing pigeon that winged its way from Saigon to Paris.

"For we have not here a lasting city, but we seek one that is to come." (Hebrews 13:14)

ᕲ O Holy Spirit, keep me ever mindful of the big purpose of my life.

A SAFETY LESSON BACKFIRED

The enterprising members of the Junior Chamber of Commerce in Minneapolis decided to do something to make the city safety warnings more dramatic.

They towed two wrecked cars to one of the busiest highways, and reconstructed a wreck. They parked an ambulance near by, and scattered wax dummies about. They felt that this should be enough to drive home a sharp lesson to drivers about the necessity for safe driving.

But their little plot backfired. A passing motorist suddenly spotted the wreck and jammed on his brakes. Four cars behind him crashed into each other!

Some who take it upon themselves to work for the good of humanity are soon discouraged by the carelessness, ignorance, apathy and general lack of cooperation that is shown by the majority of people.

If you wish to accomplish much good in life, you would do well to expect constant and continuous manifestations of such frailties on the part of most. All are handicapped by the weakness and sin of Adam, and even those who have been redeemed by Christ falter and fall at times.

In short, be ready for the worst, and you will never be surprised in playing the role of a Christ-bearer.

"For patience is necessary for you; that, doing the will of God, you may receive the promise." (Hebrews 10:36)

✍ O Lord, give me the patience to bear with the mistakes of the very ones I would help.

HE COLLECTED A 30-YEAR-OLD DEBT

Thirty years ago, a man who worked as a coal miner in Pennsylvania, found himself in need of funds. He secured a job with the Sanitation Department in New York shoveling snow.

He worked all night. But when he called for his pay the following day, he was accused of not having been on the job. He quit in disgust, without bothering to argue.

In 1933 the man moved to London, England. This past Christmas, pressed for money, he decided to take a chance and write the New York Sanitation Department asking for his long overdue pay.

To his great surprise the Commissioner sent him a check for $15, instead of the $5 he claimed, as an expression of good will and Christmas cheer.

When you stand before the Judgment Seat of God for the final reckoning of your life, you may be delightfully surprised to find that the smallest acts of love and virtue have been carefully recorded even though you may have forgotten them.

Ponder well and often the reminder of Christ that even a *"cup of cold water"* given in His name shall have its reward for all eternity.

"Work your work before the time, and he will give you your reward in his time." (Ecclesiasticus 51:38)

⋘ Thanks to Thee, O my God, for Thy great generosity to me and all mankind.

$5000 FOR AN 11-YEAR-OLD BOY

John Hayes, an 11-year-old boy in Brooklyn recently came into a $5000 fortune.

One day while in the basement of his home where he helped his mother to launder the clothes, he saw on the basement floor hundreds of tiny things that looked like the shiny snowdust that is sprinkled on Christmas trees. But these particles were hard and far more sparkly.

They were diamond chips . . . 1255 of them to be exact.

John turned them over to the police. After the usual six-month wait for claimants, they turned them back to the boy. They were worth $5000, half of which he has given to his mother. The other half is to go towards his college career.

Young John Hayes will look long and far to find another such treasure waiting for him. But if he goes through life being as generous with God by helping others in need, he is bound to enrich his life both here and for all eternity. Parents and teachers would do well to stir up and develop a generous trait in every young person.

"The things that thou hast not gathered in thy youth, how shalt thou find them in thy old age?" (Ecclesiasticus 25:5)

✑ Instill in me, O Lord, a generosity of soul that will make me eager to work for others.

RESIST BEGINNINGS

There's a small flesh-colored species of worm, about one inch long, that in one year alone destroyed $350,000,000 worth of corn in the United States.

This worm is called the European Corn Borer, and was first discovered in this country in New England in 1917. Since that time, it has been slowly spreading westward, multiplying at alarming rates, so that it now infests the entire Corn Belt and adjoining states.

Although in recent years, countless attempts have been made to destroy the Corn Borer, only a very limited degree of control has been reached.

Much of the harm that visits mankind today is caused by various destructive forces that are scarcely noticeable to the average person. Because people don't see the evil, they often jump to the conclusion that it does not exist.

While *"accentuating the positive"* in everything that affects the common good, be on the alert to observe the hidden germs in public life that can cause great harm. Encourage others likewise to be on the lookout and then to take immediate action.

"Lay not up to yourselves treasures on earth: where the rust and moth consume, and where thieves break through, and steal." (Matthew 6:19)

  Help me, O Lord, to detect and restrain evil in its beginnings.

BEAUTY ON ALL SIDES

A 40-year-old man in Boston, had his sight restored recently after fifteen years of blindness.

Dense cataracts had covered both eyes for many years, and it was thought that he would never see again. Eventually he was taken to the Massachusetts Eye and Ear Infirmary, where after two operations he regained his sight.

Of course the first things that this man wished to see were his wife and his children. He had never before seen his youngest son, aged 13. After the joyous family celebration the man was asked what he wanted most to see, now that he had seen his family. *"I would like to see flowers,"* he said. *"Flowers, and all the things that the Lord made so beautiful."*

Many who have never been deprived of the blessing of sight for even one day can go through a whole lifetime and miss the truth, the beauty and the goodness with which God has profusely endowed all creation.

Train yourself to look for the true beauty in both man and nature and you will find that you are getting a constant foretaste of the beauty of the Creator that He wants you to enjoy for all eternity.

"Consider the lilies of the field, how they grow: they labour not, neither do they spin." (Matthew 6:28)

◄§ Thank Thee, O God, for the great blessing of sight.

SUBJECT TO CHANGE

The new candidate for political office was making his first campaign speech. At first he was rather hesitant and nervous. But as he discovered that his audience was quiet and listening, his eloquence grew with his confidence. He outlined his platform in strong terms.

Feeling the power that comes with complete capture of an audience he swept to a climax. *"My friends,"* he said earnestly, *"that is what I stand for. And I want you to know that, if anyone here tonight, doesn't like these moral principles—well, I'm willing to change them."*

Trifling with the truth on the part of anyone is a sure sign of lack of character. One who shifts opinion with the winds should never have your support in taking a position where complete dedication to truth and integrity is so essential.

Do all in your power to encourage those with a high sense of honor to undertake careers in government where they can do so much for the good of all.

"Give an account of thy stewardship: for now thou canst be steward no longer." (Luke 16:2)

≈§ Let me stick to the truth at all times, O Lord, regardless of the consequences.

285

DEATHLY HASTE

Five people, four young men and a girl, were speeding along on an Ohio highway. They were headed towards Toledo. The young woman was a little disturbed at the rate at which they were going, but she didn't say much about it because it was her birthday, and she was very happy.

What she didn't know, was that the great speed was for this very reason. The young woman's parents had planned a surprise birthday party for her, and the young men had promised to get her there in time. As they were late already, the driver picked up speed. He didn't even slow down when they came to the steel bridge. Instead the speedometer mounted to eighty.

Halfway across, the driver suddenly lost control of the heavy car. It crashed through the steel railing dropping into forty feet of water, and sending all its occupants to their death.

The risks that many take for the most superficial reasons are a proof of one thing, i.e., that they have within them a tremendous power. It is a force that can be used for good rather than for evil.

Once people, both young and old, have a high and noble objective in their lives, then the driving sense of purpose within them makes them daring without becoming reckless.

"The kingdom of heaven suffereth violence, and the violent bear it away." (Matthew 11:12)

◄§ Grant me the courage, O Lord, to take many risks to protect the lives of others.

PUT IT TO PRACTICE

A photographer on a West Virginia newspaper was given his assignment. He got into his car and started out.

He hadn't been with the paper long, and he badly wanted to make a good impression. He was very engrossed in looking around for the pictures he wanted when he crashed head-on into a car coming from the opposite direction.

His face was very red when the police arrived, and photographers began taking pictures. His assignment had been to take suitable pictures for traffic safety posters!

It is easy to be very academic about what's wrong with the world and still not lift a finger to improve the very situations about which one vehemently disapproves.

Even worse, some complain bitterly about the lack of peace in the world, and yet in countless little ways they do their bit to promote confusion and hostility. A sharp reply, a catty remark, a bit of rudeness may seem small but each fault does its damage and prevents the peace and calm that God intended should be the lot of all of us during this life.

Make it your business to work even harder in putting into practice your peaceful intentions than you do in thinking up new resolutions!

"Not every one that saith to me, Lord, Lord, shall enter into the kingdom of heaven: but he that doth the will of my Father who is in heaven, he shall enter into the Kingdom of heaven." (Matthew 7:21)

⋙ Help me, O Jesus, to live Thy truth, not just talk about it.

THE WEAKNESS OF EVIL

A masked hold-up man entered a cafe in Warren, R.I. He had a gun in his hand. He marched up to the bar and in a tough voice demanded, *"Lemme have the money."*

The bartender looked at the man quietly. *"Lemme have the money,"* the man repeated. The 20-odd customers who were in the place smiled, and continued quietly eating and talking.

The would-be robber was puzzled and annoyed. *"I'm not kidding!"* he shouted at them. *"I want that money!"* To prove it he fired two shots into the wall. But still no one paid him any attention. The thug became frightened at their unconcern. He dropped his gun, and fled out the back door.

More often than not those who seem daring in crime are weak and flabby at heart. Nothing deflates them more quickly than not to be taken seriously. One takes little risk in disregarding those who shout the loudest in defiance of God. They crave attention. When no one listens, reads what they write or makes any comment about them, they invariably slink away.

To give them any attention at all, even in criticism or condemnation, is often to give them the very encouragement that can build them up to a position where they can do serious harm.

"By their fruits you shall know them." (Matthew 7:16)

◈ O my God, do not let me make the mistake of encouraging evil by giving it attention it does not deserve.

288

LITTLE DEFECTS CAUSE BIG TROUBLE

Not long ago, a letter carrier in a small New York town found himself without a job.

The *"friendly mailman"* is a sort of legend in small towns and cities. But this one overdid it.

The postmaster had become rather concerned about the fact that this mailman was so consistently late in returning from his rounds. He found that the reason was that the mailman would stop for a while at each house and pay a social call, before going to the next.

Post Office officials are not averse to mailmen being friendly with the citizens on their routes, but they sternly object to *"loitering on the route and thus causing delay to the delivery of the mail."*

Seldom do we reflect that it is the little defects and negligence multiplied many times over that weaken government in most countries the world over. They prepare the way for the greater abuses which in turn make it easier for those who would destroy a nation. These latter gain strength through the weakness of others.

By encouraging honesty, devotion and thoroughness in all levels of government, you can do much to ensure the law and order that God has ordained as the basis of freedom.

"Render therefore to Caesar the things that are Caesar's: and to God, the things that are God's. (Matthew 22:21)

⋙ Strengthen me to do my part, O Lord, in working for the good of all.

289

THE CURSE OF AVARICE

For some 30 years a man in Rotherham, England, lived alone in an old furniture store. His dwelling was not only rundown, but it lacked even the basic conveniences—heat and light.

The neighbors, feeling sorry for this obviously destitute 79-year-old man, would often provide him with food. They would pay his bus fare when he wanted to go anywhere, and offer him their used—but decent clothing to take the place of the tattered rags he held together with safety pins.

Not long ago, the man died. Upon investigation, it was disclosed that he had left $15,000 and that he was the owner of 30 homes from which he had failed to collect rent.

It is bad enough when avarice hardens a person's heart and drives him to resort to all sorts of questionable means to increase his wealth. But when he becomes so possessed by his handful of gold dust that he inflicts punishment on himself, then does he invite a foretaste of the torture that belongs to the damned.

"Gold is a stumbling-block to them that sacrifice to it: woe to them that eagerly follow after it, and every fool shall perish by it." (Ecclesiasticus 31:7)

◂§ Never let me become so attached to Thy gifts, O Lord, that I forget that Thou art the Giver.

FLOATING DANGER

A Danish ship recently was making its maiden voyage from Copenhagen. It soon became apparent that the voyage was destined to be a hazardous one.

As the ship was leaving the west coast of Jutland, it ran into a furious North Sea gale. All hands were busy keeping the ship in hand when further disaster struck—one completely unforeseen.

A magnetic World War II mine that had lain unnoticed for years suddenly exploded against the hull of the tanker. Luckily, no one was killed, and ships in the vicinity rushed to the rescue.

For nearly 9 years, since the end of the last great war, this dangerous mine has been floating on the seas a potential menace to thousands of ships.

Difficult as it is to spot such deadly threats, it is a far greater problem to detect the evil ideas that are floating around in almost every environment today. Those who spread them are very shrewd and astute in camouflaging them in such a way that they appear to be harmless.

Keep on the lookout for these dangers and warn others lest they be *"shipwrecked"* by them. Better still, make an effort to disseminate the truth and love of Christ.

"And fear ye not them that kill the body, and are not able to kill the soul: but rather fear him that can destroy both soul and body in hell." (Matthew 10:28)

◦§ Enable me, O God, to be alert in distinguishing truth from error.

KEEP YOUR EYES OPEN

A highway patrolman in Wilmington, Dela., stopped a car and scolded a driver for using his bright lights while other cars were approaching him.

"But I have always used bright lights," the man protested, *"and nothing has ever happened."*

The patrolman held on to his temper and explained that even though nothing had happened so far, something could. *"Moreover,"* he said, *"it's bad highway manners. Suppose everyone who was approaching you refused to dim his lights. What would you do then?"*

"Oh," said the driver, *"that wouldn't bother me. I always close my eyes anyway when I pass another car."*

Few people would go to the extreme of closing their eyes at any time while driving an automobile. But many invite disaster in another way by closing their eyes to the dangers that jeopardize the safety of their eternal souls.

Even trifling with a threat to one's mind, heart or soul is a risky business. It is far more sensible to keep one's eyes wide open and avoid every person, place or thing that can be even an occasion of sin.

"Be you therefore perfect, as also your heavenly Father is perfect." (Matthew 5:48)

⤜ Assist me, O Lord, in being alert to do good and avoid evil.

ONCE TOO OFTEN

A sign in a Buffalo restaurant read, *"If not delighted, dine free."* Since the management served the best they had no fear of losing money this way.

But one young man decided to take the restaurant at its word. Not that he had any complaint. He simply didn't have any money.

Walking into the restaurant, he ordered the best on the menu, and then left without paying his check. A week later, he decided to try it again. He went in, and was served. But this time the proprietor was ready. When the man tried to leave without paying his bill, the police were there. In court, the man was fined $25 for fraud.

Almighty God has been extraordinarily generous to us. But He expects cooperation on our part. One thing is certain: God will not be mocked. Those who take His gifts and then act as if He had nothing to do with them soon discover that He is a just God.

"The mercies of the Lord I will sing for ever." (Psalms 88:2)

❧ In humble gratitude, O Lord, I thank Thee for everything that I am and have.

A LITTLE CHILD SAVED A BLIND GIRL

A 19-year-old girl in Winston-Salem, N.C., is blind. But this young woman is not lonely. She has a staunch friend in the little 5-year-old girl who lives next door.

One day the young woman was watching television in the home of her little friend. Of course, she couldn't see the show, but she could hear the voices, and the child explained what was happening.

Suddenly, there was an unmistakable smell of smoke. The child ran to call her mother who, discovering that the kitchen was on fire, immediately called the fire department. But her daughter didn't wait for her to complete the call. She hurried back to the living room, and taking her friend by the hand led her out to safety.

Too often we underestimate the unusual powers that God has implanted in every young person. It often takes an emergency such as this fire to bring to the surface the keen judgment, alertness and generosity that was spontaneously shown by this 5-year-old tot.

There would be far less juvenile delinquency, thievery, brutality, drug addiction and immorality among young people if everyone of us made it our business to seize every opportunity to develop the good in every youth waiting to be nurtured.

"Suffer the little children to come unto me and forbid them not, for of such is the kingdom of heaven." (Matthew 19:14)

᪥ Let me play a part, O Lord, in bringing to blossom the beauty that Thou hast planted in every young soul.

PUT THE STEAM TO WORK

A British sailor was sentenced to a year's detention as the result of a court martial not long ago. The young man pleaded guilty to charges of smashing gauges, pipes and lightbulbs aboard the submarine depot ship *Montclare*.

The *Montclare* is stationed at Rothesay, Scotland, and rarely leaves port. The 22-year-old sailor told the court that there was no way to find any excitement in Rothesay —no way to *"blow off steam,"* and that he missed the gaiety of London. So he had used these means to have some fun.

Although the court took a dim view of the way in which he sought to let off steam, they were quite concerned about the reasons for his doing so.

As a steam engine blows up if the power generated within is not put to use, so do people *"let off steam"* with more or less violence when their energies are not channeled in the right direction.

God has given us all great powers of heart, mind and soul. But He didn't intend that they should be locked away within us. He expects us to put them to work for His glory, our own benefit, and for the advantage of others. Each and every bit of power within us has been put there for a purpose and should have a useful outlet.

"Without me you can do nothing." (John 15:5)

◄ৄ Let me serve Thee, O my God, by aiding others to put their inner power to a constructive use.

YOU CAN BE THE CONNECTING LINK

"There is no surprise more magical than the surprise of being loved," someone once said. *"It is God's finger on a man's shoulder."*

There is nobility in even the worst person. Why?—because each and every human being is made in God's image. And that divine image can never be completely effaced or lost.

Therefore never write anybody off. There's always hope!

Even the man who has decided to have nothing whatever to do with God isn't frozen in that state of mind. Deep in the very root of his being, and simply because he *is* created in the Divine Image, there is an ever-present tug toward God.

It is the privilege of the Christ-bearer to help him become aware of this tremendous tug. For this very reason, you can honestly say to anyone, *"There's a lot of good in you!"* Yes—it will be a pleasant surprise to even the worst of men to learn through you that God loves them.

"But thou sparest all: because they are thine, O Lord, who lovest souls." (Wisdom 11:27)

⋙ O Lord, let me be an instrument in carrying Thy love to those who hate.

UNEXPECTED REWARD

A former holdup man after 24 years confessed to the murder of a Brooklyn policeman, and was surprised to learn that the officer was still alive!

In 1928 while robbing a butcher shop, he shot the policeman. Later he was arrested for the robbery and acquitted, and could not understand why he had not been tried for murder, since he thought all the time he had killed the officer.

Haunted by the *"murder,"* he surrendered to the police, only to discover he was not a murderer. In releasing him the prosecutor said: *"Your conscience has punished you enough."*

God has strange ways of rewarding us. Frequently we are torn by decisions. When we make the one that seems to be against our own best interests, the Lord often blesses us much more.

"The wicked fleeth when no man pursueth." (Proverbs 28:1)

❧ Dear Lord, give me the wisdom and strength to do the right thing, especially when it does not seem to benefit me.

TO RADIATE GOODNESS

A pall of smoke 8,000 feet thick hung over New York City about a year ago, making it impossible to see further than a block or two away. This smoke came from forest fires as far off as Missouri, Oklahoma and Texas! They formed a cloud that spread over half the country.

New Yorkers were probably little aware of the fires because there was no immediate danger. And yet those fires touched their lives.

The same thing is true of the power that is within you. Little do you realize how far it can reach. You may be unconscious of it. It can be for good or for evil. But nevertheless you can exert far-reaching influence that can spread out until it vitally affects the whole world.

"So let your light shine before men that they may see your good works, and glorify your Father who is in heaven." (Matthew 5:16)

❧ O God, help me to use the power that Thou hast given me to spread Thy love and truth.

GO AND KEEP GOING

Jesus Christ was ever on the move always with the hope and prayer that as He went among the people, He would reach some who could be reached in no other way. His was with the loving purpose of bringing God to men and men to God. Jesus Christ went to dinners, to weddings, to all sorts of public and social gatherings.

He talked with all types of persons in all sorts of places. He was to be found on the roadside, on busy city streets, in village squares, in wheatfields, at the seashore, at the side of a well, in the desert, on the mountainside—anywhere and everywhere. And the people flocked to Him because He first went to them.

Only as we reach out to people, will we truly be Christophers—bearers of Christ.

We shall bring Christ's peace and truth to the world in the measure that we imitate His everlasting quest for souls.

" . . . *My delights were to be with the children of men.*" (Proverbs 8:31)

 O God, give me the strength and courage to go and keep going to all men in Thy name.

A LIFE FOR A DOLLAR

It was late October in Delaware, and the first cold winds had begun to blow. A 26-year-old poultry worker in Lewes was on his way home. He had just been paid, and he was doing some mental figuring as to how he was going to use his money. He stopped when he reached the wharf of a fish processing plant, and took the money out of his pocket to count it.

As he stood there sheafing through his bills, a gust of wind caught up a dollar bill and carried it into Delaware Bay. The young man was upset. He needed that dollar. Quickly taking off his coat and his shoes he dove into the icy water to retrieve the bill before it went below the water.

Scarcely had the young man swum more than a few feet, than he suddenly disappeared beneath the surface. Evidently he had suffered a cramp in the chill waters. Fishermen, rowing a short distance away, saw him go under and hurried to rescue him. But they were too late.

A life had been sacrificed for $1!

If you apply a bit of that hidden power within you to strive for the greatest prize of all—the salvation of your immortal soul, you will dare much to reach that precious crown.

"For where your treasure is, there will your heart be also." (Luke 12:34)

&§ O Holy Spirit, inspire me to take as many risks to win an eternal prize as others do for the insignificant gains of this world.

KEEP FIRST THINGS FIRST

A tired businessman was just settling down to his evening papers one night when his six-year-old son began to pester him. In an attempt to divert the child's attention he tore a page of the paper into small pieces. On one side was a map of the world and on the other a picture of a man. The father told his son to put the map back together again.

In ten minutes his son returned, the task completed. Since the boy had no idea of geography, the businessman wondered how he had done it so quickly. *"All I did,"* said the boy, *"was to put the man right. When I did that, the world came out right!"*

The big battle of our day is over man—the worth of man. It is a battle for man's soul. Are you doing as much to reach all men with the truth of their divine origin as are those who deny God? They are striving to eliminate all knowledge of Him from the face of the earth. Will you let them outdo you?

"For our wrestling is not against flesh and blood, but against . . . the rulers of the world of this darkness." (Ephesians 6:12)

❧ Lord, help me make the world better for my being in it.

THROUGH THICK AND THIN

A high school basketball player in Adrian, Michigan, was terribly upset. He thought the game was over. And that meant that his team had lost to their deadly rivals. In disgust he decided to wind things up by giving the ball one long fling to the other end of the court.

To the surprise of himself and everyone else it landed right in the basket. To his greater surprise that final toss tied the score. He had been mistaken in thinking the game was over.

Even though that last throw had been one of despair rather than hope, it had changed defeat into another chance for victory. In the overtime his team went on to win by two points.

In these critical times many are tempted to become cynical. It is often hard not to take a defeatist attitude. But even if you do feel discouraged, even when things look the blackest and when you think all is lost, it is still worthwhile to keep trying.

One prayer, one word, one act may be the turning point away from failure for you and countless others unknown to you.

"He that shall persevere unto the end, he shall be saved." (Matthew 10:22)

≈§ O God, give me the grace to keep trying even when there seems to be no point in trying.

OUR HAPPINESS IN OTHERS

A girl in a small California town lay in a hospital bed hour upon weary hour. Weakened by a series of recurring epileptic fits, she was forced to find relief in constant hospitalization.

She was overwhelmed with self-pity. But after some time she discovered she was even bored with this.

Looking around for something else to do, she got an idea. Maybe if she would try to forget herself and then help others . . . no, that wasn't quite it. If she tried to help others *first,* then maybe her own trouble would become smaller.

Though no literary genius, she requested the hospital authorities to contact the local newspaper, asking if she couldn't submit a little column to help people realize, as she put it, *"the good in life around them."*

The editor agreed to give her a chance and accepted her column. Within three or four weeks, letters were pouring in, thanking her and giving her a *"mental"* pat on the back for what she was doing.

And from that very first day this same girl has suffered very rarely from attacks of epilepsy!

"Give and it shall be given to you." (Luke 6:38)

⚜ O Lord, inspire me to see that in helping others I help myself even more.

PEACE OR DISASTER

Many persons feel we are at the crossroads of civilization. We may be standing on the brink of the greatest peace the world has ever enjoyed—or the most terrible nightmare of misery and chaos that mankind has ever known.

The issue is clear and narrows down to what is truth with regard to the human being. If he is not a creature of God and the noblest act of God, with rights from Him, then he is just a clod of earth or the merest tool of the almighty State.

Karl Marx, the arch-prophet of Communism, in his *"Das Kapital"* expressed this fundamental point most clearly. *"The democratic concept of man is false because it is Christian,"* he wrote. *"The democratic concept holds that . . . each man is a sovereign being. This is the illusion, dream and postulate of Christianity."*

What a challenge for you, personally and individually! You can do something, by prayer and work, to change threatening disaster into the lasting peace for which all men yearn.

"Peace be to you. As the Father has sent me, I also send you." (John 20:21)

ᴇᴈ Grant me the privilege, O Lord, of being an instrument of Thy peace.

THERE'S GOOD IN THE WORST

The weather was cold and crisp in Detroit on the day that a large hard snowball went crashing through a candy store window, accompanied by shouts of boyish laughter.

The annoyed proprietor walked to the door and looked out, but the culprit had fled. With a sigh of resignation he went about his business. That was the third window for the month!

It was late in the evening when one of his clerks brought him an envelope. *"Some kid left this for you,"* he told him. Inside the envelope the surprised storekeeper found a dollar and a note which read, *"Sir, I am sorry I broke your window. I hope this will cover the costs."*

The note was unsigned. The storekeeper told reporters that he would like to find the boy to return his dollar and to give him a box of candy. He said, *"In days like these when you hear so much about the destructiveness of kids, it's refreshing to get a note like that."*

One of the great consolations of anyone striving in Christ's Name to bring out the best in his fellowman is to find goodness, where it is not expected, and to try to encourage it.

"I came not to call the just, but sinners to penance." (Luke 5:32)

Inspire me, O Lord, to do my part in bringing out the good that is to be found in the worst of men.

WORDS, WORDS, WORDS

A lawyer in Brussels, Belgium, recently set out to discover for himself whether or not a court really listens to a lawyer's courtroom speech. For a long time he had had suspicions that such speeches are a waste of time.

One day, right in the middle of presenting his case, he switched suddenly to a law book, and read through 20 paragraphs, before anyone even mentioned it.

It appears that the prosecutor had noticed the switch, but he was at a loss as to what to do about it, for the judge had quietly fallen asleep some time before, and to awaken him would cause embarrassment to everyone. But since the lengthy reading from the law book grew even lengthier, and the judge slept peacefully on, the prosecutor was forced finally to awaken him.

Rather than talk about trouble, make it your business to do something about it. Those who are out to wreck the world are usually men of few words. They devote their time and energy to translating words into action.

On the other hand, the very ones who have in their custody the Truth that can make the world free are too frequently long on words and short on action. The Devil doesn't mind a bit if we merely pass resolutions, remain academic and never get down to the serious business of actually blending God's truth into modern life.

"Be ye doers of the word and not hearers only, deceiving yourselves." (James 1:22)

❧ O Lord, help me to be a doer, not just a talker.

306

KEEP FIRST THINGS FIRST

Not long ago, over 60 professional photographers in Dallas, Texas, got together for the purpose of forming a Photographers Association.

Proud of their numbers, and their common purpose, they proceeded to organize along accepted lines, electing officers and drawing up rules.

The only hitch came, when at the end of the proceedings, they decided to take a picture of the new president, and it was discovered that not one of the photographers had brought a camera.

Someone pointed out recently that there are three million organizations in America. Whether they be garden clubs, labor groups or church societies, they invariably begin with great enthusiasm and high ideals. But too often the original noble objective—the very purpose of the organization—is lost sight of in the techniques of procedure. The means gradually become an end in themselves. Soon most of the members lose interest and do nothing but pay dues.

A chief aim of the Christopher movement is to encourage individuals who belong to worthy organizations to attend meetings, to participate in activities, and to reduce high sounding resolutions to practical application.

"As you would that men should do to you, do you also to them in like manner." (Luke 6:31)

⋘ Remind me, O Lord, of my own personal responsibility to all men.

307

AN 8 YEAR OLDSTER AND TERMITES

An 8-year-old boy in Darwin, Australia, recently tried something entirely new in schoolboy efforts to get out of having to go to school.

He attends a small school, but disliked everything connected with it. One day in class the teacher explained how tiny little termites can little by little destroy an entire building. The boy listened raptly, an idea growing in his head.

Some days later the school superintendent caught the boy in the act of transferring some termites he had found from a bottle to the walls in the basement. The boy explained later that he had hoped that the termites would eat up the school building.

Few would think of going to such an extreme as this youngster did in trying to obstruct education. But many go almost as far by belittling the teaching profession, by discouraging their own sons and daughters from dedicating their lives to the classroom or by neglecting to give the teacher the respect and support that anyone deserves who is actually taking the place of a parent in the training and formation of youth.

It is well and good to be on the lookout for those who use the teaching profession to undermine our school system. But it is far more important to encourage more of high ideals and competence to enter this vital sphere.

"You are my friends if you do the things that I command you." (John 15:14)

&⸸ Help me, O Lord, to build up, not tear down.

IT'S YOUR WORLD

A car was wrecked on a San Francisco highway, and after the routine investigation by the police, a call was put in for a tow-truck to come to haul it away.

In a short time, the truck arrived. The driver got out and looked at the badly smashed car he was supposed to tow away.

"Say! That's a bad one!" he whistled. *"Well, I better get started."*

Suddenly he stopped, frozen in his tracks, a look of wide disbelief on his face. *"Hey!"* he breathed. *"That's my car!"*

And so it was. Investigation proved that the wrecked car had been stolen only a few hours before. The owner hadn't even had time to miss it.

Could it be that we are so busily preoccupied with the task of "picking up the pieces" over the world today that we are forgetting our primary job of extending the love and truth of Christ to all men in every part of the globe.

Once you can say to yourself: *"This is my world just as much as it is anyone's and I am going to work as hard to save it as others are striving to destroy it,"* then you will probably do more to prevent world catastrophes and not be merely content to wait to help when the next *"wreck"* takes place.

"Go ye into the whole world, and preach the gospel to every creature." (Mark 16:15)

⊷ Help me, O Lord, to extend the faith, not merely defend it.

SO RICH AND YET SO POOR

Recently in Paris, the police arrested a man who looked as rundown and bedraggled as the hotel where they found him. Yet, when he was searched they found $1,000,000 worth of diamonds hidden in his clothes.

The police were satisfied that this was the man who had perpetrated the daring jewel robbery of a few weeks before. But they were puzzled as to why with so much wealth on him the robber appeared to be so poor.

To their great surprise, the burglar confessed that he hadn't eaten for some time, and that he was very hungry. Although he had a million dollars in jewels, he didn't have enough money to buy a meal. It seems that no one would buy the jewels from him.

In a desperate attempt to find satisfaction in material things, large sections of humanity are today suffering from spiritual malnutrition. While seeking every possible physical advantage and bodily pleasure, they have neglected their souls. As a result they have developed lopsided, incomplete personalities.

Rather than condemn such persons, make it your business to bring to them in every possible way the spiritual nourishment for which they are starving. With gentleness and kindness make up for what they lack.

"As long as you did it for one of these, my least brethren, you did it to me." (Matthew 25:40)

&§ Permit me, O Lord, to serve those who are starving in soul or body.

MAKE IT YOUR BUSINESS

In 1951 Kansas City was the victim of a severe flood, causing extensive and costly damage.

Although this was regrettable, the United States Circuit Court of Appeals was somewhat surprised when suit was brought against Government agencies, including the Weather Bureau, for more than $1,000,000 in damages from the flood.

The suit was filed by six Kansas City firms. They charged the Weather Bureau with giving out misinformation about the flood crest and failing to give sufficient warning that that area was in danger of being flooded.

But the court ruled that the governmental service provided by the weather forecasts in no way relieves the individual citizen of his responsibility to exercise his own judgment in such matters.

Most tend to blame others for not giving them the proper warning when they are overtaken by trouble. Too seldom does anyone turn the light of inquiry upon himself and honestly ask: *"Why haven't I done something about it?"*

"Better to light a candle than to curse the darkness" is an expression we use frequently in the Christopher movement. Make it your business to *"light a candle"* rather than to use valuable time complaining about defects in government, education, labor relations, and in the literary and entertainment fields.

"Be not overcome by evil, but overcome evil by good." (Romans 12:21)

Inspire me, O Lord, to be a doer, not a complainer.

BE ON YOUR GUARD

A New York policeman was entering a large downtown department store when he met a man who was having quite a bit of trouble getting a large rug through the door.

The policeman smiled at the man's efforts, and held the door open for him. *"I think you need help, my friend,"* he said. The man smiled his thanks. *"I guess you're right,"* he said ruefully, setting the rug down on the sidewalk. *"And what's more, I still have another one to bring out. Look, I wonder if you'd mind watching this one till I can bring out the other. Then I'll get a cab."*

The policeman was glad to oblige. Patiently he stood guard over the rug for five minutes—then ten . . . then fifteen. Bewildered, he went inside the store to investigate. His face was very red when he found that the rug he was watching had been stolen,—and the thief had gotten away!

Anyone of us might have been fooled as this police officer was. But it is a terrible thing to realize that in most nations that have lost their God-given freedom in our day, it has been largely due to the fact that well-intentioned but very gullible persons have actually helped the very ones who were out to destroy them.

"Be sober and watch, because your adversary the devil, as a roaring lion, goeth about seeking whom he may devour; whom resist ye, strong in faith." (1 Peter 5:8, 9)

❧ Give me the good sense, O Lord, to know that to stay well is always wiser and cheaper than to try to get well.

312

FIFTY PERSONS GAVE THEIR SKIN

A 7-year-old girl in Long Island, New York, reached across the kitchen stove to get her lunch box. Her dress caught fire, and she was burned from head to foot.

The child was rushed to the hospital in a critical condition. For some time it was doubtful whether or not she would live. But when she had survived the danger line, the widowed mother was faced with a grave consideration. Her little girl would be disfigured for life unless the doctors could obtain enough skin to graft on in place of that which had been destroyed.

For such a widely burned area a great deal of skin was required. The frantic mother sent out a public appeal, hoping against hope that someone would be sympathetic enough to help. She immediately received not just one, but offers from fifty persons to give her child their skin.

Emergencies bring out the deep-seated generosity in many a person. It is proof of the good in every man despite his defects. True, he usually reacts best when emergencies occur—on a crisis-to-crisis basis. But with a little encouragement, some will dedicate themselves to the apparently difficult but deeply satisfying task of serving others in Christ's Name. Taking a temporary loss out of love of God is a guarantee of great gain for eternity. As Christ said:

"He that humbleth himself shall be exalted." (Matthew 23:12)

୶ Teach me, O Lord, the wisdom of winning by losing.

THEY ADOPTED TWO BLIND CHILDREN

A young New York couple, Mr. and Mrs. Francis Lynch, not long ago adopted their second blind child from the Boston Nursery for Blind Babies.

Mr. and Mrs. Lynch have no children of their own, and when they decided to adopt a child they decided it should be a blind baby, named Susan. Little Susan is now four years old, and perfectly healthy in all other respects.

Her parents hadn't planned to adopt another child right away. But one day when they had to make a trip to the Nursery they met two-year-old Elizabeth Ann, and immediately wanted her for their own. Nursery officials said that it was the first time in their experience that a couple had wanted to adopt two blind children.

You may not be able to imitate this unusual generosity in taking on the responsibility of giving a home to two such handicapped little ones, but there is something that you can do along these same lines.

You might, for instance, take some job (or continue in it!) that is for benefit of others but which, at the same time, is a thankless and difficult one that everyone else dodges. God blesses those in a particular way who deliberately choose the unpopular and often unpleasant tasks out of love of Him and others.

"The Son of man is not come to be ministered unto, but to minister and give his life for many." (Matthew 20:28)

۶ Teach me, O Lord, the blessedness of helping those less fortunate.

THE POWER OF TRUTH

People over the earth are beginning to realize more and more that there is a very intimate connection between truth and freedom. Sobered by the scourge of war, even those opposed to religion are more disposed to admit the inescapable conclusion of what Christ meant when He said: *"The Truth shall make you free."* (John 8:32)

Once a sufficient number of people realize that falsehood is nothing but the absence of truth, just as darkness is the absence of light, hate the absence of love, and disease the absence of health, then there is high hope that this old world of ours will one day come to know the blessing of a real, lasting peace.

Anyone can help in this task. You can. I can. And, naturally, the closer we are to God the better Christ-bearers we will be. Yes, no one is so far away from Christ that he or she cannot share in some measure in this tremendous undertaking.

"The foolish things of the world hath God chose, that he may confound the wise; and the weak things of the world hath God chosen that he may confound the strong." (I Corinthians 1:27)

⟜ O Divine Savior, grant that I may reach many with Thy truth.

315

HE ATE TOO MUCH

Police in New York couldn't help but smile when they entered the small east side restaurant very early one morning and found their suspect obligingly on hand fast asleep at a table.

The owner of the restaurant had reported that every night for a week, a burglar had entered and helped himself to a free meal, cigarettes and chewing gum. He never seemed to touch anything else however, and the police guessed that the thief was someone who was destitute and driven to steal food because of his hunger. But when they found their man they were surprised. They hadn't expected the arrest to be so easy.

The man explained sleepily, that he always left as soon as he had eaten. But that night he had eaten too much and he had become so drowsy that he had fallen asleep.

Those who spend their time living off others hurt themselves in more ways than one. Above all they cannot have much peace of heart for conscience reminds them they are cheats, both in failing to carry their share of the load, and in taking from others what does not belong to them. Sooner or later they pay the penalty of sidestepping their responsibilities.

"Depart from me, you cursed, into everlasting fire that was prepared for the devil and his angels, for I was hungry and you gave me not to eat." (Matthew 25:41, 42)

ᵃ᷍§ Keep me ever reminded, O my Saviour, that I am here to aid others, not to take advantage of them.

SO NEAR AND YET SO FAR

A cattle raiser and his son who had a thriving cattle ranch in Clear Lake, South Dakota, wanted to buy a fine bull. In fact they wanted to buy the finest bull they could find.

So they decided to attend the Western Stock Show in Denver, Colorado. For there surely they would have a wide selection from the finest animals in that section.

It was a long trip, many miles away. But they made it with no mishaps, and after a day's scouting around they finally made the choice of the finest Angus bull at the sale.

They bought the bull for $5050 and started for home. But the father and son had little to say to each other on the way back. They were both feeling a little sheepish. The bull that they had bought had been raised on their neighbor's farm up in South Dakota, less than a mile away from their own.

In our day countless persons are searching for the Way, the Truth and the Life. Little do they realize how close they are to it at all times.

A rare opportunity presents itself in our day to bring the love and truth of Christ to the countless millions who are looking in vain for someone to make it known to them. Those who are dedicated to falsehood go to endless trouble to reach everybody with their errors. Can you in conscience do any less?

"Go ye into the whole world and preach the gospel to every creature." (Mark 16:15)

⋙ Help me, Almighty God, to play the role of missioner as far as I can.

IT'S EASY TO BLAME OTHERS

In Palermo, Sicily, not long ago a sixteen year old boy found himself in serious trouble with the law.

The youngster was not a very good student, but he was possessed of an unreasonable pride and an ungovernable temper. And although he was never willing to work very hard at his studies, he nonetheless was always very put out when he failed to receive good grades.

On one occasion he became particularly furious with his instructor because he failed in one of his courses. Nothing could convince him that it was his own fault that he had failed. He was so angry that he secured a pistol, and fired four shots at the unfortunate teacher, wounding him in the arm.

It is a human tendency to blame others for our own shortcomings. Parents who neglect to give their children the proper home training too frequently take it out on teachers for what they themselves have allowed to develop. Those who fail to vote or take any interest in better government are usually the first to complain when things go wrong with the administration of public affairs.

You will never make a mistake by first looking into yourself when trouble arises to find if and where you yourself may have failed. If you examine your own conscience in this way, it will be a strong inducement for you to improve rather than merely disapprove.

"Before thou inquire, blame no man: and when thou hast inquired, reprove justly." (Ecclesiasticus 11:7)

⊷§ Help me, O Lord, to search my own heart before blaming others.

318

SHE DIDN'T REALIZE IT WAS THE KING

It was a very busy night at the big movie theater in Stockholm, Sweden. The hat-check girl was having a trying time of it. There seemed to be a never-ending line of hands holding out wraps which had to be tagged and systematically put away.

She worked steadily, automatically, without even bothering to look up at the faces. She had to hurry. It was nearly curtain-time.

A tall elderly man put his hat and coat on the counter. "That will be 25 oere," the girl said. (25 oere is about 5 cents).

"I'm sorry, I haven't any money," the man replied gently. The girl was annoyed. What did he expect? "Well, it will be 25 oere, anyway," she said shortly.

The man turned around and borrowed the coin from someone behind him. Only then did the girl look up. She gasped when she recognized her customer. It was the King of Sweden!

Christ has warned us not to overlook being kind to every human being, whether he be poor or rich, in low station or high, ignorant or educated. In each of them is the resemblance of Christ. To refuse them, therefore, is to refuse Him. Jesus put it very forcefully when He said:

"As long as you did it not to one of these least, neither did you do it to me." (Matthew 25:45)

⋖§ Guide me, O Holy Spirit, in showing love to one and all without exception.

DON'T BE FOOLED BY DOUBLE-TALK

For 25 years occupants of the city-country building in Pittsburgh, Pa., have been exasperated by the strange perversity in the temperature of the building.

In the winter, when temperatures dropped, naturally they turned the thermostats up to warm the building. But in each office it was noticed that the higher the thermostat the colder the temperature. In the summer things were no better either. Turning down the thermostats increased the heat instead of cooling the building.

Finally one day a building inspector solved the mystery. It seemed that the whole building had been supplied with defective thermostats. Not that they weren't in good working order, but that the covers had been marked in reverse reading *"hot"* when they should *"cold"* and vice versa.

This incident is a strong reminder of why much of the world is in confusion today. In the great modern deception that is being master-minded by the Devil himself, his followers find their way into positions of influence in their relentless effort to parade *"evil"* as good, falsehood as truth, slavery as freedom, and treason as loyalty.

This mass deceit can quickly be dispelled if those who are for God show as much daring for truth as others do for evil.

"Jesus therefore said to them: . . . You are of your father the devil, . . . for he is a liar, and the father thereof." (John 8:42–44)

✑ Grant me the grace, O Lord, to be a champion of truth.

THE DAY OF RECKONING

A short while ago, the FBI arrested the vice president of a suburban bank in Philadelphia. The 57-year-old man was charged with having stolen funds from the bank and having made false entries in the records to cover the amount of $146,000.

The amazing thing about this robbery is that the thefts had been made in small sums over a period of 35 years! The trusted bank official had begun defrauding his company from the age of 22, and having gotten away with it for so long he was quite certain that he would never be caught.

The discovery of his thefts was made simply enough during a routine inspection by federal bank examiners. When faced with the evidence, he confessed and told the examiners that he had taken the money *"for general daily living expenses."*

Many a person foolishly tries to convince himself that because he is *"getting away"* with a violation of God's law, he is therefore deceiving everyone. He may go to great pains to fool others—but he never completely fools himself. And, much as he would like to dodge it, he knows deep in his heart that he cannot fool his Maker. The day of reckoning must eventually come, when he will hear the Supreme Judge say to him:

"Render an account of the stewardship: for now thou canst be steward no longer." (Luke 16:2)

∽ Help me, O Lord, to live honestly all the days of my life.

HELPING OTHERS CAN MEAN INCONVENIENCE

A four-year-old boy in Brooklyn is an avid television fan. His favorite programs are those about the fantastic antics of men from other planets who fly through space as effortlessly as breathing. In fact, so greatly was this child impressed that he decided to try it for himself.

One day when his mother wasn't looking, tiny Kenneth Ward climbed up on the window sill of their second-story apartment and poised himself to fly down to earth.

But when he finally reached the outer sill and looked down at the twenty-five foot drop, Kenneth became frightened and tried to make his way back in. It was too late though. There was only room to cling to the ledge.

Fortunately, a 16-year-old girl who was passing by happened to look up and see the frightened child lose his grip and drop toward the sidewalk below. She braced herself beneath him, breaking his fall, and saving his life.

All of us can learn a lesson from this fast-thinking high school girl. It didn't take more than a quick moment for her to see that she could make up for the judgment that little Kenneth lacked, even though she might risk a broken back in the attempt. To provide others with good government, good education and good everything else must mean sacrifice for some, but it is far from in vain. It makes for fuller living here and hereafter.

"But I most gladly will spend, and be spent myself for your souls."

✎§ Let me suffer here, O Lord, that I may reign hereafter.

MUSIC WITH A PURPOSE

The jail in Dyersburg, Tennessee, is noted for its reasonable and humane treatment of prisoners. Often in the evenings, passersby may hear the sound of singing voices or of a guitar playing a merry tune.

The sheriff is of the opinion that even criminals should be allowed a little fun now and then.

But on one occasion he was not too pleased with this apparently innocent amusement. There was one prisoner who had a guitar, and who whanged away at it every night for long hours at a time.

He played very loudly, and what was worse, he played very badly. The sheriff stood it as long as he could. Then one night his nerves could suffer no more. He went to speak to the prisoner. But he found more than a noisy guitar player. Three other prisoners were keeping time to the music by sawing away with hacksaws on the bars.

Men use various ways to cover up evil. It is proof that men know the difference between right and wrong when they strive to appear as *"good"* when they are actually perpetrating *"evil."*

The most dishonest persons want honest people to handle their affairs. Those who lead immoral lives wish to appear decent and respectable. The very ones who resort to falsehood and deceit go to great lengths to make others regard them as upright.

"Deceitful souls go astray in sins." (Proverbs 13:13)

✍ Impress on me, O Lord, the importance of living honestly.

323

THE BLESSING OF TROUBLE

In Caen, France, a man was having an enjoyable meal of oysters when he suddenly bit on something hard and broke a front tooth.

He was naturally very upset. But when he searched to see what had caused the accident he found a beautiful large pearl.

In great excitement he took the pearl to a jeweler who found that it was genuine and of great value.

You may never find a pearl in an oyster, no matter how many you eat. But it is almost as certain that you will not achieve any worthwhile success, from God's point of view, without taking a loss of one kind or another. And it will probably be much worse than a broken tooth.

The reason that many fail to find any real happiness in life is that they work too hard in dodging the very trouble that would help them. When they take a job, they look for only one type of occupation—a job that pays a lot of money, requires little work and provides long vacations.

By the very nature that God gave us, we are made to work our way through life in preparation for eternity. Of course, He intends that we should have some pleasure en route. But, what many too many fail to realize, is that He gives the truest and deepest joy to those striving diligently to work for love of Him and others.

"And whosoever doth not carry his cross and come after me, cannot be my disciple." (Luke 14:27)

⊷§ O my crucified Lord, renew in me an acceptance of life's crosses.

THE EVIL USE THEIR IMAGINATION

One of the biggest fakers in the history of crime was recently exposed by the Minneapolis police force.

After some searching, they arrested a man who had had an astonishing record of success in cashing forged checks. He confessed that his success was due to his rather unique approach.

He would use onions to produce a plentiful flow of tears from his eyes. Then he would rush into some place of business with a check for $25 or less. He would explain to the proprietor that his wife had just died, and that he didn't have enough to pay funeral expenses. The sympathetic proprietors usually handed over the required amount without further question.

One seldom hears of anyone bent on mischief saying *"what can I do?"* He is usually very resourceful and alert, despite the fact that the odds are usually against him. It is one of the great paradoxes of our day that the very ones who are dedicated to enslaving the world show the most unusual daring, initiative and imagination.

You, personally and individually, can do something to change that!

"Be ye wise as serpents and simple as doves." (Matthew 10:16)

꿔 Inspire me, O Lord, to show as much imagination in laboring for Thee as others do in working against Thee.

325

FAITH IN THE WRONG WAY

A man wanted to buy a badly needed new suit. He asked a friend to go with him to the store on the corner and help him to choose one.

But the friend objected. *"No,"* he said. *"I'll be glad to go with you, but you mustn't buy it at the corner store. I know where we can get the same values for half the price."*

So, of course, the man let his friend take him to this far away spot, where believing that he was buying wholesale, he chose a suit for $50.

He was delighted with his purchase until he ran into the neighborhood butcher wearing the identical suit to church that Sunday.

"Hey!" he said grinning. *"Where did you buy that suit?"* The butcher grinned back. *"Oh, I suppose the same place you bought yours . . . At the corner store. A real buy for $30 wasn't it?"*

It is a remarkable thing that so many people put great confidence in mere hearsay and yet are so slow to show as much faith in the ageless truths of God.

But one thing is certain. However misplaced faith may be—even to the extent of being bilked, it is still an expression of trust. Channel that confidence towards supernatural truth and you will bring about a great gain for everybody.

"I do believe, Lord: help my unbelief." (Mark 9:23)

✑ Inspire me with apostolic zeal, O Lord, in helping others to believe in Thee.

SHE THREW AWAY $5000

A judge in San Francisco listened patiently while the couple before him listed their grievances. It was clear that these two had never learned to *"bear and forbear."* Small hurts had been stored away in their memories, rankling and growing, till their life together seemed to be no more than an occasion of new and better methods of revenge.

The case was brought to a climax when the husband's attorney demanded that the wife tell the court what she had done with $5000 cash which she had had in her possession, but which belonged to both.

"Oh, I threw it over the bridge into the Bay," the woman said calmly. *"You see, my husband throws away all his money gambling. So I figure I can throw mine away too."*

Rather than make a bad situation worse by becoming impatient with the faults and mistakes of others, you can do much to correct the trouble by showing greater love and forbearance than usual and thus make up for what is lacking on the part of another person.

One of the simplest ways to start to be a Christopher or Christ-bearer is to show kindness to those around you, especially to your own household. From there you can carry the habit cultivated at home into the office, classroom, shop, farm or wherever else you may be.

"By this shall all men know that you are my disciples if you have love one for another." (John 13:35)

⚜ Give me the good sense, O Lord, to lessen frictions rather than to aggravate them.

WHAT YOU DON'T KNOW

Last November a teacher in a small city in Massachusetts asked her 2nd grade students: "Why Do We Celebrate Thanksgiving Day?"

She was alarmed by the answers she received. Maybe you will be too. Here are some of the reasons the children gave:

1. *"We eat turkey."*
2. *"Our friends come to visit us."*
3. *"It's the President's birthday."*
4. *"It's Columbus' birthday."*
5. *"The teachers want a day off."*
6. *"The janitor wants to clean the school."*
7. *"It's Christmas."*

It's understandable that children may be confused about the deeper meaning of things. But it is a serious handicap for those who have every opportunity to learn the truth.

What you don't know can certainly hurt you!

Try to help those in particular who do not know the purpose of life—why they are here, where they came from and where they are going.

"What doth it profit a man,—if he gain the whole world and suffer the loss of his own soul?" (Matthew 16:26)

⊷§ Grant O Lord that I may be an instrument in bringing Thy Love and Truth to those who know Thee not.

SLOW DELIVERY

Some weeks ago, a picture postcard found its way to the Manhattan District Attorney's office. The postcard bore a one-cent Benjamin Franklin stamp and was postmarked Sunday, November 5, 1911.

The card had been mailed from a Brooklyn station six miles away, by a woman who signed herself as "Louise." It was addressed to a lady who had been the District Attorney's librarian at the time. She had retired from his service some thirty four years ago.

The message on the postcard was not important, but the Post Office hasn't yet been able to figure out where this card has been these forty-three years, or why it now suddenly found itself in the regular delivery.

This is a rare exception. Men have discovered rapid and efficient methods of communication in most parts of the earth. But occasionally even the most vaunted methods show human defects.

It is deeply satisfying to know that with God there is no chance of His communications with us—or ours to Him ever going astray. Every brief prayer that is uttered finds its way to Him. There is no chance of it getting lost for even an hour.

"Pray without ceasing." (1 Thessalonians 5:17)

❧ To Thee be praise and glory for ever and ever, O most Blessed Trinity.

A SIMPLE REMEDY

For more than five years, a woman in Vienna suffered from a mysterious chronic complaint. Although she was only 26, her hair began falling out in large quantities, she suffered a progressive loss of weight and many aches and pains.

The doctors were at a loss to diagnose her case conclusively. Remedy after remedy and operation after operation was tried. They removed her tonsils, her appendix, and her gall-bladder—all to no avail.

Finally it was decided that the woman was suffering from some sort of slow poisoning. But they had no idea how this could be happening.

After intensive investigation, the source of the trouble was finally discovered. The woman had been absorbing the lead poison from the special type of paint on the walls of her house.

Most of us tend to look far afield for the solution of the problems that confuse and trouble our lives. More often than not, they are often under our very noses.

One of the best ways to overcome the poison of hatred, for instance, is to bring the love of Christ into our own hearts and souls—and to share it as far as we can in a world that needs it so much.

"This is my commandment, that you love one another as I have loved you." (John 15:12)

&S O my Redeemer, permit me to be an instrument of Thy love.

SHARE YOUR BLESSINGS

One thing that stifles peoples' lives and makes their work meaningless, is *possessiveness*. It entangles not only the evil and the miserly, but even those who, to all outward appearances, seem closest to God.

We pity the miser because he refuses to think of anything but his money and himself. But isn't it even worse to be miserly with spiritual treasures, thinking only of self and God while failing to complete the triangle: God, self, others.

One of the easiest ways to keep your faith is to give it away. On the other hand, one of the surest ways to lose your faith or to weaken it, is to keep it to yourself.

The more you strive to enrich the lives of others, the more you enrich your own life. Christ gave us all a simple formula to follow. He summed it up in one word—love. And this is the way He spelled it out for us:

"A new commandment I give unto you: that you love one another: that as I have loved you, you also love one another. By this shall all men know that you are my disciples, if you have love one for another." (John 13:34, 35)

&ξ O God, help me to love others as Thou lovest.

A COBRA BIT HIM

When the curator at the zoo in New York City recently saw one of his cobras having a particularly hard time of it, he gently tried to loosen the skin above the snake's eyes.

Mistaking this act of kindness for one of intended harm, the cobra, lightning-like, flicked its head around and sank its fangs into the right hand of its best friend. After an anti-venom injection had been speedily administered the curator was rushed to a hospital. He barely escaped with his life.

In showing kindness to others, one does run the risk of being misunderstood. But from experience, we know that it is an exception when love is met with hate, friendliness with coldness, or a helping hand with a savage bite in return. But even when we do experience the worst ingratitude in return for a Christ-like act, it is a deep and satisfying consolation to know that God appreciates our good intent and will reward us accordingly for all eternity.

"Blessed are they that suffer persecution for justice's sake, for theirs is the kingdom of heaven." (Matthew 5:10)

~§O Prince of Peace, encourage me to persevere in kindness when ingratitude tries my soul.

THE POWER OF ONE

Two of our most famous Presidents, Thomas Jefferson and John Quincy Adams, were each elected to office by a single vote in the Electoral College. Another President, Rutherford Hayes was elected by a single vote. When his election was contested the matter was referred to an electoral commission.

Again Hayes was the winner by a single vote. The man who cast the deciding vote for him was a congressman from Indiana, a lawyer who had been elected to Congress also by a single vote. And that one vote had been cast for him by a client who, though seriously ill, insisted that he be taken to the polls for the balloting.

Going to the polls is your way of adding your voice to those that are raised in support of the justice and truth that God expects in the affairs of men. To fail to do so is to perhaps miss the opportunity to change for the better by your single vote, the tide of government.

When an undesirable person is elected to public office, it is usually not because the majority of the citizens want such a person as a leader, but that they neglected to go to the polls and lend support to one who could better replace him.

"Render therefore to Caesar the things that are Caesar's; and to God the things that are God's." (Luke 20:25)

O God, help me to do my duty to my country.

NO PRICE TOO HIGH

A Connecticut man was suddenly called to Italy on business. While he was away the November presidential elections drew near. He felt an obligation to discharge his duty as a citizen, so he flew back to the United States just to cast his vote and renew his visa. Then he returned to Italy to finish his business.

Before he began shuttling back and forth between Italy and America *"just to vote,"* someone reminded him that it would cost him at least $2000. He remarked, *"I wouldn't give up my American right to vote for a million dollars."*

By the trouble, inconvenience and expense he went to, this man proved his deep love for America. And yet there are so many who, without meaning any harm, neglect to go to the polls even though it would mean only a slight effort. We can't have self-government unless the people vote. Whether it is a national, primary or school board election your vote means more than you realize. Never forget, the absent are always wrong.

"Keep that which is committed to thy trust." (I Timothy 6:20)

᪏§ O Lord, help me always to make my voice heard by voting in all elections and reminding others to do so.

IN YOUR OWN BACKYARD

A St. Louis businessman went off on a 125 mile trip to hunt quail. During his absence his wife looked out of her kitchen window and saw a wild pheasant walking around the backyard. She hastily picked up a cardboard box and set it up as a trap for the bird. Within an hour she had succeeded in capturing the pheasant.

She kept it in a cage until her husband returned to prove to him that one doesn't have to leave home to be a hunter. Then she let the bird have its freedom.

You may never find a pheasant wandering around your backyard, but if you keep your eyes and ears open, you are bound to discover innumerable opportunities all around you through which you can help change the world for the better.

Under your very nose—in your home, office, shop, school, farm, you will find precious opportunities to spread the love and peace of Christ.

"By this shall all men know that you are my disciples if you have love one for another." (John 13:35)

O Jesus, open my eyes to all the opportunities for good that you generously send me.

BEGIN YOUR HEAVEN ON EARTH

A wealthy, socially prominent woman recently had a nervous breakdown. Her doctor told her the cause of most of her trouble was that she had spent too much thought, time and money on herself, too little on those in need.

Long before they die, those who disregard others in furthering their own selfish interests begin to pay the penalty. No matter how much of this world's goods they possess, they seem forever ill at ease, restless, and dissatisfied. Life has little real meaning or joy for them. Inside them something seems to have died.

On the other hand, those whose lives are motivated with the vital purpose of doing all they can for others, actually begin their heaven on earth. They develop a gaiety of heart that carries them through the most trying circumstances. They stay young in spirit. With St. Paul they can say:

"Charity is patient, is kind; charity envieth not, dealeth not perversely, is not puffed up; is not ambitious, seeketh not her own, is not provoked to anger, thinketh no evil; rejoiceth not in iniquity, but rejoiceth with the truth; beareth all things, believeth all things, hopeth all things, endureth all things." (I Corinthians 13:4, 7)

⁓§ O Good Shepherd, help me to realize that the way to true happiness is to live for others for love of Thee.

336

TRAIN THEM TO THINK OF OTHERS

Parents, teachers, and nearly everyone else are often so preoccupied with protecting the young that they over-emphasize self-preservation, self-sanctification, self-development, and self-enjoyment. Without intending any harm, they give their children the impression they have only one mission in life—to take care of themselves. In effect they train them to be passive, to be negative.

Little do they realize this is only part of Christianity; that by failing to teach *"love others as they love themselves"* they are clipping the wings of their own youngsters, fencing them in, depriving them of the more abundant and interesting life that God meant that all His creatures should enjoy. And in many instances they are preparing the way for the monotony, the frustration, even the tragedy which is the inevitable result of concentration on self.

Do all in your power to encourage training of the young that will bring out the great potential for good that God has put in every one of them.

"Suffer children to come unto Me and forbid them not, for of such is the kingdom of God." (Luke 18:16)

◦§ Bless all young people, O God, with a burning zeal to take an interest in others.

AN OUNCE OF PREVENTION

The American Cancer Society pointed out recently that about 70,000 persons recover each year from cancer because it has been detected in time and corrective measures taken. Twice that number of lives would have been saved, it is claimed, if cancerous patients had been given prompt and thorough medical treatment.

Experts on cancer recommend three steps in preventing or arresting the disease: 1) learn the warning signals of cancer, 2) have periodic physical check-ups, 3) do not depend upon unproved methods for the treatment of cancer.

God has put in your hands a power for good to prevent the cancer that is eating away at the vitals of civilization. Face the problem. Recognize the causes. Take steps to replace disease with health, error with truth, hate with love. As a Christopher, or a Christ-bearer, working in your own way, you can by prayer and deed, do something to stop the growth of a moral cancer that can destroy man himself.

"Fear ye not them that kill the body, and are not able to kill the soul: but rather fear him that can destroy both soul and body in hell." (Matthew 10:28)

❧ Grant me the grace, O Lord, to anticipate danger instead of sitting on the sidelines waiting for disaster.

MISPLACED ZEAL

A Detroit mother was sentenced to a five-year prison term because she embezzled money to put her daughter into the movies.

Police accountings revealed that she had taken $19,952 from the manufacturing firm where she worked as a bookkeeper. Under questioning she admitted that she had used a third of the money to promote a Hollywood career for her 19-year-old daughter, and the balance to purchase a home and also a hot-rod car for her teen-age son.

An increasing number of parents are going to extraordinary lengths to further the material success and comfort of their children. At the same time, they neglect to instill in them a sense of values that will help them to meet the joys and sorrows that are the lot of every human being. The result too frequently is a lopsided, frustrated personality that is unable to come to grips with the real problems of life.

One of the best ways to resist temptation is to seek the glory of God and the good of others in all we do. You can't do wrong, doing right!

"Seek ye first the kingdom of God and His justice and all these things shall be added unto you." (Matthew 6:33)

&ca; O Jesus, help me to be solicitous for eternal rewards as others are for the fleeting pleasures of life.

THE PENALTY OF NEGLECT

Chancellor Bismarck of Germany, before he died in 1898, said: *"What you want in the life of a nation, first put into the schools of that nation."*

In the years to come, Germany was to suffer bitterly for allowing evil ideas to get into their schools. Nazis worked hard to banish God from all spheres of education and substituted false gods. Ever since then the world has been paying the penalty.

In our own school system there is a growing tendency to forget God, to refer to the Ten Commandments as out of date or old fashioned.

This is inching closer and closer to the same point of view held by Hitler. He put it much the same way when he said, *"The Ten Commandments have lost their validity —there is no such thing as truth, either in morality or in the scientific sense."*

You, whoever you are, can do something to revive in all schools the truth upon which America is founded: *that each person is created in God's image and that he derives his rights from Him, not from the State.*

"You shall know the truth and the truth shall make you free." (John 8:32)

◦§ O Divine Savior let me be as courageous in spreading Thy Truth as others are in banishing it.

THEY NEED YOU

In a high school science class one boy asked the teacher, *"Don't you think that a hundred years from now science will take the place of religion?"*

The teacher's answer was direct. *"It never will,"* she said. *"Science cannot answer the final questions: how was the universe first started? how did life originate? for these questions do not belong to the world of matter but to the immaterial world."*

She went on to explain how religion and science were on different planes. Science tells how things happen; religion tells *why*. Science deals with the material world; religion with the *spiritual*.

The boy looked thoughtful and murmured, *"I think you've got something there."*

At heart most people are more disposed toward God than they think they are. A bit of patience and kindness in answering their difficulties can often have far-reaching results. They need *you*.

"I am the good shepherd and I know mine and mine know me." (John 10:14)

⇙ O God, instill in me a thirst for souls and allow me to be the means of drawing many to thee.

WEEK-END AROUND THE WORLD

On December 8, 1953, Pamela Martin, a young artist and copy-writer from Chicago, took a week-end trip around the world. By commercial airlines, she made the trip in 90 hours, 59 minutes. She succeeded in setting a new record as a passenger flyer.

Seventy years ago, a trip around the world traveling by everything from ships to camels would have taken at least ten weeks. This modern traveler said that her trip was the best week-end she had ever spent.

While we have made great advances in speeding our way around the world, it happens that we are still far behind in bringing peace to all men.

More than 1900 years have slipped by since Jesus Christ bade His followers to go to the *"whole world"* to *"all men"* with the divine formula for peace on earth. Today, believe it or not, more than two thirds of humanity have yet to hear that He was born, lived and died for each and everyone of them.

Until enough of us takes it upon ourselves to be a Christ-bearer and feel a personal responsibility to transmit that precious peace from the house next door to the farthermost corners of the earth, there will not be much chance of lasting peace for all men. If you live for peace, you may do much to save millions dying for peace!

"Go ye into the whole world, preach the gospel to every creature." (Matthew 16:15)

⇛ Teach me, O Lord, to see that any suffering to bring Thy peace to all the world will count for all eternity.

APPEARANCES CAN BE DECEPTIVE

When Houston, Texas, placed new aluminum trash cans on downtown streets, no one thought some people would mistake them for mailboxes.

But it was an easy error to make because the cans looked like large street mailboxes.

It wasn't long before the city garbage department began receiving calls from citizens who, supposing the trash cans to be mailboxes, had dropped letters into them. They realized their mistake only after reading in the newspapers about the new cans.

For a while, garbagemen had to look for letters in the trash they collected and deposit them where they belonged—in the mailbox.

Appearances are deceptive. Most of the trouble in peoples' lives comes from the fact that they don't take a second look. Consequently, they lose money, marry the wrong people, get involved in bad business deals and contracts. But worse—wrong decisions here can affect their eternal destiny.

"Judge not according to the appearance." (John 7:24)

⋙ O Jesus, grant that I may serve Thee by protecting others from making false choices.

343

THE BARBER STOPPED HIM CRYING

A 2-year-old in Atlanta, Georgia, was having his first haircut. The barber lifted him into the chair, and he promptly broke into terrified screams. The other customers sighed. For the next fifteen minutes they would probably have to endure an ear-splitting wait. But the barber leaned over, and whispered something to the boy, who immediately shut his eyes very tight, and stopped crying.

The customers were intrigued. Later one of them asked the barber what he had said to the child to persuade him so suddenly to hush.

The barber replied that he merely whispered to him to shut his eyes so that he wouldn't get hair in them. He said that he had found that no child can cry with his eyes closed.

Whether or not the barber is absolutely correct in that remedy, it is nevertheless true that there are a thousand simple opportunities within the grasp of all of us to alleviate the confusion and chaos that afflict most of the world.

Many persons who keep saying *"what can I do"* or *"I don't count"* are indulging in a bit of self-pity that helps no one—not even themselves. Doing one thing, no matter how small, that is positive and constructive, is far better than doing nothing at all or merely whining about how bad things are. Recall frequently our Christopher saying: *"Better to light one candle than to curse the darkness."*

"Well done, thou good servant, because thou hast been faithful in a little, thou shalt have power over ten cities." (Luke 19:19)

⋙ Help me, O Lord, not to overlook even the slightest opportunity to bring Thy peace to the world.

344

NOW AND FOREVER

Francois Mauriac, Nobel Prize-winning novelist, was once asked during the course of an interview what message he would leave to his fellow citizens if he had only a quarter of an hour to live.

Mauriac replied that he would say to them, *"Step back a little. Leave me alone, face to face with this eternity which I have not been able to face since I entered this world."*

Perhaps Mauriac spoke for many of us when he said that he had not been able to face eternity in all his lifetime. Most of us fear the thought of eternity. Whenever it presents itself we tend to switch our thoughts to other things. Yet we are born for eternity.

Each of us has already begun to lead a life that will never die. Life on earth is but a preparation for life everlasting. If we could take but a moment a day to know that each day, with its daily round and common tasks is a means to bring us closer to eternal dwelling in the Presence of God, then our lives would be much fuller and richer.

"These things I write to you, that you may know that you have eternal life, you who believe in the name of the Son of God." (1 John 5:13)

~§ Almighty God, grant that I may live in the daily knowledge of eternal life.

345

THE TRUTH CAUGHT UP WITH HER

A commercial artist had been standing in line at the bank for a long time. The young woman ahead of him had quite a good deal of business. It seemed the teller was checking her right to make a withdrawal of $7100.

The man didn't know how much longer he had to wait, so he decided to do something to pass the time. The young woman had an interesting face. He took out his pencil and a sketch pad, and made a drawing of her, completing it just as the teller handed out the money. The man put the sketch in his pocket, and took his turn at the window.

The artist had forgotten all about the incident when he returned to the bank some days later. When he heard some of the tellers talking about the fraudulent withdrawal of $7100 by a smartly dressed young woman he produced the sketch. It proved most valuable in helping the FBI to track down the woman who had forged the check.

While we can often deceive our fellowmen, we should be ever conscious of the fact that we do not fool Almighty God. Every thought, word and deed, of each day is registered with God. One day when we stand before Him in judgment we will render an account for all of them.

". . . *every idle word that men shall speak, they shall render an account for it in the day of judgment.*" (Matthew 12:36)

&⸫ O Lord, let me so live as to be always prepared to die.

346

THEY GAVE $13,000,000

During the Korean war, American servicemen gave thirteen million dollars out of their monthly allowance to help the orphans, the sick, the homeless, and countless other needy cases among the South Koreans.

This great generosity on the part of those who are far from the comforts of home is refreshing proof of the nobler side of man. It is evidence of that Christian sense of sympathy for the misfortunes of others that is seldom found where the background of a nation is godless or anti-God.

If you are truly interested in the strengthening of America you will work and pray to see that the basic truth upon which our nation is founded is kept in the foreground of both public and private life. You can be sure that those who are bent on destroying our country will leave no stone unturned to eliminate God from all spheres of life.

Despite many defects, Americans both in and out of war, have a heart for others, because they come from a country where a Christian sense of values still lives. Do all in your power to protect the *"cause"* that produces such an inspiring *"effect."*

"The fool hath said in his heart: there is no God." (Psalm 13:1)

ʘ O Creator of all, allow me to play at least a small part in keeping our nation mindful that Thou art the Author of our liberty.

347

DOES IT WORK?

A man who suffered with rheumatism consulted his doctor who immediately wrote him a prescription. As the patient was leaving the doctor called him back. *"By the way,"* he said, *"if this prescription gives you any relief, please let me know. I suffer from rheumatism myself, and I've tried in vain to cure it."*

The easiest thing in the world is to give advice to other people. Usually the advice we give is the kind we'd never take ourselves. When we stop to consider it, of course, we can see how ridiculously vain this is.

The best way to tell others what to do and how to do it is to show them by our examples. The reason that the teachings of Jesus have remained with us through the ages, is that He not only told us what to do and what not to do, but He set us a living example by proving the truth of what He said in His own life. Before we set out to advise others, let us search ourselves carefully to see if we are proving what we suggest in our own lives.

"And he spoke also to them a similitude: Can the blind lead the blind? Do they not both fall into the ditch?" (Luke 6:39)

❧ Heavenly Father, help me to live purely that I may help others.

A LIGHT IN THE DARKNESS

There was a dense fog and the officer on the bridge was becoming more and more exasperated. As he leaned over the side of the bridge, trying to pierce the gloom, he saw a hazy figure on a rail a few yards from his ship. *"What are you trying to do with your ship,"* he roared. *"Don't you know the rules of the road?"*

"This ain't no ship," came the reply, *"This here's a lighthouse."*

Isn't it true that when we are least certain, when we are most in the dark, we are most aggressive and out-spoken—like this officer?

It is hard for us to admit our ignorance and shortcomings at all times. A sure cure over the years however is to be respectful of the opinions of others, and humbly seek the opinion of others whenever there is the slightest doubt. We should not forget above all our main source of light—our Creator.

"I am come a light into the world; that whosoever believeth in me, may not remain in darkness." (John 12:46)

❧ O Lord, help us always to trust Thee.

THE ORDER OF THINGS

The sun is 93 million miles away from the earth. We are completely dependent on it for light, heat and power. If the sun were just a little closer all earth life would be destroyed by the heat; or a little farther away and the earth would freeze over.

These are scientific facts that we learned early in school and that we rather take for granted, and have long since ceased to wonder at. The fact that the entire universe is geared to run so orderly, is so daily present that we seldom stop to calculate what would happen were something to suddenly turn the order of things to confusion.

When we do pause to consider, we can find endless manifestations all about us of a Supreme Intelligence governing and ruling all. If for no other reason than that the sun is in exactly the right relation to the earth, supplying all it's needs for life and growth, and has done so for billions of years, we should be convinced of the power and goodness of God.

"The heavens shew forth the glory of God, and the firmament declareth the work of his hands." (Psalms 18:1)

Heavenly Father, Who has made heaven and earth, we thank Thee for all Thy love and goodness to us.

HE GOT PUSHED SIX MILES

A blinding snowstorm in Decatur, Ill., had one anti-climax. A motorist was cautiously making his way along a lonely road, when he came upon another car that was apparently stalled at the side of the road. He could dimly make out the figure of a man at the wheel.

"Poor man!" the motorist thought. *"To be stalled on a day like this! I suppose I ought to help him."*

He pulled his car directly behind the one standing, locking the bumpers. Then he carefully pushed it for six miles until they reached a garage. Safe in the shelter of the garage, he got out expecting the man's thanks. But he was in for a shock.

The sputtering, exasperated, and wholly ungrateful recipient of his kindness exploded into abuse. *"I wasn't having any trouble!"* he yelled at him. *"I was only waiting to make a left turn!"*

In endeavoring to be of service to others, it is well to take great care not to impose your own will upon them. The test of real charity is showing a gentle consideration for the wishes of others.

The proper approach for helping others while still avoiding intrusion or imposition was well formulated by Jesus Christ when He said:

"Behold, I stand at the gate and knock." (Apocalypse 3:20)

&⸹ Guide me, O Saviour of all, in treating with great consideration those whom I would assist.

351

DOING SOMETHING ABOUT IT

Lincoln was famous for the effective manner in which he could silence hecklers. Once while running for the Illinois legislature, he was debating a loud-mouthed, arm-waving fellow. This man, after making a lot of noise and saying little, finally sat down.

Lincoln arose and remarked quietly: *"My good friend here reminds me of a steamboat that used to run down the river when I was a lad. It had a four-foot boiler and a seven-foot whistle—and every time it whistled it stopped running."*

It's easy for any of us to spend so much energy criticizing that we have little left for doing anything constructive.

It doesn't take a thimbleful of brains to complain.

However, the slightest effort to correct abuses—to do something to rectify things instead of just talking about them—may produce great results.

God blesses the least effort we put forth to make Him known to men.

"Be ye doers of the word and not hearers only, deceiving your own selves." (James 1:22)

❧ O Divine Savior, remind me often to be a doer, not merely a talker.

THE PRICE OF FREEDOM

Captain Byron Dobbs of Clio, Mich., was one of the American pilots captured by the Communists in Korea. When he refused to sign a germ-warfare *"confession"* he was subjected to agonizing tortures.

For hours at a time, the Reds made him sit on a sharp stake, or stand rigidly at attention in 24-hour stretches. If he dared to move he was hit in the face with a bayonet.

Under such trying circumstances, one wonders what made him withstand every inducement to give in. The answer is very significant. Captain Dobbs had such a deep love of God and country that he felt he had an obligation to stand up in face of death itself for the best interests of all. When questioned he said quietly: *"I felt I should do my part."*

We are sure that if most realized how much is at stake in these critical times, they would show the same daring, bravery and generosity in protecting the best interests of all. Yet too many persons neglect to walk even a few blocks to participate in the privilege of voting to protect our God-given freedom.

Keep in mind always that freedom is everybody's business.

"It shall be given you in that hour what to speak." (Matthew 10:19)

᳘ Stir up in me a willingness to suffer much, O Lord, in bringing Thy peace and truth to all men.

SURE CURE FOR THE BLUES

The Gallup Poll made a survey to find out what methods people use to cheer themselves up when they are blue and depressed.

It seems that a large number of them turn to TV, radio, movies and dancing. Many pray, read the Bible, and count their blessings. An equally high percentage try cooking, housework, painting, study and hobbies. A very large proportion just don't do anything.

These are all good methods. There is only one thing wrong with this list. It leaves out one very important way to get rid of the blues. That is by helping others. If you will spend your time doing that for love of God, your own troubles will vanish and be replaced by great peace of heart and soul.

"By charity of the spirit serve one another." (Galatians 5:13)

➳ Help me, O God, to find all my happiness in serving Thee and my fellow men.

HALF TRUTHS OFTEN DECEIVE

For 126 years, Van Dyck's portrait of Cornelis van der Geest had hung in London's National Gallery. Considered one of the foremost art treasures of the world, the portrait measures 32½ by 26½ inches.

Recently, however, it was discovered to the dismay of the art world, that just half of it is *"the real thing"!* The head of van der Geest and the white ruff collar are authentic—the rest, the background and the black robe, is a clever forgery.

It was detected when the painting was being cleaned. The forger had carefully laid in the wood on which the original head had been painted a larger panel of wood, and smoothed them to a continuous surface. In order to prevent a careful inspection, he had covered the entire canvas with a heavily-toned varnish.

One of the greatest deceptions of our day is the practice of mixing truth and error—to present half-truths as if they were whole truths.

That is why people who are completely dedicated to *"the truth, the whole truth, and nothing but the truth"* are so much needed today in education, government, labor relations and the creative end of every channel that communicates ideas.

"They err that work evil: but mercy and truth prepare good things." (Proverbs 14:22)

⅋ O Lord, inspire me to be a champion of the whole truth.

355

HELP YOURSELF BY HELPING OTHERS

A wild-life expert in Georgia recently had occasion to put into personal practice the first aid teaching he had been giving students for eight years.

On a hunting trip he was bitten by a rather deadly snake. Without a moment's hesitation he cut across the fang marks with a pocket knife, sucked the poison from the wound and administered anti-venom serum. Although quite ill he managed to return home in his outboard motorboat and recovered in a few days.

There is a boomerang quality in doing things to benefit others.

The teacher who instructs his pupils with a real desire to help them develop as they should, finds that he in turn may learn a great deal from them. The scientist in his laboratory, searching for newer and better ways to improve human living, finds that his knowledge and understanding deepen with the search. The follower of Christ who gives of his time and his energies to help bring God's love and peace into the world, finds that in saving others he is saving himself.

"He who soweth blessings, shall also reap blessings."
(II Corinthians 9:6)

▸ O Divine Savior, grant me the grace to see that one of the best ways to protect my own salvation is to work for that of others.

BOY'S THROAT CUT TO SAVE LIFE

In Westfield, N.J., a 5-year-old boy had his throat cut in order to save his life.

He had complained of a sore throat, and the infection became so bad that it choked off his breathing. By the time the doctor arrived, his face had turned black, his windpipe was almost closed. Practically no air was getting into his lungs.

There was no time to lose. The doctor saw that the only chance of saving the youngster's life was to slit his throat and through it get the life-saving air into his little lungs.

Desperate measures must often be taken when the fate of either an individual or the multitude is at stake. Our God-given freedom is threatened in many ways. Diseases of many kinds are choking off the truth from mankind. Do your part. See that everybody has the benefit of God's truth, regardless of the cost to you.

"And you shall know the truth, and the truth shall make you free." (John 8:32)

❧ O Savior of all, let me suffer much to see that all have the truth.

357

CHRISTMAS CAROLS CHANGED A THIEF

It was Christmas Eve in Tokyo when a 28-year-old thief walked into a police station and told the astonished officers he was surrendering himself. He had committed more than 70 robberies.

Although the police had hunted this notorious thief for many years, they had never been able to catch up with him. What could possibly have made him decide to give himself up now?

The thief's explanation was even more surprising. He had been passing through the neighborhood, when he came upon a group of children singing Christmas carols. He had stopped to listen. The sweet childish voices telling of the birth of Christ had moved him so much that he had decided to end his sinful ways.

The little ones who sang the Christmas carols may never know until they appear before the throne of God how raising their voices in praise of the Prince of Peace changed the heart of a thief.

Likewise, you will probably not realize during your lifetime what far-reaching good you may have accomplished by diligently making use of every opportunity, no matter how small, to work for the glory of God and the salvation of souls. But great will be your joy if you have played your part in life well, and hear Christ Himself saying to you on your last day:

"Out of the mouth of infants and of sucklings thou hast perfected praise." (Matthew 21:16)

~§ Help me, O Lord, to seize every opportunity to help others through love of Thee.

YOU ARE IMPORTANT

The term *"Christopher"* is derived from the Greek word *"Christophoros"* which signifies *"Christ-bearer."*

It's meaning sums up our objective of encouraging individual initiative in carrying into the mainstream of life the truths that can bring lasting peace to our country and to the world—truths that have come down to us through 1900 years of Christianity, as well as those kept alive by the Jews alone for ages before the birth of Christ.

As a Christopher or Christ-bearer each of us can do something to carry the love and truth of Christ to the world.

All we have to do is play the role of messengers. God could have arranged to have it done entirely by angels, but He did not. He willed that men should be saved through their fellowmen.

He simply asks us to pass along or distribute, the simple, eternal fundamentals that are the basis of happiness for mankind in this life and the next.

He assured us He would always provide us with abundant help from on high. The more we fulfill this noble role, the more we can say with Christ:

"For this was I born, and for this came I into the world, that I should give testimony to the truth." (John 18:37)

&8 Almighty God, I thank You for the privilege of being one of Your messengers.

359

YOUR MISSION IN LIFE

Last year on the day after Christmas, a son was born to a woman in Los Angeles. She had a disease that the doctors described as incurable. She knew that to have a child would shorten her life.

"But if I can have my baby," she said, "I shall die happy. Death does not frighten me, for I shall have brought new life into the world."

This woman knew that the purpose of human existence is to give oneself to others. She was willing to sacrifice her life to bequeath God's gift of life to her child.

If you pass on life to others in a physical, spiritual or intellectual way, you are fulfilling your greatest mission on earth, for you are sharing in God's creative power, and truly reflecting His image.

"Greater love than this no man hath, that a man lay down his life for his friends." (John 15:13)

Heavenly Father, grant that while I live, I may in every way possible pass on to others the life Thou hast given me.

360

THE GOOD IN THE WORST

A blind news dealer in Riverhead, L.I., was making his way home, when he was accosted by three men.

"Hold it, Buddy," one said. *"Don't hit him,"* said another. *"He's blind."*

"I don't have any money," he told them. But he could feel the searching hands.

"Only a dollar twenty-five!" the voice that belonged to the hands exclaimed in disgust. *"Oh, a check too!"* in a happier tone.

Tears welled up in the man's sightless eyes. *"I was saving it to buy a Christmas present for my son. He's in the Army in Japan."* There was a moment's silence. Then he felt the hands again. Unbelievably, the check was being returned to him. *"A dollar twenty-five!"* the voice said again. *"Some haul! O.K., Buster. Keep the check. And Merry Christmas."*

It is a little difficult to admit that there is any good in a person who would take even a dime from a blind man. But there is, just the same, and the sooner it is developed in the right direction, the less will he be tempted to steal from the blind or anyone else.

"And God saw all the things that he had made, and they were very good." (Genesis 1:31)

↪ Give me the patience, O Lord, to find the good in those who do evil.

JUST ONE SMALL LIGHT

For safety sake during blackouts in World War II no one was permitted to strike a match. Blackouts had to be complete to be effective. Just one small light in a single window could direct an enemy bomber to its target.

Experiments had shown that the little flare from one match could be seen with the help of binoculars, for 15 miles—sometimes for 20 miles.

Some may tend to forget that God has given each of us great power for good which we can use, if we will, to light up the dark places of the earth with Christ's love and truth.

Just one small deed performed in Christ's name may be the means of pointing out the way to thousands. It may be the means of bringing them peace for time and eternity.

"So let your light shine before men, that they may see your good works, and glorify your Father who is in heaven." (Matthew 5:16)

⧢ O Jesus, grant that Your light may shine so brightly in me as to draw others to You.

SUCCESS IN SPITE OF FAILURE

A doctor's 8-year-old son went to bed one night suffering from an earache. At about 1:30 in the morning his father looked in on him and found him sleeping peacefully.

Towards dawn he heard his son in shallow, labored breathing and, rushing into his room, found him unconscious and blue in the face.

For hours he strove to save his son's life. He called for the assistance of a hospital rescue squad. They used an inhalator and resuscitator and administered every helpful drug known to medical science—but all proved useless. The little boy died.

Sometimes, in spite of our best efforts, we fail to attain our objective. But the main thing is to try and keep trying. The only real failure is not to try.

If we can go through life and enter eternity knowing that we made an honest effort to do God's will and make the world a little better place for our being in it, then it will make little difference whether we succeeded or failed in actual accomplishment. Our very failure might have brought God's blessing on someone else.

"Be thou faithful unto death: and I will give thee the crown of life." (Apocalypse 2:10)

∽§ O Lord, keep me ever mindful that I can never really lose in working for Thee.

WITH THE SIMPLICITY OF A CHILD

A little boy was saying his night prayers while his mother listened attentively. However, he was speaking so softly that she found it difficult to follow, so she said: *"Talk a little louder, Johnny, I can't hear you."*

After a moment's pause, he replied, *"But, Mother, I'm not talking to you."*

It might be well for all of us to remind ourselves from time to time that when we pray we are talking directly to God. So often prayer becomes a habit—a formality—and we forget that we are carrying on a conversation with God. If you stop and realize that your Heavenly Father is listening to you, your prayers will take on much more meaning and will be a source of comfort and joy.

"Suffer children to come to me, and forbid them not: for of such is the kingdom of God." (Luke 18:16)

◆§ O Father of all, help me to remember that when I pray I am talking to Thee.

SMALL BUT IMPORTANT

Sparta was a city in ancient Greece. Its citizens were a stoical military people who believed in decisive action and few words.

At one time when a feud was brewing between the Athenians and the Spartans, the Athenians sent a messenger to Sparta with this message, *"If we come to your city, we will raze it to the ground."*

The Spartans returned an answer composed of a single word, "IF."

A clever ruse of the Devil is to keep as many people as possible from reaching a decision about anything that concerns their eternal destiny. Good intentions are of little value if there is continual delay in putting them into practice.

Some people muddle through a whole lifetime toying with the idea of doing something worthwhile—something that will justify their existence and make the world a bit the better for their being in it.

To be a true success in this life as well as in the life to come, you must make up your own mind very positively that there is good to be done and evil to be avoided. Do not allow any *"if," "but"* or *"whereas"* to sidetrack or delay you during the coming year.

"I must work the works of him that sent me, whilst it is day: the night cometh, when no man can work." (John 9:4)

⊷ Allow me, O Lord, to be quick and decisive in doing Thy holy will.